S

WATCHMAN NEE

A Seer
of the
Divine
Revelation
in the
Present
Age

W i t n e s s   L e e

Living Stream Ministry
Anaheim, California • www.lsm.org

First Edition, November 1991.
Softbound Edition, October 2007.

Library of Congress Catalog
Card Number: 91-77171

ISBN 978-0-87083-625-1 (hardcover)
ISBN 978-0-7363-3576-8 (softcover)

Published by

Living Stream Ministry
2431 W. La Palma Ave., Anaheim, CA 92801 U.S.A.
P. O. Box 2121, Anaheim, CA 92814 U.S.A.

Printed in the United States of America

22   23   24   25   26   27   /   10   9   8   7   6   5   4

CONTENTS

A SHORT INTRODUCTION

The Bible contains many biographies. The Old Testament shows us the portraits of Abraham, Moses, David, and many others, and the New Testament presents to us the lives of Peter, John, Paul, and others. These biographies convey much of the divine revelation concerning God and His dispensations. As I had a close and spiritual contact with Brother Watchman Nee for twenty-five years, and as I was involved in the same unique work with him for the Lord's recovery for such a long time, I felt burdened to write a biography for him that the life and work of such a witness of the Lord might not disappear from those after him, but rather might be kept, as it should be, to minister Christ according to God's desire to the generations to come.

But to write a biography of a certain person is not an easy and simple matter. Could what is written about that person be a genuine picture of him? Is the motive for writing proper? Is the writing accurate? What will the influence be? What will the issue be? After much consideration, my solution to all these points is this: Since I have been under Brother Nee's teaching, edifying, and perfecting, and since he was a brother I respected, observed, and weighed for a quarter of a century, the accuracy of my writing about him should be guaranteed. As to the motive, the heart-searching God is the Judge! As to the influence and issue, the merciful Lord is the blessing. Much endeavor has been exercised to avoid flattery, exaggerations, and the exaltation of men, and the Holy Spirit has been the Guide and Controller of this writing. Thus, I desire to see this writing accomplished unto the good pleasure of the Triune God for His rich blessing.

This volume, except chapter thirty, was consummated for publishing in 1977. But at that time, though many were expecting to see a book concerning Brother Nee's life, within

my spirit I did not feel pleasant to release it. So I concealed
it for fourteen years. This corresponds with the apostle
Paul's experience in 2 Corinthians 12:2. After such a long
period of concealment, I now have the sensation—as many
others do—that I should no longer conceal it, but publish it
according to the Lord's leading. May such a slave and witness
of Christ as Brother Nee, still speak and shine through the
lines of this inadequate writing, under the anointing of the
Holy Spirit, for the edification of the saints and the building
up of the Body of Christ, and for the glory of the One whom he
loved and lived for his whole life.

The author
July 22, 1991
Anaheim, California

CHAPTER ONE

RAISING UP A UNIQUE GIFT TO THE AGE

THE LORD'S MOVE TO CHINA

In creation God ordained that man should replenish the earth and have dominion over all created things (Gen. 1:28). In redemption the Lord commissioned His disciples to go into all the world to preach the gospel and disciple all the nations for His kingdom on earth (Mark 16:15; Matt. 28:19). Following Pentecost, the territory around the Mediterranean Sea was evangelized in less than half a century, and the gospel was spread to Europe within the first two centuries. However, it was confined there for over ten centuries. Following the discovery of America the gospel was brought to the Western Hemisphere through European immigration, but it never properly spread to the Far East before the defeat of Spain.

The Nestorians brought their religion from Persia to China in the seventh century. Nestorianism was a deviation from the divine revelation. It was not the pure gospel of life. Three emperors of the Tang Dynasty in China received this religion. However, after two centuries Nestorianism was banned and vanished because of its inaccuracy and lack of life. After that, there was no trace of Christianity in China in any form until the arrival of the Franciscans in the thirteenth century and the Jesuits in the sixteenth century. They, with their Western learning, were also lifeless and full of traditional ordinances. They were not prevailing in winning the conservative Chinese, who were saturated with the ethical teachings of Confucius and misled by the superstitions of Buddhism. It was only from the beginning of the nineteenth century that the pure gospel and the Bible were brought to China.

After the defeat of Spain, which was the power of the Catholic-dominated world in the sixteenth century, many Protestant missions under God's sovereign grace were raised up both in Europe and in America to send hundreds of

missionaries to heathen countries. More missionaries were
sent to China than to any other country. Robert Morrison
landed in Canton, capital of the southernmost province of
China, in the early years of the nineteenth century. The
Congregationalists, Methodists, and Anglicans came to the
southern province of Fukien. The American Presbyterians
and the Southern Baptists arrived in the northern province of
Shantung. The Christian and Missionary Alliance reached the
international port of Shanghai. The China Inland Mission
pioneered a number of inland provinces, and other missions
settled in many other territories. Many of these missionaries,
especially the pioneers, were men of God. They sacrificed
much for the Lord's commission and suffered a great deal for
the gospel. Through their pioneering work, many doors in
China were opened and thousands of people who were in darkness and sin were led to the Lord and received the Lord's
salvation. These missionaries brought with them three trea-
sures: the Lord's name, which is the Lord Himself, the gospel,
and the Bible. We thank the Lord for this! However, the gospel
was not adequately presented to the educated Chinese class,
and the truth concerning life and the church was not effectu-
ally released until the first decade of the twentieth century.

In 1900 Satan instigated the Boxer Rebellion. In this
uprising many missionaries and a great number of Chinese
believers were martyred. Satan's intention was to terminate
the Lord's move in China. But under God's sovereignty this
persecution aroused a great burden among the saints in the
Western world to pray desperately for the Lord's move in
China. We believe it was through the Lord's answer to those
desperate prayers that some prevailing evangelists among
the Chinese believers were raised up after the Boxer
Rebellion. These "native" preachers became prevailing in
gospel preaching, and their preaching reached the students of
China's new generation. Around the year 1920 the gospel
penetrated many schools, and a good number of high school
and college students were captured by the Lord throughout
the country from the far north to the far south. A number
of brilliant ones were called and equipped by the Lord to do
His work.

Raising Up of Watchman Nee

One of these outstanding students was Nee Shu-tsu. His English name was Henry Nee. His paternal grandfather, Nee Yu-cheng, studied in the American Congregational College in Foochow and became the first Chinese pastor in northern Fukien among the Congregationalists. Nee Shu-tsu's paternal grandmother was a student in the American Congregational Girls' College in Foochow. His father, Nee Wen-shiu, a second generation Christian, studied in the American Methodist College in Foochow. Nee Wen-shiu was well trained in classical Chinese and became an officer in the Chinese customs. Nee Shu-tsu's mother, Lin Ho-ping, also a second generation Christian, studied in the Chinese Western Girls' School in Shanghai. This school maintained a high English standard. Nee Shu-tsu, a third generation Christian, studied in the Anglican Trinity College in Foochow. This school was a two-year college which maintained a high standard both in Chinese and English. After being raised up by the Lord to carry out His commission, he adopted the new English name Watchman Nee and the new Chinese name To-sheng, which means, the sound of a watchman's rattle. As a newly regenerated Christian, called by the Lord, he considered himself a watchman, raised up to give the sound of a rattle to people in the dark night. He eventually became, by the Lord's bountiful mercy and grace, a unique gift to this age. Watchman Nee was given by the Lord to His Body for His move of recovery on the earth, not only in China but also throughout the entire world.

CHAPTER TWO

SAVED AND CALLED

THROUGH DORA YU'S PREACHING

Among the evangelists whom the Lord raised up in China was a young sister whose English name was Dora Yu and whose Chinese name was Yu Tzu-tu. She had been saved at an early age and later was sent to England by her family to study medicine. On the way to England her ship docked at Marseilles in southern France. At that point she became greatly burdened and told the captain that she could not continue the voyage and that she must return to China to preach the gospel of Christ. The captain was perplexed but could do nothing except send her home. Her parents were extremely disappointed by her return, and though they attempted to change her mind regarding the preaching of the gospel, their efforts were unavailing. Eventually they gave up. She soon left home, wandering about preaching the Lord Jesus on the streets. No one hired her. She simply trusted in the Lord. Through means supplied by the Lord, she rented a storefront in a suburb of Shanghai for preaching the gospel. From then on she was invited by denominations to hold many gospel preaching meetings. She traveled extensively through many provinces doing gospel work and became a prevailing witness for the Lord. She continued to preach for the rest of her life, leading hundreds to the Lord.

In February of 1920 Dora Yu was invited to Foochow, the capital of Fukien province, where she preached the gospel in the Methodist auditorium. Her preaching was so convincing and full of power that following every meeting rows of tears could be seen on the floor from the weeping of the audience. Many were saved. Among the converts was a well-educated Chinese lady, Watchman Nee's mother. She and her husband were Methodists but without the experience of salvation. After being saved, she returned home and made a thorough confession to her husband and children. Her oldest son, Shu-tsu, was greatly surprised and inspired by her confession. He felt that he must go to Dora Yu's meeting and see what it was that had brought about such a change in his mother. The next day he went, and the Lord caught him. Later the same night he saw a vision of the Lord Jesus hanging on the cross. Through this experience the Lord called him to be His servant.

<hr />

WATCHMAN NEE'S PERSONAL TESTIMONY GIVEN AT KULANGSU, FUKIEN PROVINCE, OCTOBER 18, 1936[1]

I was born into a Christian family. I was the third child preceded by two sisters. Because I had an aunt who had borne six daughters in succession, my paternal aunt was displeased when my mother bore two girls. According to Chinese custom, males are preferred over females. When my mother gave birth to two girls, people said she would probably be like my aunt, bearing half a dozen girls before bringing forth a boy. Though at that time my mother was not clearly saved, she knew how to pray. So she spoke to the Lord, saying, "If I have a boy, I will present him to You." The Lord heard her prayer and I was born. My father told me, "Before you were born, your mother promised to present you to the Lord."

I was saved in 1920 at the age of seventeen. Before being saved I experienced some mental conflict concerning whether or not to accept the Lord Jesus as my Savior and whether or not to become the Lord's servant. For most people, the problem at the time of salvation is how to be delivered from sin. But for me, being saved from sin and my life career were linked together. If I were to accept the Lord Jesus as my Savior, I would simultaneously accept Him as my Lord. He would deliver me not only from sin but also from the world. At that time I was afraid of being

---

[1] Translator's note: The following excerpts are translated directly from the original manuscript of K. H. Weigh and are slightly different from the published version.

saved, for I knew that once I was saved I must serve the Lord. Of necessity, therefore, my salvation would be a dual salvation. It was impossible for me to set aside the Lord's calling and to desire only salvation. I had to choose either to believe in the Lord and have a dual salvation or forfeit both. For me to accept the Lord would mean that both events would take place simultaneously.

On the evening of April 29, 1920, I was alone in my room. I had no peace of mind. Whether I sat or reclined, I could find no rest, for within was this problem of whether or not I should believe in the Lord. My first inclination was not to believe in the Lord Jesus and not to be a Christian. However, that made me inwardly uneasy. There was a real struggle within me. Then I knelt down to pray. At first I had no words with which to pray. But eventually many sins came before me, and I realized that I was a sinner. I had never had such an experience in my life before that time. I saw myself as a sinner and I also saw the Savior. I saw the filthiness of sin and I also saw the efficacy of the Lord's precious blood cleansing me and making me white as snow. I saw the Lord's hands nailed to the cross, and at the same time I saw Him stretching forth His arms to welcome me, saying, "I am here waiting to receive you." Overwhelmed by such love, I could not possibly reject it, and I decided to accept Him as my Savior. Previously, I had laughed at those who believed in the Lord, but that evening I could not laugh. Instead, I wept and confessed my sins, seeking the Lord's forgiveness. After making my confession, the burden of sins was discharged, and I felt buoyant and full of inward joy and peace. This was the first time in my life that I knew I was a sinner. I prayed for the first time and had my first experience of joy and peace. There might have been some joy and peace before, but the experience after my salvation was very real. Alone in my room that evening, I saw the light and lost all consciousness of my surroundings. I said to the Lord, "Lord, You have really been gracious to me."

In this audience there are at least three schoolmates of mine. Among them is Brother Weigh Kwang-hsi, who can testify concerning what an ill-behaved student I was, as well as what a wonderful student I was in school. On the evil side, I often violated the school rules. On the good side, I was always first in every examination, because God had bestowed intelligence on me. My essays were frequently posted on the bulletin board for exhibition. At that time I was a youth with many grand dreams and many plans for the future. I considered my judgments sound. I can humbly say that had I worked hard in the world, it would have been quite possible for me to have had great success. My schoolmates can also testify to this. But following my salvation many new things happened to me. All my previous planning became void and was brought to nothing. My future career was entirely abandoned. For some this step might be easy, but for me, with many ideals, dreams, and plans, it was exceedingly difficult. From the evening I was saved, I began to live a new life, for the life of the eternal God had entered into me.

My salvation and calling to serve the Lord took place simultaneously. Since that evening, I have never once had any doubts about being called. During that hour I decided on my future career once and for all. I realized that, on the one hand, the Lord had saved me for my sake, and at the same time, He did so for His own sake. He wanted me to obtain His eternal life, and He also wanted me to serve Him and be His co-worker. As a boy I did not understand the nature of preaching. When I was older, I considered it the most trifling and base of occupations. In those days most preachers were employed by European or American missionaries. They were servile subordinates to the missionaries and earned merely eight or nine dollars per month. I had no intention of becoming a preacher nor even a Christian. I could never have imagined that I would choose the profession of a preacher, a profession which I despised and considered trifling and base.

CHAPTER THREE

EDIFIED AND PERFECTED

UNDER DORA YU

After being saved, Watchman Nee had a strong desire to serve the Lord. Although still in high school, he longed to be trained by Dora Yu in Shanghai. His mother agreed, and Dora Yu accepted him into her Bible school. However, because he had certain habits of which she did not approve, such as sleeping late, Dora Yu decided not to keep him. On one occasion she sent him to deliver mail to the downtown post office in Shanghai. Because of the long distance and the poor condition of the road, it took him longer than she expected. She assumed that he had gone to some amusement, which was actually not the case. But she dismissed him, and he returned home and finished his two years of college.

His Personal Testimony
Given at Kulangsu, Fukien, October 18, 1936

After being saved, I continued on in school, though I had little interest in books. Others read novels in class, but I diligently studied the Bible. Later, desiring to pursue spiritual things further, I left school and entered Dora Yu's Bible Institute in Shanghai. However, before long she politely dismissed me, and I returned home. The reason she gave for her action was that it was inconvenient for me to stay there any longer. I realized that my flesh had not been dealt with. I was still fond of good food and fine clothing, and I enjoyed sleeping until eight o'clock in the morning. Dora Yu felt I was good material for the Lord's interest and had good prospects, but when she discovered my laziness, she sent me home.

At that time I was thoroughly disappointed and felt my future was doomed. At that time I even questioned my salvation. But surely I was saved! I even considered that I was quite good and that I had been transformed in many ways, not realizing that there was much yet to be learned and much to be dealt with. Confident that the Lord had saved me and called me, I could not be disappointed. I admitted that I was not yet good enough, but I felt that with the passing of more time I would improve.

Since the time was not ripe for me to continue my spiritual pursuits, I decided to return to school. When my schoolmates saw me, they recognized that I had changed, but I had not changed thoroughly, for I still occasionally lost my temper and did some things wrong. There were times when I seemed very much like a saved person, but at other times I seemed very much like an unsaved person.

UNDER MARGARET BARBER

During his school days Watchman Nee's seeking after the Lord brought him into frequent contact with Margaret E. Barber. Miss Barber, an Anglican missionary, was sent to Fukien, China, in the latter part of the last century. Her co-missionaries became jealous of her and fabricated a serious charge which caused her to be recalled from the field. Miss Barber had come to know the Lord in a living way. She had deeply experienced the cross and practiced continually the lessons of the cross. For this reason, she decided not to vindicate herself concerning the charges made against her. She remained at home in Great Britain for a number of years. At a certain point, the chairman of the mission board became aware that the case against her was misrepresented, and he asked her to tell him the truth. He said he realized that she was seeking to learn the lesson of the cross and that she would say nothing in her own defense, but as one in authority over her, he commanded her to tell the truth. Miss Barber then told the whole story. She was fully vindicated before the mission board, and the decision was made to send her back to China. However, she resigned from the mission, considering that it was the right time to do so, even though she still had the burden to return to China for the Lord's interest.

Before this time Miss Barber had come in contact with
D. M. Panton. Mr. Panton was both a great student of the
Word and one who had learned the evils of denominationalism. Through her relationship with him, Miss Barber also
became clear concerning the denominations.

After spending much time in prayer, she felt the Lord
Himself was sending her back to China. She did return to
China, but this time not in connection with any mission. From
a human standpoint, she went back on her own in the early
part of this century. She settled in a suburb of Foochow,
Watchman Nee's home city. She lived there with little
traveling and no publicity. She simply remained at home,
praying much for the Lord's move in China and helping those
who sought her counsel in seeking after the Lord. She was,
no doubt, a seed sown in China by the Lord for His recovery.
She composed a number of poems, many of which have been
adapted for inclusion in our hymnbook (*Hymns*, published by
Living Stream Ministry). All of them exhibit a deep experience in Christ.

Margaret Barber lived by faith. She had no outward
means of support. According to Chinese custom, all bills must
be fully paid at the end of the year. But at the end of one year,
she discovered she was short one hundred twenty Chinese
dollars. With only two days remaining until the Chinese new
year, she prayed desperately to the Lord for this need. On the
last day of the year, a cable arrived from D. M. Panton in
London through the British bank in Foochow. The amount
sent was exactly one hundred twenty Chinese dollars.

Through his relationship with Miss Barber, Watchman
Nee was greatly edified and perfected. Whenever he had a
problem or needed spiritual instruction or strengthening, he
would go to her. She treated him as a young learner and
frequently administered strict discipline.

At that time over sixty young brothers and sisters received
help from Miss Barber. Being deep in the Lord and exceedingly
strict, she frequently rebuked the young people concerning
many things. After a short time most of these young people
stopped going to her. The only one who continued to see her
was Watchman Nee. When he visited her, she rebuked and

reproved him. Frequently she pointed out that as a young man
he could not serve the Lord in this way or that way. However,
the more she rebuked him, the more he returned to be rebuked.
By deliberately putting himself before her to be rebuked, he
received untold help.

On February 7, 1950, in his fellowship with the church
in Hong Kong, he said, "There were sixty-six young people
under Sister Barber's training. In the first letter I received
from Brother D. M. Panton, he said that it would be considered good if after ten years six of those young people would
still remain. Now, after a long period of time, only four
remain."

Margaret Barber was very much in the Lord's presence.
One day Watchman Nee went to see her. While he was
temporarily delayed in being received by her, he waited in her
living room. He said that even though she was not yet there,
he had a deep sense of the Lord's presence.

Day by day Miss Barber anticipated the Lord's return. On
the last day of a certain year, as the two of them walked
together, they neared a street corner. She said, "Perhaps as we
turn the corner we will meet Him." She eagerly anticipated
the Lord's coming back. She lived and worked under the hope
of the Lord's return.

In 1933 Watchman Nee visited Europe. Throughout all his
travels he said that he scarcely found one person in the
Western world who could compare with Margaret Barber. It
was through this sister that he obtained the foundation of the
spiritual life. He frequently told others that it was through a
sister that he was saved and that it was also through a sister
that he was edified.

Margaret Barber went to be with the Lord in 1930. In her
will she left all her belongings to Watchman Nee. These
included little more than her old Bible with all the precious
notes. Though he intended to write her biography, time did
not allow.

In his open letter in the March 1930 issue of *The Present
Testimony,* Watchman Nee made the following remarks concerning Miss Barber's departure: "We feel most sorrowful
concerning the news of the passing away of Miss Barber in

Lo-Hsing Pagoda, Fukien. She was one who was very deep in the Lord, and in my opinion, the kind of fellowship she had with the Lord and the kind of faithfulness she expressed to the Lord are rarely found on this earth."

Miss Barber always put Watchman Nee under Leland Wang (Wang Tsai), one of his co-workers. Leland was five years his senior and was continually disagreeing with Watchman's concept. This caused Watchman a great deal of suffering. When appealing to Miss Barber for the solution to their problems, she would continually put him down, saying that Leland was older than he. On one occasion a baptism was scheduled. Who should be the baptizer became a problem to them. Watchman referred the matter to Miss Barber. Her answer was that Leland should be the baptizer. When Watchman asked why, she answered, "Because he is older than you." Dan-wu, another brother with them, was older than Leland Wang. Watchman thought he could defeat Leland Wang by bringing up Dan-wu and suggested to Miss Barber, "Since Brother Wu is older than Brother Leland, he should be the baptizer." However, she still answered that Leland should be the baptizer. She would not yield him any ground so that he might learn the lesson of the cross and learn not to reason but to submit.

His Personal Testimony
Given at Kulangsu, Fukien, October 18, 1936

In 1923 seven of us worked together as co-workers. Two of us took the lead, a co-worker who was five years my senior and myself. We had a co-workers' meeting every Friday in which the other five were often forced to listen to the arguing between the leading two. We were all young then, and each had his own way of thinking. I often charged the elder co-worker with being wrong, and vice versa. Since my temperament had not been dealt with, I frequently lost my temper. Today in 1936 I do sometimes laugh, but I seldom laughed at that time. In our controversies I admit that many times I was wrong, but he was also at times in the wrong. It was easy for me to forgive my own faults, but not easy to forgive others. After having

a dispute on Friday, I would go to Sister Barber on Saturday and accuse the other co-worker. I would say, "I told
that co-worker that he should act in a certain way, but he
would not listen. You should speak to him." Sister Barber
replied, "He is five years older than you; you should listen
to him and obey him." I answered, "Am I to listen to him
whether he is reasonable or not?" She said, "Yes! The
Scriptures say that the younger should obey the elder." I
replied, "I cannot possibly do this. A Christian should act
according to reason." She answered, "Whether there is
reason or not, you need not care. The Scriptures say that
the younger should obey the elder." I was angry at heart
that the Bible would say such a thing. I wanted to give vent
to my indignation, but I could not.

Each time following the controversy on Friday, I would
go to her to state my grievances, but she would again
quote the Scriptures, demanding that I obey the elder.
Sometimes I wept Friday evening after the dispute on
Friday afternoon. Then I would go to Sister Barber the next
day to state my grievances, hoping that she would vindicate me. But I would weep again after coming home
Saturday evening. I wished I had been born a few years
earlier. In one controversy I had very good arguments. I
felt that when I pointed them out, she would see how my
co-worker was wrong and would support me. But she said,
"Whether that co-worker is wrong or not is another matter.
While you are accusing your brother before me, are you
like one who is bearing the cross? Are you like a lamb?"
When she questioned me in this way, I felt very ashamed
and I could never forget it. My speech and my attitude that
day revealed that I was indeed not like one bearing the
cross, nor like a lamb.

In such circumstances I learned to obey an elder co-
worker. In that year and a half, I learned the most precious
lesson in my life. My head was filled with ideas, but God
wanted to see me enter into spiritual reality. In that year
and a half, I came to realize what it is to bear the cross.
Today in 1936 we have some fifty co-workers. Had it not
been for the lesson of obedience which I learned in that

year and a half, I fear that I could not work together with anyone. God put me in those circumstances that I might learn to be under the restraint of the Holy Spirit. In those eighteen months I had no opportunity to put forward my proposals. I could only weep and painfully suffer. But had it not been for this, I would never have realized how difficult it was for me to be dealt with. God wanted to polish me and to remove all my sharp, projecting edges. This has been a difficult thing to accomplish. How I thank and praise God, whose grace has brought me through!

Now I must speak a word to the young co-workers. If you cannot stand the trials of the cross, you cannot become a useful instrument. It is only the spirit of a lamb that God takes delight in: the gentleness, the humility, and the peace. Your ambition, lofty purpose, and ability are all useless in the sight of God. I have been down this path and must often confess my shortcomings. All that pertains to me is in the hand of God. It is not a question of right or wrong; it is a question of whether or not one is like the bearer of the cross. In the church, right and wrong have no place; all that counts is bearing the cross and accepting its breaking. This produces the overflowing of God's life and accomplishes His will.

CHAPTER FOUR

TAUGHT AND ENLIGHTENED

Watchman Nee did not attend a theological school or Bible institute. Most of what he learned concerning Christ, the things of the Spirit, and church history was acquired through studying the Bible and reading the books of spiritual men.

STUDYING THE BIBLE

From the beginning of his Christian life, Watchman Nee diligently studied the Bible. The methods he used for Bible study were as follows:

1) A general study of all the books of the Bible consecutively to acquire an overall view.

2) The study of a particular book, such as Genesis, Daniel, Matthew, Romans, or Revelation, to probe the depths contained in that part of the Word.

3) The study of particular subjects, such as the better covenant, the dispensations, the second coming of Christ, the kingdom, and the rapture, to apprehend the full scope of certain truths.

4) The study of single words, such as redemption, forgiveness, justification, reconciliation, salvation, righteousness, and holiness, to learn the basic meaning of certain crucial words.

5) The study of types, such as the tabernacle, the altar, the ark, the temple, and the offerings, to get a clear picture of Christ, the church, and spiritual things.

6) The study of allegories, such as Sarah and Hagar (Gal. 4:24), Jacob's well (John 4:12-14), and the rivers of living water (John 7:38), to realize the significance of such spiritual matters.

7) The study of the parables, such as the seven parables in Matthew 13, the parable of the ten virgins, and the parable

of the talents, to understand the depths of these deeper mysteries.

8) The study of numbers, such as the numbers three, five, seven, eight, and twelve, to understand their significance in the Scriptures.

9) The study of prophecies, such as prophecy concerning Israel, prophecy concerning the church, and prophecy concerning the Gentiles, to understand the truth in the Bible concerning the ages.

10) The study of the lives of certain biblical characters, such as Abraham, David, Daniel, Peter, and Paul, to learn from the example of their lives in the Scriptures.

11) The study of history, such as the history of Israel and the history of the church, to see how God administrates in His government.

12) The study of psalms and songs, such as psalms in the book of Psalms and songs in other books, to learn how to praise and pray.

13) A study comparing one portion of the Bible with another similar portion or dissimilar portion.

14) A study referring to the original Hebrew or Greek text to acquire the accurate meaning of a certain word or phrase.

15) A study using the writings of others to receive their help, inspiration, and balancing point of view.

16) A study to acquire knowledge and to receive light from the Bible. He used a special copy of the Bible for making notes and remarks for this purpose. He instructed others to study the whole Bible once a year, reading three chapters of the Old Testament and one chapter of the New Testament daily for this purpose.

17) A study for life, to receive daily bread for the spiritual life. For this purpose he used a different Bible without any remarks or notes that he might receive new light for spiritual nourishment. He instructed others to do the same every morning by reading a few verses and digesting them thoroughly while contacting the Lord with a praying spirit.

18) A study done by speed-reading, to acquaint himself with the Bible. Around the age of twenty, he read through the New Testament weekly for approximately one year.

19) A study done by reading slowly to ponder over certain portions of the Word.

20) A study done by memorizing certain crucial verses or portions to store the Word in the heart for constant and instant needs.

By studying the Bible in so many different ways, Watchman Nee became fully familiar with the Word and enlightened concerning the purpose of God, Christ, the church, and the things relating to salvation and life.

READING SPIRITUAL BOOKS

Watchman Nee was not only an excellent student of the Bible; he was also a studious reader of spiritual books. He was brilliantly gifted in being able to select, comprehend, discern, and memorize appropriate material. He could easily grasp the points of a book at a glance. Through reading Christian publications, he was not only helped to receive spiritual light and life; he also became knowledgeable regarding church history and Christianity in the Western world. Through Margaret Barber he became familiar with the books of D. M. Panton, Robert Govett, G. H. Pember, Jessie Penn-Lewis, T. Austin-Sparks, and others. He also collected the writings of the Brethren teachers, such as John Nelson Darby, William Kelly, and C. H. Mackintosh. In addition to these he also collected the writings of many others. In the early days of his ministry, he spent one-third of his income for personal needs, one-third for helping others, and the remaining third to buy books. He had an arrangement with some used bookstores in London that whenever they acquired a book for which he had placed an order, it was to be sent automatically. In this way he collected nearly all the classical Christian writings from the first century on. He acquired a collection of more than three thousand of the best Christian books, which included books on church history, biographies and autobiographies of outstanding Christians, and the central messages and commentaries of spiritual writers. When he was twenty-three years of age, his bedroom was nearly filled with books. There were books on the floor and a row of books on either side of his bed, with only a narrow space in the middle to lie down. It was often said that he was buried in books. By reading these books, along with diligently studying the Bible, he not only acquired much learning concerning the content of the Bible; he also became balanced in his views. By such study he was also helped to realize more truths than all his predecessors. This greatly strengthened and enriched his ministry for the Lord's recovery. He picked up all the good, scriptural points from the church fathers' writings through the writings of all the prominent writers of all the centuries down to the present and put them together into his practice of the Christian life and of the church life.

Watchman Nee studied the hymnals of different Christian groups along with the songs and poetry of many authors. He became familiar with ten thousand hymns, songs, and poems. From these writings he also received light and spiritual help.

The help he received from reading books can be classified as follows:

1) He received help concerning the assurance of salvation from the works of George Cutting, a Brethren writer.

2) John Bunyan's *Pilgrim's Progress* and Madame Guyon's biography, along with Hudson Taylor's biography and the writings of other mystics, helped him in the matter of life.

3) He was greatly helped on the matter of Christ from the writings of J. G. Bellett, Charles G. Trumbull, A. B. Simpson, T. Austin-Sparks, and others.

4) Andrew Murray's book, *The Spirit of Christ*, was a great help concerning the Spirit.

5) The writings of Jessie Penn-Lewis and Mrs. Charles McDonough assisted him in understanding the three parts of man.

6) He found George Müller's autobiography enlightening concerning faith.

7) Light concerning the matter of abiding in Christ was received from the books of Andrew Murray and the biography of Hudson Taylor.

8) He received help on the subjective aspect of Christ's death and on spiritual warfare from the books of Jessie Penn-Lewis.

9) The writings of T. Austin-Sparks and others were especially helpful concerning the truths of Christ's resurrection and His Body.

10) Concerning God's plan of redemption, Mary McDonough's book by the same title was a great help.

11) Light concerning the church was received from the writings of John Nelson Darby and other Brethren teachers.

12) The writings of Robert Govett, D. M. Panton, G. H. Pember, and other Brethren writers were helpful in the matter of prophecy.

13) The insights of John Foxe, E. H. Broadbent, and others were especially helpful in the matter of church history.

14) Watchman Nee especially received help on expounding the Bible and on many other truths, in general, from the writings of Darby and the Brethren.

CHAPTER FIVE

BURDENED AND COMMISSIONED

Watchman Nee's study of the Bible and his reading of many spiritual books greatly enlightened him regarding God's economy. It was according to the revelations which he received from the Lord that he was burdened to work for the Lord. This burden was actually the Lord's commission to him for His recovery in this age. His burden fell into several categories.

TO PREACH THE GOSPEL

Watchman Nee's initial burden was to preach the gospel. Shortly after he was saved, he began to love the Lord and was intensely burdened to preach the gospel to his schoolmates and countrymen. He did this in season and out of season. For a period of time, he fasted every Saturday that he might have power to preach the gospel in the Sunday morning preaching meeting. Through his preaching nearly all his schoolmates were led to the Lord, and a revival was brought into his school. This revival, with the help of his co-workers' preaching, spread extensively to the people of his hometown in 1923. Hundreds were saved and had their lives changed. During this same period he also wrote a number of long gospel messages for publication. Through these endeavors he not only brought many sinners to the Lord and helped the church in Foochow increase; he also laid a solid foundation and a good example of gospel preaching for us. Through the years, wherever the Lord's recovery has gone, gospel preaching has been stressed and practiced. This is why hundreds of unbelievers among the Chinese people have been brought to the Lord for the spread of His kingdom.

TO EDIFY THE YOUNG BELIEVERS

Following gospel preaching, Watchman Nee was burdened

to help young believers in the following five areas: 1) in their Christian walk, 2) in the growth of life, 3) in knowing the Bible, 4) in knowing the errors of denominationalism, and 5) in knowing the church. He instructed them in how to make a thorough confession of their sins to God, how to be reconciled with others, how to make a full clearance of the past, how to overcome sin, how to forsake the world, how to consecrate themselves to the Lord, how to study the Bible, how to pray, how to lead others to the Lord, how to meet and fellowship with the saints, how to seek the Lord's will, how to follow the inner anointing, how to live by faith, how to renounce the sects, and how to keep the unity of the Body. To fulfill this purpose he dedicated his time for two years to publish a monthly magazine entitled *The Christian* which received wide circulation. Thousands of copies of each issue were printed, and hundreds of young followers of the Lord were immensely edified by these messages.

TO TEACH THE TRUTHS

Watchman Nee was also burdened to help believers have a right understanding of spiritual things concerning the Lord's interest and to teach them the truths of the Bible. In his early ministry he held a study on the book of Revelation. Following that, he held a thorough study with the church in Shanghai on the Gospel of Matthew, on the rapture and tribulation, on how to meet, and on a number of other subjects. Since he knew the Bible thoroughly, he desired to expound the Bible book after book, but the Lord frustrated this intention. He then realized that the Lord was burdening him and commissioning him concerning two things: 1) to bear a specific testimony of the Lord, and 2) to establish local churches.

TO BEAR A SPECIFIC TESTIMONY OF THE LORD

First, he himself learned to know the Lord in a deep way by experiencing His all-inclusive death and resurrection. Because of his own experience along this line, he was specifically burdened and commissioned by the Lord to bear testimony to this truth. For the discharge of this burden, he released spoken messages and also issued a magazine, called *The Present Testimony,* in which he published messages on the subjective aspect of the Lord's crucifixion and resurrection, on the principles of life, on the supremacy of Christ, and on God's eternal purpose. He also held conferences and special meetings through the years to release messages on these deeper themes. In his open letters (chapter twenty-five of this book) he made this more than clear.

TO ESTABLISH LOCAL CHURCHES

Second, Watchman Nee's ultimate burden was to establish and build up local churches for the satisfaction of God's desire. This was his ultimate commission from the Lord, based on what he had seen and experienced of the Lord. His vision was that the preaching of the gospel, the edifying of believers, the teaching of biblical truth, and the bearing of a specific testimony of the Lord should be according to God's economy for the establishment and building up of local churches. These things are not God's goal; they are only procedures to accomplish God's goal, which is the establishment and building up of local churches. God desires to have local churches according to His New Testament economy; this is His eternal purpose. This is clearly and emphatically revealed in the New Testament, and this is the central point of the New Testament revelation. Watchman Nee, like the apostle Paul, was fully burdened and commissioned with this revelation. He was very much welcomed by all Christians in preaching the gospel, in edifying believers, in teaching biblical truths, and in bearing the specific testimony of the Lord. However, he was rejected by the majority of Christians in the matter of establishing and building up local churches. Some Christian leaders and teachers not only opposed him but also condemned him in this matter. Even some of his admirers say in their writings that Watchman Nee was wrong in his view of the church. Today, throughout the whole world, nearly all Christian bookstores carry his books, but very few stock his books on the church. This is due to the ignorance prevailing in the Christian world concerning the importance of the church in God's economy. Watchman Nee suffered a great deal because of his faithfulness to the Lord's commission concerning the church. He definitely saw a vision and received a commission concerning this matter. Because the vision was so clear and the commission so real, he did not care that he was rejected, opposed, and condemned. He anticipated this response and was determined to pay the price for the commission he received of the Lord. His faithfulness to this commission cost him his life.

HIS PERSONAL TESTIMONY GIVEN
AT KULANGSU, FUKIEN, OCTOBER 20, 1936

During the period between 1921 and 1923, revival meetings were held to lead people to the Lord. At that time preaching the gospel was believed to be the unique work for God. But God opened my eyes to see that His purpose requires that those who have been saved by grace stand upon the ground of oneness in local churches to represent and maintain God's testimony on earth. Some of my co-workers had different views of the truth concerning the church. But when I carefully studied the book of Acts, I realized that God's wish is to establish local churches in each city. At that time the light shone upon me so clearly that I recognized that this is His purpose.

At the same time I received this light, a problem arose with some co-workers who held different views regarding important points of our work. This resulted in friction among us. They felt that we should be zealous in revival and gospel preaching work and that the fruit of such work could be easily seen. My view, however, was to establish local churches with less stress on the revival and preaching side. When an older co-worker went out to hold gospel meetings, as he frequently did, I was at times tempted to secretly hold revival gospel meetings of my own. However, instead of doing this, when he was away, I immediately acted according to the vision I had received. Upon his return, he would undo what I had done and work according to his concept. But when he was again absent, I would go back to my previous way. Consequently, we oscillated back and forth on this matter all the time. Since the light each of us had received in respect to the work was different, our ways of working were also different. One way was that of revival and evangelism, while the other way was that of establishing local churches. What the Lord revealed to me was extremely clear: Before long He would raise up local churches in various parts of China. Whenever I closed my eyes, the vision of the birth of local churches appeared....

When the Lord called me to serve Him, the primary objective was not to hold revival meetings, help people hear more scriptural doctrines, or for me to become a great evangelist. The Lord revealed to me that He desired to build up local churches in various places to manifest Himself and to bear the testimony of unity on the ground of the local churches. In this way, each saint is able to function in the church and live the church life. What God wants is not individuals trying to be victorious or spiritual; He wants a corporate glorious church presented to Himself.

CHAPTER SIX

OBEYING THE SCRIPTURES
AND DROPPING THE TRADITIONS

One year after being saved, Watchman Nee began to obey the Scriptures and drop the traditions in the matters of baptism and the breaking of bread; he also left his denomination. The following is an excerpt from an account given by him in Shanghai on December 4, 1932, and published in the thirty-third issue of *Notes on Scriptural Messages* in 1933.

QUESTIONING

I was saved in the spring of 1920. During the first year following my conversion, I was unclear regarding the truths of the church, except that the sister who led me to the Lord had told me that unfortunately there were too many nominal Christians in the church today. I also felt that the character of the pastors I knew was too poor, for one did not ordinarily see them except when they came to ask for donations. Before my family was revived, we frequently had several mahjong games going on at home. When the pastor would come for donations, we conveniently handed him money from the mahjong table. Although he knew quite well where the money came from, he still accepted it. From this observation, I felt that the character of the pastors was very poor, for as long as they had money all was well. Besides this, it seemed that so many members in the church were merely nominal.

BAPTIZED

In March 1921 the Lord showed me the truth of baptism. I saw that baptism by sprinkling as practiced by the denominations was not scriptural. As I studied the Bible in those weeks, I found that when the Lord Jesus was baptized in the Jordan River, He came up out of the water. In the denominations, however, when a person was baptized, a small bowl was used to contain the water. How then could one come up out of the water? When I was young, I was baptized by a bishop of the Methodist Church. He sprinkled cold water on my head and pressed it down with his two big hands. I became impatient and cried, wishing he would get it over with quickly. After being sprinkled, I received a certificate of baptism, which bore my name and the bishop's signature. This certificate I considered absolutely meaningless. If I had not come to believe in the Lord, even though I had that certificate, I would still dare to do anything. Fortunately, I was later saved and my life was changed. My mother had arranged for me to be sprinkled before I believed in the Lord. About a year after I was saved, I realized that the baptism I had received was wrong and that according to the Scriptures baptism should be by immersion.

On the morning of March 28, 1921, my mother asked, "If I were to be baptized by immersion, how would you feel?" I replied, "That is just what I have been waiting for." She asked, "Where can we go to be baptized by immersion?" I answered, "I inquired about it quite some time ago. We can go to Mawei (which is two hours away from Foochow by small steamer) and find out from Miss Barber. When Dora Yu came to Fukien, she was baptized by immersion at Miss Barber's place." We felt that rather than choose a date, it was better to do it that same day. So my mother and I decided to depart that very same day. Upon arriving at Miss Barber's, we told her of our intention and she fully agreed. Thus, on the same day we went hurriedly to the countryside of Yangchi and were immersed there.

When I was baptized by immersion, I experienced a great turn in my life. The first thing I did was tell my friend Leland Wang. I came to know him during the first year after my salvation through a Bible study class held in our home. Since most of the attendants were elderly folk, and I was a young kid, I was unable to find anyone my age to talk to. Two or three weeks later, Brother Wang came.

Since he was closer to my age, I began to communicate with him. So on the following day after being baptized by immersion, I went and told him, "I went to Yangchi yesterday and was immersed there." He said, "Very good, very good. Formerly, I was also baptized by sprinkling in Nanking, but later in Amoy I met a brother who told me the truth concerning baptism. Due to this further light I was baptized by immersion in Kulangsu." We were quite happy because we had both seen the same light.

The second thing I did was tell the old pastor who led our Bible study. In Foochow he was the most advanced in knowing the Bible. I especially desired to tell him because he had taught us that we should do everything according to the Scriptures. However, though I was quite excited when I told him, his attitude was quite cold. So I asked, "Is baptism by immersion scriptural or not?" He replied, "Yes, it is scriptural, but do not be so legal." I thought this was peculiar. Having taught us the Bible for a year, he continually said that as long as it is the teaching of the Scriptures, it should be followed. Since baptism by immersion is scriptural, why did he say, "Do not be so legal?" I had obeyed the truth, yet he said, "Do not be so legal." I realized then that in his teaching there was compromise. If concerning this matter he would say do not be so legal, it was unlikely he would be bold to say that any other truth concerning the church should be obeyed. From that point on, I began to have doubts regarding the truths of the church which he taught. I also realized that I must put man's authority aside, and I determined that from then on I would carefully study the Bible.

BREAKING BREAD

In this same year (1921) I went to the Bible regarding a number of questions. I said to myself, "There are so many nominal Christians in the present day church, yet the Bible says that only the saved ones are in the church. There are so many denominations today, yet there is no Methodist Church, Presbyterian Church, or any other denomination in the Bible. Why then am I a member of the Methodist

Church? Since God's Word is not saying it, why am I doing it?" The Methodist bishop was a good friend of our family. Being a personal friend of the bishop was one thing, but the fact that denominations are unscriptural was another thing. I saw that the system of pastors was not scriptural and that meetings should be practiced according to scriptural principles. In the beginning the light I had on these matters was small. I was like the blind man in Mark 8 who, although he could see men, could only see them as trees walking. I had seen a little, but I did not see clearly.

One afternoon in the first half of 1922, I was much troubled concerning the matter of the breaking of bread. I had seen from the Bible that believers should often come together to break bread in remembrance of the Lord. For this reason I said to myself, "Why is it that in the church today the breaking of bread is held only four times a year?" Besides, among the ones who came to break bread, some were regular movie-goers, some were habitual mahjong players, some even questioned whether or not the Lord Jesus could be considered a good man, and some were evidently not even children of God. When I saw such people going to receive Holy Communion, I began to consider whether or not I could go. No! I could not go. Following my salvation, up to 1922, I had never been to receive the so-called Holy Communion. For many days I searched the Bible concerning this matter of breaking bread. Was a pastor required to preside over it? Was it true that only those who had received ordination could break it, while those who had not received ordination could not? I spent much time studying but found nothing like this in the Scriptures. This matter of a pastor presiding over the breaking of bread was not in the Bible. At this point I was very troubled. Though I wished so and though the Bible said that we should often break bread in remembrance of the Lord, I had no such place to break bread.

One Thursday afternoon following the Bible study, I sought out my friend, Leland Wang, for a little talk. I shared my feeling that according to the Bible we should break bread often in remembrance of the Lord, but that I had not done it once since being saved. I also mentioned that there were some in the denominations who were clearly not the children of God and with whom I could not break bread, and that there was the further problem that according to them no one could break bread except the pastor. I told him, "Neither you nor I are pastors; so even if we gathered all the true believers together, we would be considered unqualified to break bread. Isn't this puzzling?" Brother Wang took my hands and said, "God has been leading me exactly the same way. Last night I could not sleep, but was continually praying and searching concerning this very matter of whether or not believers should break bread, and whether or not it is necessary for a pastor to preside over it. I realized from my prayer and searching that in no place does it say that only ordained pastors can break bread." When I heard this, I thanked the Lord because He had been leading us in the same way. Since we had clearly seen the principles of meeting in the Bible, I said, "No day is better to begin than today; let us begin breaking bread on the coming Lord's Day."

Since we were settled on the time to begin, we began to discuss the place. Our house was larger, but I had not told my mother how I felt about this matter, lest she think that we young people were rebelling. Leland Wang was living in a house borrowed from a girls' school and was moving soon, so he felt it would not be too convenient. I said, "It does not matter; let us meet at your place." After we had made that decision, I was exceedingly happy on Friday and Saturday, for I was anticipating the happy day which was soon coming. When the evening of the Lord's Day came, I informed my mother that I was going to Leland Wang's home. She asked, "What for?" I replied, "To take care of something very important." That night three of us (Leland Wang, his wife, and I) met in his little house to break bread and drink the cup together. As long as I live, and even into eternity, I will remember that experience. I was never so close to the heavens as on that night! That night the heavens came near to the earth! All three of us could not help but weep! On that day we knew what it meant to break bread in remembrance of the Lord. As a young boy, after being sprinkled, I had partaken of the Holy Communion. My response at that time was, "The bread is rather sour and the grape juice is rather sweet." I understood nothing regarding the significance of breaking bread; I only realized that the bread was sour and the juice was sweet. But when the three of us broke bread that night in Leland Wang's home, I knew that this was a most precious matter to God. On that first occasion we learned what it meant to worship and remember the Lord. We could do nothing but give praise and thanks to Him.

After the first meeting we asked ourselves, What about the next meeting? Some denominations observed the breaking of bread every three months, but what about us? The Bible tells us to remember the Lord often. We felt from reading Acts 2, that at that time the breaking of bread was probably a daily matter. Acts 20:7 says, "And on the first day of the week, when we gathered together to break bread." This is very clear. On the basis of the word, therefore, we decided to observe the breaking of bread every Lord's Day. From that time on, except when I was ill, traveling on the road, or prevented by some unexpected event, I always broke bread every Lord's Day. Shortly afterward, my mother discovered what we were doing. She did not object; she only commented that we were too bold. Several months later, she also joined us in breaking bread.

Gradually the way the Lord was taking us began to have its outside effects. There was talk that several members of the Nee family were baptized by immersion. The district superintendent of the Methodist Church came to inquire of us concerning this matter. I said, "The only question is whether or not baptism by immersion is scriptural. If it is not scriptural, I am willing to stand before the congregation and confess my error; if it is scriptural, then I must obey." He only said, "Yes, it is scriptural, but you should not be so legal." If there was no need to be legal in one matter, there was no need to be legal in any matter. It surprised me to find that while the Methodists had originally been our good friends, now because of baptism by immersion, they turned quite cold toward us. From that day on I realized what it means to obey the Lord and that there is a price to do it. I also realized that people do not ordinarily consider baptism important; however, after one is baptized in a different way, they do consider it important.

LEAVING THE DENOMINATION

During the latter half of 1922, I uncovered another problem from the Bible—the problem of denominations. Do the Scriptures say that I should be a member of the Methodist Church? In 1 Corinthians 1 Paul exhorted the Corinthian believers not to be divisive by saying, "I am of Paul, and I of Apollos, and I of Cephas, and I of Christ." I began to consider: Was Wesley greater than Paul? If Paul rebuked the Corinthian believers for saying, "I am of Christ," surely for you to say that you are of the Presbyterian Church, while I am of the Methodist Church, and he is of the Baptist Church, is not scriptural.

At this time I was studying in a mission school. The school sent me as a delegate to a spring retreat and required on the application form that I state in what denomination I held membership. I wrote, "I am a Christian and I belong directly to Christ." They said, "Nevertheless, you are still a member of a denomination." I replied, "No, I am simply a Christian. The Bible does not say that I should be a member of any denomination." At that time I was determined not to confess with my mouth that I belonged to the Methodist Church. Whenever I was asked concerning this matter, I always replied, "I am a Christian."

One day while reading the Bible I was pondering this problem: Could I simply leave the denomination? Shortly after this I heard someone say that a certain department store went bankrupt. The conversation went like this: Whenever several people go into a business partnership, regardless of whether or not they are personally involved in the business of the store, once the business goes bankrupt, none can escape the consequences; everyone must share the responsibility of the bankruptcy. I realized from this conversation that as a member of the Methodist Church I was in a sort of partnership. Although in reality I did not take part in the system of the Methodist Church, in name I could not escape the consequences. If I wished to follow the Lord, not only must I refrain from being a member of the Methodist Church in deeds, but also I must have my name removed from the Methodist Church. Having become clear concerning this matter, I felt it necessary to discuss it with my mother, since originally it was she who placed my name there. My mother did not immediately approve of my intention, for she feared that the Western missionaries who were considered our good friends would be offended. My feeling was that we should not be afraid of people being offended by us; rather, we should be afraid of the One who is greater than men being offended by us.

One day I went by boat to Mawei to see Margaret Barber. I asked how she felt about my name being in the Methodist Church's book of life (what they called the church register). She replied, "I am afraid that among the names in that book of life many are dead and not a few are perishing." I said, "Should I have my name in a book of life on earth?" She replied, "If your name is recorded in the book of life in heaven, what good will an earthly book of life do you? And if your name is not recorded in the heavenly book of life, what will this earthly book of life profit you?"

I spoke to my mother persistently for two months regarding this matter, but still she would not agree. One day while my whole family was in the garden, I took the opportunity to speak to my parents. I said, "Is it scriptural to leave our name in the denomination?" They answered, "No." Again I said, "Is it our duty to obey the Bible?" "Yes," they replied. Then I pressed on, saying, "Then why do we delay and not obey the Scriptures?" They replied, "Very well. Do it; do it." Immediately, I drafted a letter, and my father personally wrote out the letter. After each of us signed it, I dispatched it by registered mail. In essence, the letter said this: "We have seen that sects are unscriptural and that denominationalism is sinful. Therefore, from this day on please remove our names from your book of life. We are doing this not because of any personal animosity, but simply because we wish to obey the teaching of the Scriptures. Our decision is final, and it will not be necessary to bring it up again. We still consider ourselves your friends. Besides our desire to obey the Bible, there is no other reason for our action."

Four days after the letter was mailed, several Western missionaries came to our home. They said, "One only hears of a church excommunicating its members, never of a member excommunicating himself from a church. What is the reason for your action?" We answered, "We have already explained our reason, and there is no need to discuss it further." The following day they asked the principal of a certain school to come speak to us. We said, "We have nothing to say. We are still your friends, but we wish our names to be removed from the record." Later, our pastor, the district superintendent, and the bishop all came asking whether we had taken this action because of baptism by immersion. They explained that if members of the Methodist Church wished to be baptized by immersion, there was no problem. We replied, "The Lord led us to do what we have done. You feel there is no need to be legal, but we feel we must obey the Lord at all cost."

It is not a question of arguing with others about baptism by immersion or about leaving the denominations. The only question is whether or not men are willing to obey the Scriptures. *To be baptized by immersion and to leave the denominations are not great things; they are but two items among thousands that require our obedience.* The main thing in the Scriptures is obedience.

CHAPTER SEVEN

LEARNING HOW TO
BRING PEOPLE TO THE LORD

WATCHMAN NEE'S PERSONAL TESTIMONY
GIVEN AT KULANGSU, FUKIEN, OCTOBER 18, 1936

After I was saved, I spontaneously loved the souls of sinners and hoped that they would be saved. To this end, I began to preach the gospel and to bear testimony among my schoolmates. After nearly a year's work, however, no one was saved. I thought the more words I could speak and the more reasons I could present, the more effective I would be in saving people. But though I had much to speak concerning the Lord, my words lacked power to move the listeners.

Prayer for Others' Salvation

About this time I met a Western missionary, Miss Groves (Margaret Barber's co-worker), who asked me how many persons I had brought to the Lord in the year following my salvation. I bowed my head, hoping to forestall further questioning, and shamefully admitted in a low voice that, although I had preached the gospel to my schoolmates, they did not like to listen, and when they did listen, they would not believe. My attitude was that, since they would not heed the gospel, they would have to bear the consequences. She spoke to me frankly, "You are unable to lead people to the Lord because there is something between God and you. It may be some hidden sins not yet completely dealt with, or something for which you are indebted to someone." I admitted that such things existed, and she asked if I were willing to settle them immediately. I answered that I was willing.

She also asked how I went about bearing testimony. I replied that I pulled people in at random and began to speak, regardless of whether they were listening or not. She said, "This is not right. You must speak to God first, before you speak to people. You should pray to God, make a list of your schoolmates' names, and ask God which of them you should pray for. Pray for them daily, mentioning them by name. Then when God affords the opportunity, you should bear testimony to them."

After that conversation, I immediately began to deal with my sins by making restitution, paying debts, being reconciled with my schoolmates, and confessing offenses to others. I also entered in my notebook the names of about seventy schoolmates and began praying for them daily, mentioning their names individually before God. Sometimes I prayed for them once every hour, praying silently, even in class. When opportunity arose, I would bear testimony to them and try to persuade them to believe in the Lord Jesus. My schoolmates often said jokingly, "Mr. Preacher is coming. Let us listen to his preaching." The fact was that they had no intention to listen.

I called on Miss Groves again and said to her, "I have fully carried out your instructions. Why is it not effective?" She replied, "Do not be disappointed. Keep praying until some are saved." By the Lord's grace, I continued to pray daily. When opportunity arose, I bore testimony and preached the gospel. Thank the Lord, after several months, all but one of the seventy persons whose names were in my notebook were saved.

To Be Filled with the Holy Spirit

Though some had been saved, I was still not satisfied, because many in the school and in the town were still not saved. I felt the need to be filled with the Holy Spirit and to receive power from above that I might be able to bring more people to the Lord. Then I called on Miss Margaret Barber. Being immature in spiritual matters, I asked her if it was necessary to be filled with the Holy Spirit in order to obtain power to bring many to salvation. She answered, "Yes." I asked her concerning the means to be filled with the Holy Spirit. She said, "You must present yourself to God that He may fill you with Himself." I replied that I had already presented myself. But when I considered, I knew that I was still my old self. I knew that God had saved me, chosen me, and called me. Though I had not yet attained absolute victory, I had been freed from sins and evil habits, and many matters hitherto entangling me had been abandoned. However, I still felt the lack of spiritual power to cope with spiritual work. Then she told me the following story:

Brother Prigin was an American who had been to China. He had obtained a master's degree and was studying for a Ph.D. Feeling the condition of his spiritual life unsatisfactory, he sought the Lord and prayed. He said to God, "I have very strong unbelief; some sins I cannot overcome, and I have no power to work." For two weeks he asked God specifically to fill him with the Holy Spirit that he might lead a victorious life with power. God said, "Do you really want this? If so, do not take the Ph.D. examination two months from now, for I have no need of a doctor of philosophy." He felt he was in a dilemma. The Ph.D. degree seemed a sure thing; it would be a pity not to sit for the examination. He knelt down to pray and ask why God would not allow him to get the degree and be a minister as well. But here is a strange thing: Once God has made a demand, He sticks to it and never compromises with anyone.

The following two months were most painful. On the last Saturday of that period he experienced real conflict within. Did he want the degree or did he want to be filled with the Holy Spirit? Which was better: a doctor's degree or a victorious life? Others could be doctors and yet be used by God as well— why couldn't he? He was struggling and reasoning with God and was at his wits' end. The Ph.D. was dear to him and so was the filling of the Holy Spirit.

But God would not give way. To choose a doctor's degree would make it impossible to live the spiritual life. To live the spiritual life would require forfeiting a doctor's degree. At length, with tears in his eyes, he said, "I submit. Despite my two years' study toward a Ph.D. degree, a goal which I have cherished for thirty years, ever since childhood, I have no alternative but to relinquish sitting for the examination for the sake of submission to God." Following this decision he wrote to notify the university authorities that he would not sit for the examination on Monday, thus abandoning hope for a Ph.D. degree once and for all. He was so exhausted that night that he could find no message to deliver the following day. So he simply told the congregation the story of his surrender to the Lord. On that day the congregation was revived. Three-quarters of them were in tears. He himself also gained strength. He said, "If I had known before that the result would be like this, I would have submitted earlier." His subsequent work was greatly blessed by the Lord, and he was one who had the deepest knowledge of God.

When I visited England, I intended to go on to the United States to meet him, but the Lord took him before I had the opportunity. But when I heard this testimony, I said to the Lord, "I am willing to remove anything standing between God and me in order to be filled with the Holy Spirit." Between 1920 and 1922 I went to at least two or three hundred people to confess offenses. After a further strict scrutiny of past events, I felt there was still something between God and me; otherwise, I would have had spiritual vitality. But despite further dealings in many ways, I still could not gain strength.

Dealt With by God

One day while seeking a theme from the Bible before delivering a message, I randomly opened the Bible and Psalm 73:25 appeared before my eyes: "Whom have I in heaven but thee? And there is none upon earth that I desire besides thee." After reading these words I said to myself, "The writer of this psalm can say that, but I cannot." I discovered then that there was something between me and God.

Since my wife is not present today, I will relate the story to you. About ten years before our marriage, I was in love with her. She was not then saved, and when I spoke with her about the Lord Jesus and tried to persuade her to believe, she laughed at me. I must admit that I did love her, but at the same time I suffered her laughter at the Lord I believed in. I also questioned at that time whether she or the Lord would have first place in my heart. I must say that once young people have fallen in love, they find it very difficult to give up their beloved. I told God of my willingness to give her up, but deep in my heart I was not willing. After reading Psalm 73 again, I said to God, "I cannot say that there is none upon earth that I desire besides Thee, because there is one on earth whom I love." At that instant, the Holy Spirit indicated clearly that there was something between God and me.

On that day I delivered a message, but I did not know what I was talking about. I was actually speaking to God, asking Him to be patient and impart strength to me until I could give her up. I asked God to postpone dealing with this matter. But God never reasons with people. I considered going to the frontier of desolate Tibet to evangelize and suggested many other enterprises to God, hoping that He might be moved not to raise again the question of my giving up the one I loved. But once God's finger has pointed to something, He will not withdraw it. No matter how hard I prayed, I could not get through. I had no enthusiasm for my studies in school, and at the same time I failed to acquire the power of the Holy Spirit, which I was earnestly seeking. I was in great distress. I prayed constantly, hoping that my earnest supplication might change God's mind. Thank the Lord that all along He wanted me to learn to deny myself, to lay aside human love, and love Him with a single heart. Otherwise, I would be a useless Christian in His hand. He cut down my natural life with a sharp knife so that I might learn a lesson which I had never learned before.

On one occasion I delivered a message and returned to my room with a heavy heart. I told God that I would return to school the following Monday and seek for the filling of the Holy Spirit and the love of Christ. During the following two weeks, I found that I still could not say with conviction the words of Psalm 73:25. But thank the Lord, soon afterwards I was filled with His love, and I was willing to lay my loved one down and loudly declare, "I will lay her aside! Never will she be mine!" After this declaration I was at long last able to utter the words of Psalm 73:25. On that day I was in the second heaven, if not the third. The world appeared smaller to me, and it was as if I were mounting the clouds and riding the mists. On the evening of my salvation, the burden of my sins rolled away, but on that day, February 13, 1922, when I laid aside my beloved, my heart was emptied of everything that previously occupied me.

[At that time Brother Nee wrote the following hymn:

> How vast, immense, and measureless
>   The love of Christ to me!
> How else could such a wretch as I
>   Be blessed so graciously?
>
> To bring me back unto Himself,
>   My Lord His all did spend;
> So I would gladly bear the cross
>   And follow to the end.
>
> My all I have forsaken now,
>   This blessed Christ to gain;
> Now life or death is no concern—
>   What else can me restrain?
>
> My dear ones, wealth, ambition, fame—
>   What can they offer me?
> My gracious Lord for me was poor;
>   For Him I poor would be.

My precious Savior now I love,
    Him only would I please.
For Him all gain a loss becomes,
    And comfort holds no ease.

Thou art my comfort, gracious Lord!
    I've none in heav'n but Thee.
And who but Thee is there on earth
    With whom I love to be?

Though loneliness and trials come,
    My griefs I'd rise above.
This only would I ask Thee, Lord:
    Surround me with Thy love!

O gracious Lord, I now beseech,
    Guide me through every stage;
Stand by and strengthen me to go
    Through this dark, evil age.

The world, the flesh, and Satan too,
    Do tempt my soul apace;
Without Thy love and strength'ning power
    I may Thy name disgrace.

The time, dear Lord, is running short;
    From earth my soul set free.
When Thou dost come, I'll sing with joy,
    Hallelujah to Thee!]

In the following week, people began to be saved. Brother Weigh, who was my classmate, can testify to the fact that up to this time I had been very particular about my dress. I used to wear a long silk gown with red dots. But on that day, I removed my refined clothing and shoes. I went to the kitchen, made some paste, and with a bundle of gospel posters in my arms, went to the street to post them on the walls and to distribute gospel tracts. In those days in Foochow, Fukien, this was a pioneer act.

From my second school term in 1922, I began the gospel work, and many of my schoolmates were saved. I prayed daily for those whose names were in my notebook. From 1923, we began to borrow or rent places for meetings to expand the work of evangelization. Several hundred people were saved at the same time. All but one of those whose names were in my notebook were saved. This is evident proof that God listens to such prayers. It is His way that we must first pray for sinners before they can be saved. In those few years there were many instances to confirm this fact.

CHAPTER EIGHT

LIVING IN THE PRESENCE OF GOD

Following his salvation, Watchman Nee first began bringing people to the Lord, and second he began learning to live in the Lord's presence. He discovered that anything between him and God was a hindrance to receiving answers to prayer. It was also a frustration to trusting God for his needs and kept him out of God's presence. At the same time he saw that he must make thorough confession of sins to God and fully rectify any wrongs regarding people. He was very strict in these two matters in order to maintain a good conscience without offense (1 Tim. 1:5; Acts 24:16). Whenever he was having a transaction with God regarding a certain matter, God would deal with him regarding the elimination of certain things to maintain his fellowship with God. He went on with God in this way through his entire life.

DEALING WITH SINS

In order to stay in God's presence, he repeatedly wrote to the saints confessing his wrongs, offenses, and faults, asking for forgiveness. He dealt with sins both before people and before God. Many times at the Lord's table he was heard to confess in prayer that he was sinful and to ask the Lord to forgive him. This indicated a conscience sensitive to anything sinful before God. His conscience was so keen because he always kept it pure by dealing with sins before men and God, leaving nothing undealt with. By keeping his conscience free of offense, he was able to maintain an intimate fellowship with God.

DEALING WITH WORLDLINESS

In order to live in the presence of God, Watchman Nee eliminated everything worldly from his life. He was absolutely separated from the world. There was no sign of worldliness in his home, in his manner of dress, or in anything related to his living. Although he did not do it in a legal way, he lived in an unworldly manner throughout his entire life. He would not observe any festival or celebrate a birthday because to his enlightened understanding these things were worldly.

He kept himself from worldliness not only in his living but also in his work. The way all his publications were designed bore no impression of the world, nor did any of the practices he introduced into the church have any flavor of the world.

Because he dealt with worldliness in such a strict fashion, he was continually kept in the presence of God. His manner of life exercised a strong influence upon all of us who were close to him and upon all the churches in the Lord's recovery which were benefited from his ministry.

DEALING WITH THE FLESH

The flesh is the worst part of fallen man and always fights against the Spirit of God (Gen. 6:3; Gal. 5:17). Watchman Nee fully realized this and always stood against his flesh and natural temperament in order to maintain an unbroken fellowship with the Lord and remain in the presence of God. His flesh was continually suppressed by simply living in the spirit and behaving according to the inner anointing. By living and behaving in this way, he was continually exercised in prayer for the Lord's deliverance. He feared his flesh and would do nothing according to his flesh, but continually walked according to his spirit that he might not lose God's presence.

DEALING WITH SELF

It was revealed to Watchman Nee that fallen man is saturated with Satan and can easily become the very embodiment and expression of Satan. This was Peter's experience in Matthew 16:21-23. In following the Lord Watchman Nee continually denied the self (Matt. 16:24) in order to continually enjoy the Lord's presence. He feared the self and condemned it more than any other negative thing. In his daily life, in his work, and in his contact with others, no trace of self could be found. Rather, his behavior and his work always left the impression that he was a person bearing the cross and denying the self. It was by such a living that he maintained the enjoyment of God's presence.

DEALING WITH SELF-PREFERENCE

Watchman Nee was fully aware of the self-preference which exists in the fallen nature of man. His conscience would not allow him to have any self-preference in spiritual things or in the Lord's work. He knew that King Saul lost his kingship and throne because of his self-preference (1 Sam. 15:1-28). Realizing that self-preference was more subtle than either sin or worldliness, he frequently touched people's conscience in this matter when speaking to them. He would not tolerate any self-preference to exist between himself and the Lord in order to maintain the presence of God.

DEALING WITH DISOBEDIENCE

Disobedience was another thing Watchman Nee dealt with in order to maintain fellowship in the Lord's presence. His experience was that nothing, not even good and spiritual things, can substitute for obedience. For him to obey the Lord meant to cleave to the Lord's purposed will; it did not mean to take His permissive will as Balaam did (Num. 22:2-35). Anything which deviates from the Lord's purposed will is a form of disobedience. For him disobedience was a veil which would separate him from God's presence. He stressed that for him to receive light and revelation from the Lord he needed an unveiled face. Margaret Barber told him, and he passed it on to his close associates, that a small leaf on a tree can block out the full moon from one's sight. Since he realized that disobedience would cause the loss of God's presence, he made it his purpose to obey the Lord's will and the Lord's revelation at any cost.

APPLYING THE BLOOD OF CHRIST

In order to keep his fellowship with the Lord untarnished, Watchman Nee learned how to apply the blood of Christ to his situation. He told me that once his conscience was strongly condemning him before God concerning certain things. He could not get through, so he was compelled to seek out Miss Barber for help. After relating his story to her, she said to him, "The blood of Jesus His Son cleanses us" (1 John 1:7). When he told her that he was still under condemnation she repeated to him several times, "The blood of Jesus His Son cleanses us." Eventually, he received light that only the blood of the Lord can keep one's conscience from any kind of condemnation before God. By that fellowship with Miss Barber, he learned that through the cleansing of the Lord's blood it is possible to keep oneself always in the presence of God.

In 1940 while I was attending his training in Shanghai, I heard him confessing sin and applying the Lord's blood in his prayer at the Lord's table. I was greatly impressed with his prayer. This indicated that he relied upon the cleansing of the Lord's blood to maintain a continual practice of God's presence.

ABIDING IN THE LORD

Watchman Nee also thoroughly learned the lesson of abiding in the Lord according to the inner anointing (1 John 2:27-28). To him this was vital for the practice of the presence of God. He realized that the inner anointing was the Lord's moving and working within him. To disobey the anointing was to disobey the Lord Himself. Only by obeying the inner anointing could he have the closest and most intimate walk with the Lord. He realized that even a little negligence regarding the inner anointing would keep him away from the presence of God.

By all the above practices, he kept himself continually in the presence of God. No shadow whatsoever was allowed to come between him and God, and his fellowship with the Lord was constantly maintained. It was in this kind of uninterrupted fellowship with the Lord that he continually received heavenly light and spiritual revelation. He greatly treasured God's presence. To him God's presence was life, light, power, and victory. In His presence he enjoyed all the riches of God's provision. It is obvious that he received much help from the book *The Practice of the Presence of God* by Brother Lawrence. In this matter he was also helped very much by the biography of Hudson Taylor.

CHAPTER NINE

LIVING BY FAITH

From the very beginning, Watchman Nee realized fully that he should live by faith, not only for his living, but also for the Lord's work. Thus he learned to trust in the Lord for all his needs. This forced him to pray much, to consecrate himself to the Lord absolutely, to thoroughly deal with the Lord, and to obey the Lord in everything. In order to trust God in a living and practical way, he needed to keep his conscience free of offense. He would often say that a hole in our conscience would cause our faith to leak out.

Living by faith kept him in the Lord's will. When living and working by our own means, we do not need to be restricted and limited by the Lord's will. We can do whatever we like, whenever we like, without needing to seek the Lord's will or to wait for His guidance. But to live by faith requires us to be restricted to the Lord's will; otherwise, when we pray in faith He will not answer. He will never support us and supply our need in anything we are doing according to our own preference. Through living by faith, Watchman Nee was preserved from being distracted by the outward appearance of the work. What he cared for was the Lord's will, not a booming work. His desire was to live by a faith that God would honor. He knew that if he performed any work which was not done in life and according to God's will, God would never respond to his faith. For this reason, both his personal life and his work were continually under restriction.

Down through the years, he continually exercised himself to live such a life of faith. In China he pioneered such a life. He became a strong example for all his close associates who had been called by the Lord to live and work for Him by faith.

WATCHMAN NEE'S PERSONAL TESTIMONY
GIVEN AT KULANGSU, FUKIEN,
OCTOBER 20, 1936

While praying last night, it seemed that the Lord wanted me to testify once again. Those who know me are aware that I seldom testify regarding my own affairs. It has been my observation that people often abuse others' testimonies, treating them as news for circulation. It is also true that some testimonies are not sufficiently founded. The third heaven experience of the apostle Paul was not disclosed to others until after fourteen years. Regarding many spiritual testimonies, an appropriate length of time should be allowed to elapse before they are divulged. Many, however, would speak them forth not in fourteen years, but in fourteen days.

Matters concerning Money

The matter of money can be either a small or a big problem. When I began to serve the Lord, I was somewhat anxious about the question of my livelihood. Had I been a preacher in a denomination, I would have been on a large monthly salary. But since I was to walk in the Lord's way, I would only rely upon Him to support me; I could not depend upon a monthly salary. In the years 1921 and 1922, very few preachers in China lived in sole reliance on the Lord. It was difficult to find even two or three; the great majority lived on salary. At that time many preachers were not bold enough to devote their entire time to serving the Lord; they felt that if they were not receiving a regular salary, they would not know how to face a situation in which they had nothing to live on. I also had such thoughts. In China today [1936] there are approximately fifty brothers and sisters in fellowship with us who live by relying solely on the Lord. Such a situation is more common now than it was in 1922. Brothers and sisters in various places today also care for the workers more than before. I think that after ten years or so, brothers and sisters will show even greater concern for the need of the servants of the Lord. But it was not very common ten years ago.

Declaring to My Parents
My Desire to Live by Faith

I have pointed out in a previous testimony that after I was saved I continued to study in school and at the same time work for the Lord. One evening I spoke with my father concerning the matter of receiving financial assistance. I said, "After praying for several days, I feel that I must tell you that I will no longer spend your money. I appreciate that you have spent so much on me in accord with your sense of fatherly responsibility. But you will expect me to earn money in the future and support you in return, and I must tell you beforehand that since I am going to be a preacher, I will not be able to repay you in the future nor pay you interest. Even though I have not completed my studies, I wish to learn to depend solely upon God." When I said this, my father thought I was joking. However, from then on, when my mother would occasionally give me five or ten dollars, she would write on the envelope: "To Brother Nee To-sheng." She was not giving me money as a mother.

After I had expressed myself thus to my father, the devil came to tempt me by saying, "Such an act is very dangerous. Suppose one day you are unable to maintain your living and you again approach your father for money. Won't that be disgraceful? You have spoken to your father too soon; you should have waited until there was more progress in your work, until many people had been saved and you had many friends, before you began to live a life of faith." But thank the Lord, ever since I expressed my decision to discontinue receiving my father's support, I have never asked him for money.

Looking to God for
Sustenance while Working

To the best of my knowledge, Sister Dora Yu was the only preacher at that time who did not receive a salary and

who depended wholly upon God for her living. She was
my spiritual elder sister, and we knew each other very
well. She had many friends, Chinese and foreign, and the
field of her work was very wide since she preached everywhere. But my condition was just the opposite; few cared
for me, so I found it rather difficult. Yet when I looked to
the Lord, He said to me, "If you cannot live by faith, you
cannot work for Me." I knew that I needed living work and
living faith to serve a living God. When once I found that
there was only about ten dollars in my wallet, which before
long would be fully spent, I suddenly recalled the widow
of Zarephath, who had only a handful of meal in the barrel
and a little oil in the cruse (1 Kings 17:12). There were not
two handfuls of meal. I did not know by what means God
sustained her, but I knew He had the means.

In 1921 two co-workers and I went to a place in Fukien
province to preach, intending to go from there to another
place. In my pocket were only four dollars, an insufficient
amount for three bus tickets. But, thank the Lord, a brother
gave us three tickets.

Again, at Kulangsu, in the south of Fukien province,
my money was stolen from my pocket, so that I had no
traveling expenses to return home. We were then staying
in someone's house and preached once a day in a small
chapel. We finished and were ready to leave. My two
co-workers had money to return home, but mine had been
stolen. (At that time each of us was spending his own
money.) They made the decision to leave on the following
day. When I heard this I was embarrassed, but I was not
willing to borrow money from them. That evening I prayed
to God, beseeching Him to provide the needed money for
traveling expenses. Nobody knew this. That afternoon
some people had come to speak with me about the Word,
but I was in no mood to do so. At that time the devil came to
tempt me and shake my faith, but I was firm in believing
that God would not let me down. I was then merely a
youth, just embarking on serving the Lord by faith; I had
not yet learned the lesson of living by faith. I continued
praying to God that evening, thinking that perhaps I had

done something wrong. The devil said, "You could ask the co-workers to buy your ticket, then repay them when you reach the provincial capital." I did not accept this suggestion and continued looking to God. When the time came for us to leave, there was still no money in hand. I packed my luggage as usual and hired a rickshaw. At that moment, I recalled the story of a brother who had no train ticket when the train was about to leave, but at that very instant, God ordered someone to give him a ticket. We were all ready and boarded the rickshaws, of which there were three. I took the last one. When the rickshaw had been pulled about forty yards, an old man in a long gown came from behind shouting, "Mr. Nee, please stop!" I ordered the rickshaw boy to halt. After handing me a parcel of food as well as an envelope, the old man departed. I was then so grateful for God's arrangement that my eyes were filled with tears. When I opened the envelope, I found four dollars inside, just sufficient for a bus ticket. The devil kept speaking to me, "Don't you see how dangerous it is?" I replied, "I was indeed a little anxious about it, but it is by no means dangerous, for God has supplied my need in time." After arriving in Amoy, another brother gave me a return ticket.

In 1923 Brother Weigh Kwang-hsi invited me to preach in Kien-ou in the north of Fukien province. I had only about fifteen dollars in my pocket, one-third of the traveling expenses. I decided to leave on Friday evening and continued my prayer on Wednesday and Thursday. The money, however, did not come in. I prayed again Friday morning. Not only was no money forthcoming, but also I had a feeling within that I should give five dollars to a certain co-worker. I recalled the Lord's words: "Give, and it will be given to you." I had not been a money lover, but on that day I really loved money and found it extremely difficult to give. I prayed to the Lord again, "O Lord, if You really want me to give away five dollars, I will," but I was still rather unwilling inwardly. I was deceived by Satan into thinking that after praying I would not have to give away the five dollars. That was the only time in my life that I shed tears over money. Eventually, I obeyed the

Lord and gave the five dollars to that co-worker. After the money was given, I was filled with heavenly joy. When the co-worker asked why I gave him the money, I said, "You need not ask; you will know later."

Friday evening I prepared to begin my journey. I said to God, "Fifteen dollars was already insufficient, and You wanted me to give away five dollars. Won't the sum be even more inadequate? Now I don't know how to pray." I made up my mind to go first to Shui-Kow by steamer and then to Kien-ou by a small wooden boat. I spent only a little for the journey to Shui-Kow. As the steamer was about to arrive, I felt that if I would not pray according to my own concept, the result would be much better. So I said to the Lord, "I do not know how to pray; please do it for me." I added, "If You will not give me the money, please provide a boat for me with a little fare." When I arrived in Shui-Kow, many boatmen came to solicit business. One asked only seven dollars for my passage. This price was beyond expectation; the usual fare was several times more. I asked the boatman why his price was so low, and he replied, "This boat is hired by the magistrate, but I am allowed to take one passenger only for the space at the stern, so I do not care how much the fare is. But you have to provide your own food." Originally, I had fifteen dollars in my pocket. After giving five dollars to a co-worker and spending a few dimes for the journey by steamer, seven dollars for the small wooden boat, and a dollar or so for food, there was still a dollar thirty left when I reached Kien-ou. Thank the Lord! Praise Him that His ordering is always good.

After I completed my work at Kien-ou and was ready to return to Foochow, the problem arose again: I did not have sufficient funds for traveling expenses to return. I had decided to leave on the following Monday, so I continued praying until Saturday. This time I had a feeling of certainty in my heart, recalling that before I left Foochow, God had asked me to give five dollars to a co-worker, which I then begrudged giving. At that time I read Luke 6:38: "Give, and it will be given to you," and I laid hold of this sentence. I said to God, "Since You have said this, I beseech You to provide me with the necessary money for traveling expenses according to Your promise."

On Sunday evening a British pastor, Mr. Philips, a true brother, assuredly saved and loving the Lord, asked Brother Weigh and me to dinner. At dinner Mr. Philips told me that he and his church had received great help through my messages, and they offered to be responsible for my traveling expenses both ways. I replied that there was already someone who had accepted this responsibility, meaning God. Then he said, "When you get back to Foochow, I will give you *The Dynamics of Service* written by Mr. Paget Wikes, a gospel messenger greatly used by the Lord in Japan." I soon felt that I had missed a great opportunity; what I needed then was money for traveling expenses, not a book. I somewhat regretted that I had not accepted his offer. After dinner Brother Weigh and I returned home together. I had refused Mr. Philips's offer for my traveling expenses so that I might look solely to God for help; nevertheless, there was joy and peace in my heart. Brother Weigh was unaware of my financial situation. I had a slight thought of borrowing money from him for my expenses and then reimbursing him when I returned to Foochow, but God would not allow me to divulge this matter to him. I was under full conviction that God in heaven is forever dependable, and I wished to see how He was going to provide for me.

When I left the following day, I had only a few dollars in my pocket. Many brothers and sisters came to see me off, and some carried my luggage. While walking I prayed, "Lord, surely You wouldn't bring me here without taking me back." Halfway to the wharf, Mr. Philips sent someone with a letter. The letter read, "Though someone else has assumed the responsibility for your traveling expenses, I feel that I should have a share in your work here. Would it be possible for me, an aged brother, to have such a share? Please be good enough to accept this small sum for this purpose." After reading the letter, I felt I should accept the money, and I did. It was not only sufficient for my return expenses to Foochow, but also for printing one issue of *The Present Testimony*.

Upon my return to Foochow, the wife of the co-worker who received the five dollars said to me, "I have the feeling that when you left you did not have enough money yourself. Why did you suddenly give five dollars to my husband?" I then asked her what had occurred in connection with the five dollars, and she replied, "We had only one dollar left in the house on Wednesday, and that had been spent by Friday. On Friday we prayed all day. Afterwards my husband felt that he should go for a walk, and then he met you, and you gave him five dollars. The five dollars lasted us through five days; then God provided for us from another source." At this point she continued with tears, "If you had not given us the five dollars on that day, we would have suffered hunger. It does not matter that we suffer hunger, but what about God's promise?" Her testimony filled me with joy. The Lord had worked through me to supply their need with the five dollars. The Word of the Lord is indeed faithful: "Give, and it will be given to you."

This is the lesson I have learned in my life. I have now experienced that the less money I have in my hand, the more God will give. This is a difficult path to follow. Many people may feel that they are able to live the life of faith; but when the trial comes, they are in fear. Unless you can believe in the real and living God, I do not advise you to take this path. I can bear testimony today that God is the One who gives. To be sustained by means of ravens as Elijah was at his time is still possible today. I am going to mention something to you which you may find difficult to believe. It has been my experience that God's supply arrives when I have spent my last dollar. I have had fourteen years of experience. In each experience God wanted to get the glory for Himself. God has supplied all my needs and has not failed me once. Those who used to give do not do so now. There is a constant change of offerers; one lot of people replaces another. All this does not matter, for God in the highest is a living God. He never changes! I say this today for your benefit. I must say this that you may go straight forward in the path of living a life of faith. There are ten to twenty more cases like these that I have already related to you.

Concerning the matter of offering the Lord money, one ought to set aside a definite amount—a tithe of your income or a half of your income—and put it in the hand of God. From her natural being, the widow who gave two half-farthings might have grudged doing so, but she was praised by the Lord. We have to be an example for others; we need not fear, for God will not fail. We should learn to love God, to believe Him, and to serve Him as is His due. We ought to thank Him and praise Him because of His unspeakable grace! Amen.

Looking to God for Sustenance for the Publication Work

Some people would never enter a meeting place to listen to the gospel. For this reason, in 1922 I began printing gospel tracts. The gospel must be delivered to them. After writing the tracts, I began praying and asking for provision for the printing and distribution expenses. God said to me, "If you wish Me to answer your prayer, you must first rid yourself of all hindrances." On the following Sunday, I preached on the theme, "Removal of All Hindrances." At that very time many people were criticizing the wife of one of my co-workers, who was a sister among us. After the meeting she stood at the door. When I entered the meeting to deliver the message, I looked at her and inwardly criticized her, considering others' criticism of her to be true. When I left the meeting hall after delivering the message, I greeted her. Later, when I again supplicated God for printing expenses, saying that I had removed all hindrances, God said to me, "What is the message which you have delivered? You have criticized that sister; that is a hindrance to prayer, a hindrance which you ought to deal with. You must go to her and confess your guilt." I replied, "It is not necessary to confess to others sins that are in the mind." God answered, "Yes, that is right, but your condition is different." Afterward, when I considered confessing to her and came face to face with the issue, I hesitated five times. Even though I wished to do it, I was concerned that she, who had always greatly admired me, would then despise me. I said to God, "If you order me to do anything else, I will do it, but I am unwilling to confess to her." I continued to ask God for the printing expenses, but He would not listen to my reasoning. Rather, He insisted on my confessing. The sixth time, through the Lord's grace, I confessed to her. With tears we both confessed our faults and then forgave each other. We were filled with joy and thereafter loved each other all the more in the Lord.

Shortly after this, the postman delivered a letter containing fifteen U. S. dollars. The letter read, "I like to distribute gospel tracts and feel constrained to assist you in the matter of printing gospel tracts. Please accept my gift." As soon as all hindrances were removed, God answered my prayer. Thank the Lord! This was my first experience of God's answering my prayer in the matter of printing. We were then handing out more than a thousand tracts daily. Two or three million copies were printed and distributed annually to supply the churches in various places. In the few years after the publication work was begun, God always answered my prayers and supplied all our needs.

The Lord also wanted me to publish the magazine *The Present Testimony* and to give it out free of charge. At that time all spiritual periodicals throughout China were for sale; only what I published was free. The editing room where I wrote the manuscripts was a small cubicle. When the manuscripts were completed, they were sent to the press. When there were no funds available, I would pray to God for His provision for printing. When I considered what I was doing, I laughed because the manuscripts were being sent to the press without the necessary funds. As long as I live, I will never forget the time when I had no sooner finished laughing than there was a knock at the door. Upon opening the door, I saw a middle-aged woman who constantly came to the meetings but to whom my heart was unusually cool. She was wealthy, but she loved money and treated a dime as a dollar. I wondered how she could possibly be the one who would give money for printing the magazine. Then I asked her why she had come. She replied, "About an hour ago I began feeling inwardly uneasy. When I prayed to God, He told me that I am not like a Christian, for I have never done well in the matter of offering, and that I love money too much. I asked Him what He wanted me to do, and He said, 'You should offer some money for the use of My work.' " Then she took out thirty silver dollars and placed them on the table, saying, "Spend it on whatever you feel the need is." Then as I looked at the table, I saw two things, the manuscripts and the money. I thanked the Lord without thanking her. She left, and I went immediately to the printers to negotiate the printing. The money she had given was sufficient to print fourteen hundred copies of the magazine. Others gave money for the packing expenses and postage. Now about seven thousand copies of each issue are being printed. All the finances required are provided by God at the right time and in the way I have been relating. I have never solicited contributions from anyone. At times people have even begged me to accept money. In all of these matters I have been looking solely to Him.

In Watchman Nee's *Narration of the Past*, given in a meeting on the Lord's Day, December 4, 1932, he related the same matters in more detail.

By the end of 1922 I had a burden to publish a magazine, because a number had been saved in Foochow, and the number was increasing. At that time, Brother Leland Wang was away in the Yangtze region doing evangelistic work. Only his wife and children were at home. He asked me to move into his house to help take care of the family. Daily, Sister Wang and I prayed for the magazine. I was at that time extremely pressed financially. After praying for more than a month, there was not a single dollar on hand. One morning I arose and said, "There is no need to pray further—that would be a lack of faith. What I must do is start writing. God need not put the money into our hands before we begin to write! Henceforth, I will no longer pray for this matter, but will proceed with the preparation of drafts."

When everything was ready and the last word had been written, I said, "Now the money will come." Eventually, I knelt down to pray again, saying, "O God, the draft is ready for printing, but there is still no money." After praying thus, I felt wonderfully confident that God would certainly give the money. We began to praise God.

The amazing thing was that we had no more risen to our feet than there was a knock at the door. I thought someone was coming with the money. That house being Sister Wang's, I let her answer the door. To my surprise, the one who came was a wealthy yet stingy sister. "Oh, since it is she," I thought, "there could be no money." But she said to me, "I have something extremely important to see you about." "Please tell me," I replied. Then she asked, "How should a Christian donate?" I replied that we should not adopt the Old Testament way of paying tithes, but follow the word in 2 Corinthians 9:7, which says that each person should give according to the order of God. He may donate a half, a third, a tenth, or a twentieth of his income. She then asked, "Where should the donation be made?" I answered, "Do not give it to a church which opposes the Lord, nor to those who do not believe the Bible or the redemption of the Lord's shed blood. If no one contributes to them, they will not be able to carry on their preaching. Pray before each donation; then give it either to the poor or to some work, but never to an improper organization." She said, "The Lord has been speaking to me for many days concerning my excessive devotion to money. At first I could not reconcile myself to this, but now I can do so. When I was praying this morning, the Lord said to me, 'There is no need for you to pray anymore. Just start giving away your money.' I was rather disconcerted, but now I am here with thirty dollars for you to use for the Lord's work." This money was just sufficient for the printing of fourteen hundred copies of *The Present Testimony*. Later, another person gave an additional thirty dollars, which was sufficient for the postage and incidental expenses. This is how the first issue of *The Present Testimony* was published.

In his personal testimony given at Kulangsu on October 20 concerning the above incident, he concluded with the following words:

If a person fails in dealing properly with money, he will also fail regarding many other things. We must, with a single heart, look to God and never do anything which will bring disgrace upon Him. When people give us money, we must accept it on behalf of Christ, but never ask anyone for such a favor. Thank God that after I declared to my parents that I would spend their money no longer, I could still go on studying in school for two more years. Though I did not know from where my sustenance would come, whenever there was a need, God always provided. Sometimes the situation appeared extremely difficult, yet God never let me down. We often place our hope in other people, but God does not want us to look to them. We must learn this lesson: Spend as we receive and never be like the Dead Sea, with an inlet and no outlet. We ought to be like the River Jordan with inlets on one end and outlets on the other. The Levites in the Old Testament devoted themselves to serve God, yet they too had to offer tithes.

MORE PERSONAL TESTIMONIES

In his *Narration of the Past*, given on December 4, 1932, he gave more personal testimonies concerning living by faith:

After we had been holding meetings for about a month, some young brothers among us felt that we should have a proper place to meet in the future. But since we were short of money, it was beyond our means to do so. I went to school to talk the matter over with several brothers, that

is, with brothers Faithful Luk, Simon Meek, and Wang
Tze, and we agreed that we should continue our work
among the students. Then for the first time I rented some
premises, a place owned by a family named Ho, all the
members of which had been saved. They agreed to rent the
place to me for a monthly amount of only nine dollars.
I then prayed with several brothers, asking God to supply the three months' rent which was needed in advance
before we could move in.

Every Saturday I went to Ma-Kiang, Fukien, to listen to
Miss Margaret Barber's preaching. This time when I saw
her, she said, "Here is twenty-seven dollars, which a friend
asked me to give you for your work." This sum was
exactly sufficient for three months' rent at nine dollars per
month—not too much and not too little. On my return,
without hesitation, I paid the three months' rent in
advance. Later, we prayed again, and the Lord provided
again.

In his second testimony given at Kulangsu, Fukien, on
October 20, 1936, he testified of the following:

I wrote *The Spiritual Man* during my long illness.
When it was ready for publication, about four thousand
dollars were needed. Since there were no means on
hand, I asked God to fill the need. Only four co-workers
knew of this need. No one else knew. Before long the
Lord provided four hundred dollars, and we entered
into a contract with a printer to commence printing the
book. It was agreed that should we fail to pay the subsequent installments, we would not only forfeit the cash
down payment of four hundred dollars, but we would
also pay for the default. We therefore prayed concerning
this matter with one accord. At that time I was still
confined to bed. Whenever the printer came for his
payment, the Lord had always provided us with the
means. Seeing that we were able to maintain good faith,

the printer said, "No one but you church people make payments so punctually."

In his open letter in the nineteenth issue of *The Present Testimony*, published in January-February of 1931, he gave the following testimony:

We have no lack of money for printing, although we have asked contributions from no one, and no one has given us an endowment fund. The Lord Himself has put the need of this work in the hearts of men, and little contributions given here and there enable us to accomplish what He wishes us to accomplish. We really thank Him!

He gave the following words of gratitude in his open letter in the twelfth issue of *The Present Testimony*, published December 19, 1929. This was a word of appreciation to the brothers and sisters for their faithfulness, but may also be considered his testimony concerning the Lord's supply:

I feel very grateful concerning this one thing: While I was perplexed on every side, a number of brothers and sisters in the Lord came to help me in my trouble. At the resurrection of the just, may the Lord reward them richly. Many brothers and sisters are aware that I do not have a constant livelihood. So for the Lord's sake, from the north and from the south, they deprived themselves, generously and voluntarily supplying me with abundant gifts, that I need not be anxious during my illness concerning my lack. Their excellent kindness and favor toward me has been overflowing. Surely I am not worthy. I am one of the most useless servants of the Lord. I quote Paul's words: "You sent both once and again to my need...I seek the fruit which increases to your account." My only prayer is that your kindness toward me would not be for nothing. I hope that when I am up again, I may be able to accomplish a

small portion of my work in God's enterprise. Besides their
financial supply, many brothers and sisters have written to
show me their concern, and I express my thanks. I say to all
who have ministered to me in such a way: Please accept my
grateful, heartfelt thanks.

CHAPTER TEN

LIVING A CRUCIFIED, RESURRECTED, AND OVERCOMING LIFE

Through his fellowship with Margaret Barber, Watchman Nee realized from the very beginning that to be a Christian is altogether a matter of life. Miss Barber herself was an excellent example of this principle. She cared for nothing but life. As a seed of life, she was sown into Watchman Nee. From her he learned to live by Christ as his life.

LIVING A CRUCIFIED LIFE

To live by Christ as life, one must see the subjective aspects of Christ's death. Watchman Nee received the revelation that he had been crucified with Christ, that it was no longer he that lived, but Christ that lived in him. He also saw that to experience the death of Christ in a subjective way, he needed to bear the cross. He was crucified with Christ, but he had to remain in Christ's crucifixion. To remain in Christ's crucifixion is to bear the cross, not letting the old man or the flesh leave the cross. He realized that for him to have such an experience, God must sovereignly arrange his environment, making it a practical cross for him to bear. This is exactly what God did. From the very beginning of his ministry, God arranged situations in which he could deny his self by bearing the cross and living by Christ as life.

Throughout the years he was a person under the cross, willing to be opposed, rejected, criticized, and condemned. He would not vindicate himself, excuse himself, reason with people, or explain things in order to reduce his sufferings. He always shunned disclosing things about himself which would let people know what good work he had done for the Lord or what good things he had done for others. He truly lived a crucified life.

In the early years of his ministry, he was excommunicated by his six co-workers. At that time his temperament and his flesh rose up to react to their action, and this inclination was reinforced by the fact that most of the saints who met with them took sides with him. While he was on a trip ministering, letters and cables were sent telling him that he had been excommunicated. At the time he received them, he was restricted from reading them. But while on a boat returning to Foochow, he read the letters and cables and was much provoked. He felt that his six co-workers had unfairly excommunicated him, and he intended to return and vindicate himself. Immediately, however, the Holy Spirit within him made him clear that the Lord would not allow him to vindicate himself, and he was silenced by the Lord. Upon his arrival many brothers and sisters were waiting for him at the pier. They simply could not help telling him how unfairly the six co-workers had dealt with him. They followed him from the pier to his home later that night, and all of their sympathy aroused his temperament, but the Lord strongly forbade him to do anything. Then, as the brothers and sisters crowded around, waiting for a definite word, he told them that the Lord would not allow him to vindicate himself and that he would leave home the next morning for another place in order to stay away from that situation. He asked them to be quiet about it, and this made them all the more disappointed. In that difficult situation he learned a great deal about how to remain in the Lord's death practically and bear the cross in order to live by Christ and for Christ. During that time of suffering, he wrote the following hymn:

1 If I would only stray a bit,
    Then ease my lot would be;
    But I recall how Christ my Lord
    Did suffer faithfully.

2 The world I have forever left
    And severed all its ties;
    The way may yet more narrow grow
    And all against me rise.

3   But though the worldlings glare in rage;
    I seek His smiling face.
    Though outward glory others choose,
    I, His "well done" through grace.

4   My heart's desire is not for fame
    Nor profit in these days;
    I humbly wish to serve my Lord
    And gain that day His praise.

5   Unto the judgment seat of Christ
    I daily look away;
    May all my living and my work
    Abide the fire that day.

6   You may your reputation hold,
    Wealth, friends, and glory gain;
    You may win all success and praise,
    A following great obtain.

7   But I would be but lonely, poor,
    With no prosperity;
    My heart desires to follow Him
    And finish faithfully.

8   My Lord, when here on earth, I know,
    Gained nothing but the cross.
    I only hope to be like Him
    And for Him suffer loss.

9   My glory's in the coming age,
    Today I'll patient be.
    I'd ne'er enjoy ahead of Him
    This world's prosperity.

10 That day I shall receive the crown,
    He'll wipe away my tears.
    So faithfully I'll journey on
    Till He at length appears.

While staying in Shanghai as an unmarried person, his mother came to stay with him for a period of time. Rumors circulated that a woman was living with him. Miss Groves, a sister who had previously been a help to him, heard the rumor and came to ask, "Is it true that you have a woman living with you?" He answered, "Yes." Then she rebuked him. Years later when he related this incident to me, I asked, "Why didn't you tell her that that woman was your mother?" He replied, "Miss Groves didn't ask who that woman was." He simply did not like to explain things to people in order to vindicate himself.

Following his marriage, his wife's aunt threatened to take some steps to damage his reputation if he would not come to pay her the courtesy of a visit. This actually stopped him from paying her a visit. If she had not threatened him in such a way, he would have done it. Under such threatening, however, he would not meet her demand. He refused to do anything to reduce the attack of others upon him. He believed that everything was from God's hand and was willing to bear any kind of opposition or attack as a cross, in order to live a crucified life with Christ.

In 1942 in the church in Shanghai, there was a big disturbance concerning him. He did not say a word to vindicate himself; neither did he take any steps to appease the situation or reduce his suffering. Again, he was learning the lesson of the cross, living the crucified life by the Christ who was living in him.

Because of that disturbance he was frustrated from continuing his ministry for six years. During that six-year period of suffering, he did nothing to attempt to recover his ministry, nor did he attempt to start any other kind of work. He remained fully silent, under God's sovereign hand, learning the lessons of the cross. He kept himself fully in the confinement of Christ's death and experienced Christ as his life during that long trial. Following that long dark night of six years, when the day dawned and the Lord came to recover his ministry in 1948 through a revival in Shanghai, he asked us to sing the following hymn on the life of the grapevine. This hymn portrays how the grapevine is continually under certain kinds of hardship and dealing, yet it still continues to bear fruit and to cheer others. Three stanzas of the hymn say:

Yet its wine throughout the winter
  Warmth and sweetness ever bears
Unto those in coldness shiv'ring,
  Pressed with sorrow, pain, and cares.
Yet without, alone, the grapevine
  Midst the ice and snow doth stand,
Steadfastly its lot enduring,
  Though 'tis hard to understand.

Winter o'er, the vine prepareth
  Fruit again itself to bear;
Budding forth and growing branches,
  Beauteous green again to wear;
Never murmuring or complaining
  For the winter's sore abuse,
Or for all its loss desiring
  Its fresh off'ring to reduce.

Breathing air, untainted, heavenly,
  As it lifts its arms on high,
Earth's impure, defiled affections
  Ne'er the vine may occupy.
Facing sacrifice, yet smiling,
  And while love doth prune once more,
Strokes it bears as if it never
  Suffered loss and pain before.

(#635, *Hymns*)

This hymn indicates that Watchman Nee was continually under hardships and dealings in order to produce spiritual fruit for cheering others. After that long winter, he prepared himself to bear fruit, not murmuring or complaining about anyone's abuse nor desiring to reduce his fresh contribution. Yet he was still willing to face any sacrifice by being pruned once more, as if he had never suffered any strokes before.

He told those of us who were his close co-workers that when criticized in our behavior and character, we should not vindicate ourselves, although we must without hesitation contend for the truth.

In Shanghai in 1948 there was a brother in the church who opposed Watchman Nee, because this brother's longstanding ambition for position in the church was not fulfilled. This brother gave financial assistance to a traveling preacher who wrote a long article criticizing and accusing Watchman Nee on a number of counts. The article was widely circulated, but Watchman did nothing to vindicate himself concerning this article.

In 1950 we were both in Hong Kong. One evening after the meeting, two young men standing at the front gate of the meeting hall were distributing flyers criticizing him. These two young men were standing directly in front of us, yet he did not react. He only smiled a little at them and walked away.

During my long association with him, I never once saw him quarrel, dispute, or fight with anyone. One always received the impression that he was following in the footsteps of the Lamb and living under the putting to death of Jesus in order that the life of Jesus might be manifested in him (2 Cor. 4:10).

HIS PERSONAL TESTIMONY
GIVEN AT KULANGSU, FUKIEN, OCTOBER 20, 1936

A believer may read, study, or expound a teaching concerning the cross, while at the same time not necessarily receive the lesson of the cross or know the way of the cross. When I was being tempered together in the service with my co-workers, the Lord ordered many crosses for me. Many times I felt embarrassed. I would not accept the dealing of the cross and found it difficult to submit. Inwardly, however, I knew that if the cross were ordered by the Lord, it would be the right thing, though it would still be difficult to obey and accept it. While the Lord was on the earth, He learned obedience by the cross which He suffered (Heb. 5:8; Phil. 2:8). How could I be an exception? In the first eight or nine months, when the lesson of the cross began to come, I would not obey. I knew that I should yield without resistance to the cross ordered by the Lord. When I would make up my mind to obey, my determination would last only a short time. When some event would arise where I should obey, I found it difficult to obey and was full of rebellious thoughts. This made me very uneasy.

Once I recognized the cross which the Lord had ordered for me, I found it very beneficial. Among my co-workers, five had been my schoolmates since childhood. Another one came from a different city and was five years older than I. The five always sided with him and opposed me. No matter what I did, they would invariably condemn me. They received the credit for many things I did. Sometimes when they rejected my views, I went to a lonely hill to cry before God. At these times I wrote some hymns on bearing the cross. For the first time I experienced the significance of "the fellowship of His sufferings" (Phil. 3:10). When I could not have fellowship with the world, I could enjoy heavenly fellowship. The first two years after my salvation, I did not know what the cross was. But at this time I was beginning to learn its lesson.

I was always ranked first in my class as well as in my school. I also wanted to be first in serving the Lord. For this reason, when I was made second, I disobeyed. I told God repeatedly that it was too much for me to bear; I was receiving too little honor and authority, and everyone sided with my elder co-worker. But today I worship God and thank Him from the depths of my heart that this all happened to me. It has been the best training. God wished me to learn obedience, so He arranged for me to encounter many difficulties. Eventually, I told Him I was willing to be placed second. When I became willing to yield, the joy I experienced differed from the joy I experienced at the time of my salvation; it was not a broad joy but a deep one. After another eight or nine months, on many occasions I was willing to be broken and did not do what I wished. On my spiritual path I was filled with joy and peace. The Lord submitted to the hand of God, and I was willing to do the same. The Lord, existing in the form of God, did not consider being equal with God a treasure to be grasped, but emptied Himself (Phil. 2:6-7). How dare I rank myself above the Lord? When I first began to learn obedience it was difficult, but as time went on I found it easier and easier. Eventually, I told God that I would choose the cross, accept its breaking, and put aside my own ideas.

LIVING A RESURRECTED LIFE

Watchman Nee saw that he had been crucified with Christ and that he had risen with Christ. The resurrected Christ with the fullness of the Spirit had become his life. It was by the resurrection life of the indwelling Christ that he was able to bear the cross and to participate in the fellowship of His sufferings and be conformed to His death. By the resurrection life of Christ, he abandoned the world, forsook his future, denied himself, was freed from sin, overcame besetting sins, subdued Satan's temptations, conquered Satan's evil wiles, and defeated Satan himself. It was also by the resurrection life of Christ that he served the Lord, worked for Him, and carried out His commission. He consistently rejected his natural strength in the Lord's service. He feared the intrusion of himself into the Lord's work. He dared not minister apart from the indwelling Christ. In delivering messages, contacting people, writing articles, corresponding with the saints, and in all trifling things, he acted not by himself but by the resurrected life.

He further saw that the church as the Body of Christ was simply the enlargement, expansion, and expression of the resurrected Christ. His vision that Christ in resurrection was the life and content of the church was unique. He not only ministered by the resurrected Christ, but also ministered the resurrected Christ to the saints for the building up of His Body. He frequently emphasized that anything which is not Christ in resurrection is not the church, and anything not done by the resurrected Christ is something foreign in the Body. He would serve the church with nothing but the resurrected Christ. The more he continued his ministry, the more he ministered the resurrected Christ to the saints and to the churches. The resurrected Christ became not only his life and living, but also his message and ministry. He was one who not only knew resurrection life and who lived and ministered by and with the resurrected Christ; he was also one who bore the cross, participated in His suffering, and was being conformed to His death. I believe it was by living such a resurrected life that he was able to pass through the long martyrdom of twenty years' imprisonment which finally ended in death.

LIVING AN OVERCOMING LIFE

Watchman Nee received a clear vision of what it means to be an overcomer by studying the Scriptures and reading the writings of Jessie Penn-Lewis. He saw the principle in both the Old Testament and the New Testament that whenever God's people failed Him, He called some back to His original standard to overcome the defeated situation and fulfill His purpose. This is emphasized repeatedly by the Lord in the seven epistles to the seven churches in Revelation 2 and 3. He saw that the church was in a defeated condition, and he felt called by the Lord to be an overcomer in this age so that the Lord might recover His original purpose concerning His church. The rich provision of God's sufficient grace enabled him to live such an overcoming life by the power of the resurrected Christ. His overcoming life was the result of living a crucified and resurrected life. By the crucified and resurrected life, he overcame sin, the world, self, self-pity, natural temperament, the flesh, and Satan. By the crucified and resurrected life, he also overcame defeated, degraded, and deviated Christianity with all its forms and traditions. He equally overcame Christianity's criticisms, rejections, oppositions, and persecutions by the crucified and resurrected life. By living such a life, he followed his Master as the Lamb and bore His reproach outside the camp of Christianity in an overcoming way. In living such an overcoming life, he followed in the footsteps of the apostle Paul by filling up what was lacking of the afflictions of Christ for His Body's sake (Col. 1:24). Ultimately, by living such an overcoming life, he became a living witness of Christ, bearing "the testimony of Jesus" (Rev. 1:9) not only in the sin-stricken world but also in Satan-stricken Christianity. The overcoming life which he lived eventually became his testimony of the Lord for His recovery.

The following words by Sister Ruth Lee in her open letter published in the sixth issue of *The Present Testimony*, dated December 24, 1928, testifies how Watchman Nee labored in his work by living an overcoming life:

In the last issue's open letter, our brother Watchman Nee told how he completed the work on that issue even though he was being stretched out in different ways. In spite of the situation he was in, he proceeded to prepare the current issue of *The Present Testimony* for publication. This period of our brother's life has been filled with fierce conflicts and perilous fightings. While writing *The Spiritual Man*, his days were spent in the crevices of Satan's teeth. Since its completion Satan has been fighting even more with all the power of hell, attempting to completely wipe our brother out and make void the testimony of his book. This kind of warfare has occupied us and made us inactive for many days. These have been days of chanting lamentations. But at this very hazardous moment, our loving Father, our victorious Savior, has led our brother to the ascended position in the heavenlies to overcome Satan's fierce attack. With tears of joy we thank the Lord today that He has enabled us to put out this issue of *The Present Testimony* in His victory.

Watchman Nee lived an overcoming life, worked by such a life, and ministered such a life to the saints and to the churches. One of the burdens of his ministry was to hold a number of overcomer conferences. The goal of the messages given in these conferences was to sound the call for overcomers. His intention was to help the saints to become overcomers in this age for the recovery of the Lord's testimony by living an overcoming life, which is the living of a crucified and resurrected life.

All through the years of his life and ministry, Watchman Nee so cleaved to the crucified and resurrected Christ that he lived in the reality of an overcoming life. In the final period of his life, to all appearances he was taken away from his ministry by a change in the political situation. Actually, however, he was sovereignly put into an environment which afforded him a long period of twenty years to live an overcoming life. He did live such a life, overcoming even unto death. This is a strong testimony of the Lord, not only to us who are his followers, but also to all the children of God in this age.

CHAPTER ELEVEN

PAYING MORE ATTENTION TO LIFE THAN WORK

THE EXAMPLE OF MARGARET BARBER

Margaret Barber was a great example to Watchman Nee in the one matter of paying more attention to life than to work. He realized that God cares for what we are more than what we do, and his work was according to this principle. He observed how Miss Barber continually stressed the matter of life, paying almost no attention to her work.

From time to time, he and Miss Barber would go together to listen to a Christian speaker. He always admired either the speaker's eloquence, knowledge, zeal, ability, or natural power of persuasion. Then Miss Barber would point out to him that what he admired was neither of life nor of the Spirit. What he admired might be able to stir people up and motivate them to perform certain works, but it could never minister life to people. Through such spiritual diagnosis, he was educated to discern and distinguish the difference between life and work. He began to realize that most of the sermons given by preachers and Christian teachers were not grains of life but flakes of chaff. He also observed that in most Christian work, supposedly carried out for Christ, there is very little life ministered to people.

FOOTSTEPS OF THE LORD JESUS

Watchman Nee pointed out to his co-workers that according to the four Gospels, the Lord in His ministry did not care for popularity; rather, He frequently withdrew when a crowd was seeking Him. Brother Nee often said that the Lord Jesus sowed Himself as a seed of life (Matt. 13:3) and fell into the ground as a grain of wheat, that the life within Him might be released to bring forth many grains (John 12:24).

THE PERIL OF BEING POPULAR

He told me that when his co-worker, who was five years older than he, was traveling through the country conducting evangelistic meetings, Margaret Barber, realizing the peril of popularity, warned him by saying, "If you continue to travel for evangelistic work, I will not pray for you any longer." She had the foresight to realize that such work would bring shipwreck to his spiritual life. Eventually, that is exactly what happened. That other co-worker was distracted from spiritual life to popular work.

Watchman Nee was afraid of being popular. He was fearful of making a name for himself and of being highly praised and uplifted by people. He looked upon such popularity as an instrument of seduction to tempt the young co-workers away from the right track of life in following the Lord. He was never bothered by the depreciation, opposition, rejection, and accusation of others. Rather, he considered these things a sort of safeguard to preserve him in life and cause him to grow more in the Lord. Such a vision made it easier for him to be one with the Lord in His work and to obey the Lord's leading. He carried out the revelation he received from the Lord, not in the way of work, but in the way of life.

NOT QUANTITY BUT QUALITY

Watchman Nee saw through 1 Corinthians 3:12-15 that the important thing regarding our work is not its quantity but its quality. Gold, silver, and precious stones are always small in quantity but high in quality, whereas wood, hay, and stubble are always high in quantity and low in quality. Wood, hay, and stubble cannot stand the test of fire, but gold, silver, and precious stones can. We will be judged at the judgment seat of Christ not according to the quantity but according to the quality of our work.

OUTFLOW OF LIFE

When he would hear that a certain preacher had success-fully gained a large following or that a certain Christian worker was doing a big work, he would frequently tell us, his trainees, that the real work is the outflow of life.

With the gifts, knowledge, and ability he had, he could easily have acquired a large following in Christianity. Watchman Nee, however, did not misuse his gifts and knowledge in this way. He always took pains to restrict himself in the function of his gifts and the use of his knowledge in order to ensure that his work was fully in life, of life, with life, and was life itself. As long as he had the assurance that his ministry was the outflow of life, he was satisfied.

His ministry began from the year 1922, and the church in Shanghai, which was fully under his ministry, was raised up in 1927. By the end of 1933, when I first visited him in Shanghai, the number of saints meeting there in the Lord's recovery was slightly over one hundred. In February 1928 he held an overcomer conference in Shanghai. The attendants at this conference included all the co-workers and seeking ones throughout the country. The attendance was a little over three hundred. After he had been in his ministry for over six years, the number of saints in the Lord's recovery at that time was still so small. However, he was not disappointed; rather, he was strongly encouraged because he realized that that small number was the issue of his ministry. Praise the Lord! Because Watchman Nee was not interested in the outward work, the life-issue of his ministry has flowed throughout the whole earth. That part of his ministry which has flooded today's Christianity through his books was not his work but rather the very life that issued from his work. To him work did not mean much; life meant everything. In my whole life, he is the only person I have known who paid more attention to life than to work.

The following is an excerpt from his open letter in the fourth issue of *The Present Testimony,* published in July 1928:

We firmly believe that God is not seeking a great work which would shock heaven and shake earth. Men only care for what is seen, but God is not so near-sighted. We do not trust in the kind of work which publishes photos and issues reports. It is a sad thing that while the children of God realize that God is not in excitement, they still are bent on having excitement. Hence, we have to be careful that we do not consider everything that sounds good as from God. I feel that the unprecedented need today is to discern between the work of the spirit and that of the soul.

CHAPTER TWELVE

EXPERIENCING GOD
AS THE GREAT PHYSICIAN

Because of overwork and lack of adequate physical care, Watchman Nee became sick with tuberculosis of the lungs in 1924. It became so serious that in some of his open letters to the readers of his papers he said that the pegs of his tabernacle on earth were shaken. Several times rumors were spread that he had died. During this time of illness, he was greatly exercised to trust in God for his existence, and God faithfully cared for him. He suffered with this illness for about five years. Eventually, however, he was graciously healed by experiencing God as his Great Physician. The following is his personal testimony regarding this matter given at Kulangsu, Fukien, October 20, 1936:

SICK BUT NOT CEASING FROM WORK

When I first became aware of my illness in 1924, I was feeling feeble, there was pain in my chest, and I had a slight fever. I did not know what was wrong. Dr. H. S. Wong said to me, "I know you have faith and that God can cure you, but allow me to examine you and diagnose your disease." After the examination he spoke to Brother Wong Teng-ming for some time in a very low voice. At first, even though I asked, they would not tell me the result of the examination. But when I informed them that I was not afraid, Dr. Wong told me that I was afflicted with tuberculosis and that my condition was so serious that prolonged rest would be necessary.

I could not sleep that night; I did not want to meet the Lord without having completed my work. I was very depressed. I decided to go to the countryside for a rest and have more fellowship with the Lord. I asked the Lord,

"What is Your will for me? If You wish me to lay down my life, I am not afraid to die." For half a year I could not grasp the Lord's will, but there was joy in my heart, and I believed the Lord could never be wrong. The many letters I received during this time did not convey encouragement or consolation; rather, they rebuked me for overworking and for not taking adequate care of my life. One brother reproached me by quoting Ephesians 5:29, "For no one ever hated his own flesh, but nourishes and cherishes it, even as Christ also the church." Brother Cheng Chi-kwei of Nanking invited me to his home where I could rest and at the same time help him translate Dr. C. I. Scofield's Bible correspondence course. At this time some thirty brothers and sisters came to me for fellowship. I spoke with them regarding the question of the church. I came to realize that God's hand was on me for the express purpose of turning me back to my first vision; otherwise, I would have ended up walking in the path of a revival preacher.

Day after day passed without my tuberculosis being cured. Though I exerted myself to write and to study the Bible, I found it exceedingly strenuous. I had a slight fever each afternoon, I could not sleep at night, and I frequently experienced night sweats. Upon being advised to take more rest, I replied, "I am afraid that I might rest to such a degree that I become rusty." I felt that even though I might not live long, I should believe that God would increase my strength and that I must work for Him. I asked the Lord concerning any unfinished work He had for me to do. Whatever He wanted me to do, I would ask Him to spare my life to do it; otherwise, I felt there was nothing upon earth worth living for. For awhile I was able to arise from bed, but eventually I could not even do that. On one occasion I was asked to conduct a gospel meeting. I exerted myself to arise and asked the Lord to strengthen me. While walking to the meeting, I was forced to lean against a lamp post every now and then for rest. Each time this happened I would say to the Lord, "It is worthwhile to die for You." Some brothers who knew that I had done this rebuked me for not sparing my health. To this I replied that I loved my Lord and would give up my life for Him.

THE SPIRITUAL MAN WRITTEN IN SICKNESS

After praying for over a month, I felt that I should write a book concerning what I had learned before God. My concept had been that one should not write books until he was old, but when I considered that I might be leaving this earth, I felt I should begin writing. I rented a small room in Wusih, Kiangsu province, where I shut myself up and spent my days writing. At that time my disease became so aggravated that I could not even lie down. While writing I sat on a chair with a high back and pressed my chest against the desk to alleviate the pain. Satan said to me, "Since you will soon be dying, why not die in comparative comfort rather than in pain?" I retorted, "The Lord wants me just like this; get out of here!" It took four months to complete the three volumes of *The Spiritual Man*. The writing of this book was a real labor of blood, sweat, and tears. I despaired of life, yet God's grace brought me through. After completing each time of writing, I would say to myself, "This is my last testimony to the church." Though the writing was done in the midst of all sorts of difficulties and hardships, I felt that God was unusually near to me. Some felt God was ill-treating me. Brother Cheng wrote saying, "You are exerting yourself to the uttermost; some day you will regret it." I replied, "I love my Lord and I would live for Him."...

SICKNESS WORSENED

Following the publication of the book, I prayed, "Now let Your servant depart in peace." At the same time my disease worsened. I could not sleep peacefully at night, and when I awoke I turned incessantly from side to side. Physically, I was a bag of bones. I had night sweats, and my voice became hoarse. People had trouble hearing me speak, even when they placed their ear to my mouth. Several sisters took turns waiting upon me, one of whom was a veteran nurse. Whenever she saw me, she would weep. She testified, "I have seen many patients, but I have never seen one whose condition was as pitiful as his. I am afraid that he can live only three or four more days." When someone told me of this, I said, "Let this be my end. I realize I am going to die soon." One brother telegraphed the churches in various places, telling them there was no more hope for me and that they need pray for me no more.

HEALED

One day I asked God, "Why are You calling me away so soon?" I confessed my trespasses before God, fearing that I might have been unfaithful concerning some matter. At the same time I told God that I had no faith. On that same day I devoted myself to fasting and praying and presented myself to Him once more. I told Him that I would do nothing but what He assigned me. From morning until three o'clock in the afternoon I fasted. At the same time the co-workers earnestly prayed together for me in Sister Ruth Lee's home. As I prayed to God to grant me faith, He spoke His words to me, words which I could never forget. The first sentence was, "The just shall live by faith" (Rom. 1:17). The second sentence was, "By faith you stand" (2 Cor. 1:24). The third sentence was, "We walk by faith" (2 Cor. 5:7). These words filled me with great joy, for the Bible says, "All things are possible to him who believes" (Mark 9:23). I immediately thanked and praised God because He had given me His words. I believed that God had cured me.

The test came immediately. The Bible says, "By faith you stand," but I was still lying in bed. A conflict arose in my mind: Should I get up and stand or remain lying down? We all know that human beings love themselves and consider it more comfortable to die in bed than to die standing. Then the word of God manifested its power, and ignoring all else, I put on my clothing, clothing which I had not worn for a hundred and seventy-six days. As I left the bed to stand, I perspired so profusely that it was as though I had been soaked through with rain. Satan said to me, "Are you trying to stand when you can't even sit up?" I retorted, "God told me to stand," and I rose to my feet.

Being again in a cold sweat, I nearly fell down. I kept repeating, "Stand by faith, stand by faith!" I then walked a few steps to get my trousers and socks. After putting on my trousers, I sat down. No sooner was I seated than the word of God came to me that I should not only stand by faith but also walk by faith. I felt that the ability to rise and walk a few steps to get my trousers and socks was already something marvelous. How could I expect to walk further? "Where do You want me to go?" I asked God. He answered, "Go downstairs to Sister Lee's home at number 215." A number of brothers and sisters had been fasting and praying for me there for two or three days.

Walking within the room might be all right, I thought, but how could I walk downstairs? I prayed to God, "Oh God, I can stand by faith, and by faith I am also able to walk downstairs!" Immediately, I went to the door leading to the staircase and opened it. I tell you honestly that when I stood at the top of the staircase it seemed to me to be the tallest staircase I had ever seen in my life. I said to God, "If You tell me to walk I will do so, even if I die as a result of the effort." But I continued, "Lord, I cannot walk. I pray that You will support me with Your hand while I am walking." With one hand holding onto the rail, I descended step by step. Again I was in a cold sweat. As I walked down the stairs, I continued to cry out, "Walk by faith, walk by faith!" With each step down, I prayed, "Oh Lord, it is You who enable me to walk." While descending those twenty-five steps, it seemed I was walking hand in hand with the Lord in faith.

Upon reaching the bottom of the stairway, I felt very strong and went quickly to the rear door. I opened the door and headed straight for Sister Lee's home. I said to the Lord, "From now on, I will live by faith and will no longer be an invalid." I knocked at the door just as Peter did in Acts 12:12-17, but without Rhoda to open the door. When the door was opened and I entered the house, seven or eight brothers and sisters gazed at me. They were speechless and motionless. For about an hour everyone sat quietly as if God had appeared among men. I also sat there full

of thanksgiving and praise. Then I related all that had
happened in the course of my being graciously healed.
Exhilarated and jubilant in spirit, we all praised God aloud
for His wonderful work. That same day we hired a car to go
to Kiangwan in the suburbs to visit Dora Yu, the famous
woman evangelist. She was greatly shocked to see me, for
she had received recent news of my imminent death. When
I appeared, I was looked upon as one who had been raised
from the dead. That was another occasion of joyful thanksgiving and praise before the Lord. On the following Sunday,
I spoke on the platform for three hours.

WHAT A WONDER

About four years ago, I went to an auction at the house
of a German doctor. Upon inquiring I found that this
doctor was the one who had taken x-rays of my chest many
years ago. He had taken three pictures and told me that
there was no hope. When I asked him to take another
picture, he said that there was no further need. He then
showed me another person's chest x-ray and said, "This person's condition was better than yours, yet he died at his
home two weeks after this picture was taken. Don't come
to see me anymore; I don't want to make money out of
you." When I heard this, I went home extremely disappointed. Then, four years ago, I read an advertisement in
the newspaper concerning the auction of a building and
furniture of a certain famous German doctor who had died.
When I discovered that this doctor was the one who had
taken x-rays of my chest many years ago, I lifted up my
hands to praise the Lord. I said, "This doctor has died. He
said that I would die soon, but now he is dead. The Lord
has shown me His grace." Under the Lord's blood, I said,
"This doctor, who was stronger than I, has died, but I have
been healed by the Lord and am still alive." On that day I
bought many things from his house for memorial.

GOD'S FURTHER SUSTAINING CARE

While Brother Nee was seriously sick with tuberculosis,

his heart was stricken with angina pectoris in 1927. God graciously healed him of tuberculosis, but sovereignly left him with the angina pectoris. He suffered this heart disease for forty-five years, until the end of his life. It often caused him to suffer severe pain and experience cold sweat. Sometimes, while delivering a message, the pain would hit, and he would be forced to lean upon the stand. He could have died at any moment. This spontaneously ushered him into a full trust in the Lord for his existence. Moment by moment he existed by faith in God, and all through the years God sustained him with His gracious care and resurrection life until he died. Through such physical hardship, he experienced and enjoyed God much more than would have been possible if he had not had such an entangling and exhausting disease.

The kind of divine healing Watchman Nee experienced is different from the so-called gift of healing. It was not merely a miraculous act of God; it was the working out of the resurrection life through the procedure of grace by the exercise of living faith in the faithful Word of God for edification and growth of life. It was not merely a miracle of divine power; it was absolutely a matter of grace and of the divine life.

CHAPTER THIRTEEN

MARRIED AND ENGAGING IN BUSINESS

MARRIED

When Watchman Nee was a teenager, he fell in love with a young girl by the name of Charity Chang. Their two families had been friends for three generations. After Watchman Nee had turned to the Lord, Charity was still unsaved. At times she ridiculed the Lord in Watchman's presence. This bothered him. How could he who loved the Lord marry one who despised the Lord? At the time he sought to be filled with the Holy Spirit, the Lord required him to give her up. He struggled for some time with this matter. Eventually, the Lord forced him to give her up. At that time he made a thorough consecration of himself and his future to the Lord. He experienced the reality of Psalm 73:25 in a practical way, to have no other love in heaven or on earth but the Lord.

Ten years later, after finishing her university education, Charity turned to the Lord and began to attend the church meetings in Shanghai in 1934. Through those ten years she was sovereignly kept by the Lord from marrying. Eventually, the Lord brought her back to Watchman Nee. Charity's aunt, however, strongly opposed the marriage. She looked upon Watchman Nee as simply a poor preacher. On the one hand, this caused Watchman to hesitate in going ahead with the wedding; but on the other hand, his mother was very much concerned for his marriage, since he was thirty years of age. In 1934, during his fourth overcomer conference held in Hangchow, all the co-workers were present. His mother grasped this opportunity to speed up the wedding. As a result, immediately following the conference, the wedding took place. Charity's aunt was extremely unhappy about her niece's marriage. She made a threat that if Watchman Nee would not pay her the customary courtesy call she would cause him trouble. He would have surely paid her such a visit if she had not made such a threat. However, her threats caused him not to do so. He felt he could not comply with her desire under such duress. People would think he was playing politics to please her. For this reason he refused to do what she asked. Through this conflict, a great turmoil burst out in Shanghai caused by Charity's opposing aunt. This caused Watchman a great deal of suffering. However, this marriage was the provision of the Lord. Charity was the helpmate he needed to take care of him in his sickly condition. She was the only one permitted to visit him during his twenty-year imprisonment. The Lord took her away one year before Watchman died. It was God's sovereign arrangement that they had no children to burden them while undergoing such a long trial.

ENGAGING IN BUSINESS

Watchman's second brother was a qualified chemist. In 1938 he began a small pharmaceutical factory. He was experienced in pharmaceutical production but was inexperienced in business management. Watchman was blamed by his parents for helping many other brothers, but not helping his own brother in business. Due to this family feeling, Watchman began to help his brother in the management of the pharmaceutical factory in the latter part of 1939. At this time he was also burdened with the supply of his co-workers. He felt that some profit could be made through the business to meet their needs. He therefore picked up the full management of the factory and reorganized it. Because of this unavoidable involvement, some brothers employed in the factory became unhappy with him. Through this whole situation, Satan stirred up turmoil among the saints in Shanghai against Watchman. This resulted in his inability to function in the ministry. At the same time the occupation of the invading Japanese army compelled him to move the factory far to the interior, from Shanghai to Chungking. Chungking was the Chinese capital during the Sino-Japanese war. There he carried on the business and was also employed by the government. After the war, he brought the pharmaceutical factory back to Shanghai. Through the profits derived from this business, he was not only able to care for the need of a number of brothers and sisters; he was also able to purchase a training center with approximately twelve bungalows on Kuling Mountain, close to his hometown. In 1948 a revival was brought to the church in Shanghai, and he resumed his ministry. At the same time he also handed over the factory to the work as an offering to the Lord. That act influenced many brothers and sisters to also hand over their possessions to the work.

TESTIMONY OF BROTHER SAMUEL CHANG

The following is a testimony of Samuel I. L. Chang, Mrs. Nee's brother, concerning Watchman as a businessman:

I received my college degree in the field of chemistry, and in 1938 I engaged in the pharmaceutical enterprise as an assistant to Watchman Nee's second brother, Hwai-tsu (George). From the time Watchman Nee began to manage the enterprise late in 1939, I worked with him for about ten years, until I left the China mainland in 1949.

Due to the Japanese invasion, our factory was moved from Shanghai to Chungking. In 1943 Watchman Nee went back to Foochow. At that time he cabled me to come there. After arriving, he told me that there was a brother who needed approximately ten thousand dollars to clear his debt. I was quite puzzled at the time that he was exercising such generosity to unconditionally pay off this brother's large debt. But this incident made me clear that he was running the business, not for his own needs, but for the needs of others.

Sometimes the Lord provided for Watchman's needs; sometimes He did not provide. Then he would work with his own hands to supply his own needs as well as the needs of others.

As time went on, the restriction on obtaining raw materials from abroad became acute, and there was no way to develop the pharmaceutical business on a large scale. The saints still needed to be provided for, yet the income was limited. This situation forced Watchman to work at a government job in order to not become a burden to others. He worked not only in order to provide help for others but also to meet the need of his own living expenses.

After the war he returned to Shanghai with the pharmaceutical factory. He built the business on a sound foundation, and there was such blessing from the Lord that another factory, which produced dye, was added to the business. From the financial blessing of these two factories, Watchman was able to offer a large sum to the church in Shanghai for the building of the meeting hall. He was also able to maintain the training center on Mount Kuling, Foochow, with a number of living quarters.

I believe I was the only one with him from the beginning to the end of his time in business. I can bear witness that his motive was absolutely not to make himself rich. He was utterly captured by the Lord. Although he was criticized for going into business, I must testify that he did not spend the profit for his own enjoyment. The money he made was for the Lord, and he spent it in the way the Lord desired.

Because of his rich experience in the Lord, he was enabled to work with government officials in a very efficient way. All his superiors admired him. He never attempted to prove that he was superior; rather, he lived and worked in the spirit of submission and took orders from those above him. For this reason, when the war was over and the government returned to Nanking, he was offered a high position. However, because of his relationship with the Lord and his ministry with the co-workers and the churches, it was necessary to give up the government job.

CHAPTER FOURTEEN

HELPED

Four sisters were vital to Watchman Nee in his life and work. He was saved through the preaching of Dora Yu, perfected under Margaret Barber, and sustained by two elderly co-workers, Ruth Lee and Peace Wang. Dora Yu and Margaret Barber were of the older generation, whereas Ruth Lee and Peace Wang were of the same generation as Watchman Nee.

RUTH LEE

Ruth Lee was born in the province of Hupei in 1894, about nine years before Watchman Nee. Her Chinese name was Lee Yuan-ru.

Saved

The following excerpts are from her personal testimonies given at different times and recorded by Dr. Chang Yu-lan and Weigh Kwang-hsi.

I was born and raised in a non-Christian family. I considered myself a good person who had no need of salvation. During my first year in the Girls' Normal College in Wuchang, I experienced some fear of sinning against God, although at that time I was not sure there was a God. After passing through some years of schooling and acquiring more knowledge, I became careless.

Later I taught in a school in Tientsin, established by a relative. My maternal uncle was a believer, and I respected his character and learning. Yet I considered him somewhat superstitious. I learned English under a Western lady missionary but would not attend her Bible study. When I was dean of Nanking Public Normal College, I frequently advised the students not to believe in Christ.

In March 1918 while sailing on the Yangtze River, I was enjoying the scenery. At that time I realized that there must be a Supreme Being superior to mankind, who was wise and almighty, as mentioned in Romans 1:19-20.

One day one of my colleagues, a Miss Cheng, opened her Bible and called my attention to Romans 2:28-29. She also read Romans 3:29. At that time I realized that there was a God and that He was also my God.

At the end of April, Miss Cheng invited me to a luncheon held at the home of Miss Mary A. Leaman, an American missionary, where I discovered that my friend had been praying for me. After lunch Miss Leaman admonished me to believe in the Lord and asked me to kneel down and pray with her. After the prayer some of those present sang the following hymn for me: "That my Savior were your Savior too! For you I am praying, For you I am praying" (#933, *Hymns*).

From then on I read a few verses of the Bible every day. One day I knelt down and prayed that if God was true and if the Bible was true, He must enable me to believe the Bible. After rising up, I was able to believe.

I then desired to learn how to pray and how to sing the hymns. I secretly asked one of my Christian students to copy the words and music of a hymn for me. How wonderful when I sang the first stanza of the hymn: "O happy day that fixed my choice on Thee, my Savior and my God!" I determined to believe that Jesus was my Savior. I sang the chorus, "When Jesus washed my sins away," and rejoiced exceedingly. I felt that God had told me that Jesus had washed my sins away. On that day I was saved.

Later the light of God came to me again. I realized how sinful and heavily burdened with sins I was. I confessed all my sins to God and received His forgiveness. From that time on, whenever I remembered having wronged anyone, I would confess it to them. Thus, in my daily life and in my inward desire, there was a great change.

One day I read Luke 12:8. I determined to confess before men that I believed in Jesus. However, I simply did not have the nerve to confess the Lord before men. I struggled with this for a long time and was greatly troubled. One day I heard a voice within me saying, "Are you willing to forsake everything and follow Me?" At first I did not know what it meant, but later I knew. When I realized what this word meant, I told the Lord, "Lord, I am willing." After I made the decision, I went to the principal and resigned my job.

Called

Not long after this a certain Christian girls' high school offered me the position of dean. I considered employing some methods of my own to improve the religious life in the school. After two weeks I became sick and knew it was the Lord's discipline. I realized that I was not right, for I was ambitious and was depending on my strength to work for the Lord. I began from that time to learn to know God. A short time later God again demanded that I leave my teaching job and serve Him with my whole heart. I resigned in March of 1920. Eventually, I answered the Lord's call to serve Him.

After leaving my job, I worked with an American lady missionary for seven years, receiving much help and edification.

Seeking the Lord's Way

During these years I frequently contacted the various groups in Christianity. I discovered that most of them had fallen into organizations of human opinion. I desired to seek for a straight way. Finally, the Lord brought me to Nanking. There I met some spiritual brothers and sisters who helped me. I began to learn the difference between what was of man and what was of God.

Contact with Watchman Nee

At the end of 1922 Ruth Lee was invited to visit Foochow for evangelistic work. The brothers and sisters in Foochow were preparing to meet her at the pier. The night before her arrival, Watchman Nee was considering whether or not to join the reception, thinking that although she might be a good evangelist, since she was a female, she should not be too highly esteemed. However, during the night he had a dream. In that dream he and others met her at the pier. When he saw her in the dream, the Lord told him that she would be his co-worker. The next morning he awoke and seriously considered the dream. He realized that if that dream was of the Lord, he would miss the Lord's will if he did not meet her. So he went. When her boat arrived at the pier, many brothers and sisters went on board to welcome her, but Watchman Nee stayed somewhat behind. They shook hands with Sister Lee and introduced her to Brother Nee. He said, "I have seen her already." Of course, they did not understand what he meant. In 1926 Ruth Lee and Cheng Chi-kwei invited Watchman to Nanking for some rest. At that time he had further contact with Ruth Lee and some others. In his *Narration of the Past,* given in a meeting in Shanghai on December 4, 1932, Watchman Nee referred to Ruth Lee's situation as follows:

A year before I went to Nanking, I fellowshipped with Sister Lee concerning the truth of the church. However, since her attitude was very rigid and since she was not at all receptive, I made no further mention of it. Later she read a book on church history, saw that the origin of the denominations was not scriptural, and became somewhat clear. Eventually, I heard that she was baptized by immersion. Later she and several other sisters began holding bread-breaking meetings every Lord's Day. When I arrived in Nanking, naturally I attended the meeting to remember the Lord with them.

At that time Ruth Lee was invited to be the editor of *The Spiritual Light,* a leading spiritual magazine, published by the outstanding Christian writers of the country. She accepted the position, but through her contact with Watchman Nee, she received light concerning the proper way of the Lord's move and determined to turn to the Lord's recovery. She therefore presented her resignation as editor of *The Spiritual Light*. The chairman of its committee turned down her request and wished to keep her at any cost. Since she was a person with a deep sense of responsibility, she had no way at that time to carry out her desire to resign.

In 1927 Nanking was occupied by the revolutionary army. Several of the church buildings and the office of *The Spiritual Light* magazine were desolated by those who opposed Christianity. The magazine was terminated, and Ruth Lee was released under the Lord's sovereign arrangement.

A Huge Help

Being now free from her editorial responsibility, she traveled to Shanghai to meet with some sister co-workers. In the same year Watchman Nee moved his gospel bookroom to Shanghai and asked Ruth to help him in the editorial work.

She had an excellent command of the Chinese language, and from 1927 on, all of Watchman's writings were edited by her. She was a great help in his publication ministry.

In 1933 he decided to publish *The News Letters* for communications and fellowship between the saints and the churches. He asked Ruth to be his acting editor. She was a great help and saved much of his valuable time.

In 1937, because of the Japanese invasion, the brothers and sisters were scattered. At that time Watchman began to publish *The Open Door* magazine to facilitate the flow of information among the saints and the churches. Because of his need to visit Europe, Ruth Lee was again asked to be his acting editor. Her editorials provided much help to all the churches throughout China and the Southeast Asian countries.

In the years 1950 to 1952, Watchman Nee was desperately burdened to speed up the publication of messages from his 1948 and 1949 trainings. In this task Ruth Lee was of immeasurable assistance to him. Through her help, most of those messages were published in book form before his imprisonment and have become a great heritage to the Lord's recovery today. How we thank the Lord for this!

Moreover, Ruth Lee not only had a solid foundation in spiritual life and knowledge; she was also adequate in knowing and experiencing human life. She was a very able person with deep insight coupled with a disciplined character. She was able to supply much care not only to the sisters but also to the brothers, both in the churches and in the work.

The following excerpts from her open letters, published in *The Present Testimony* while substituting for Brother Nee, show to some extent her spiritual weight. She wrote the following in the seventh issue of March 27, 1929:

The more our vision is enlarged to see the eternal will of God, the more joyful and hopeful we are, and the more we need to recognize clearly the boundaries which God has measured to us. If God has raised up some to do another kind of work, we ask the Lord to bless it and our hearts rejoice for it. But we, in ourselves, dare not start a work in order to meet the pressing need in our environment. What we pray for and hope for is that we may be faithful to the Lord within the limits which He has measured to us. When we consider that the church shares the same life as Christ and will ultimately grow up fully into Him, the Head, we simply cannot refrain from praising with singing this mystery of the gospel. Oh brothers and sisters, may the Lord stir up our fervent and loving heart to rise and pray. Pray to hasten the completion of the building of the Body of Christ and the coming of His kingdom.

The following excerpt is from the eighth issue of *The Present Testimony*, published May 18, 1929:

We do not want the truths of God to be stored only in the heads of men, nor to always be displayed on bookshelves. Rather, we want them to be assimilated into the human spirit and to be manifested in human living. Hence, although every issue contains only a few pages, the messages therein are important. We hope that with every issue you receive you do not merely read it through, but rather spend time to comprehend it in depth. It is not simply by knowing the truth that it becomes yours. Rather, it is after you have experienced the truth that you obtain its deliverance and freedom.

This last quotation is from the ninth issue of *The Present Testimony*, published June 20, 1929.

None of the articles in this issue is vain theory. If we will humble ourselves and give diligence, we will see the truth of "Christ in us." How real, how significant, and how glorious! We shall also see how much prayer we need in order to be fellow workers with God, and what attitude we need in order to cause Satan to be cast out of heaven.

Oh readers, now is really the time that we need the Lord to revive us. However, we must discern the difference between a revival of human works and a revival of the Holy Spirit. If it is an artificial revival, even though grandiose and noisy, it is but the flesh in another form. When we learn to put ourselves aside and only exercise our faith to identify with Christ in His fullness, how restful it is. We already have too many ways, and we already have too many failures. God does not want us to save the situation, nor does He want us to be discouraged and shrink back. Rather, He wants us to admit that we have come to the end of our road and that the goodness of our flesh is but vanity. Thus, we must turn to Him to seek His will. Our greatest dangers are that we are not willing to ask God to examine all our lives and works, that we are not willing to lay aside our natural ability and opinions and wholly trust in God, and that we are not willing to stop struggling in our failures and weaknesses and look to God alone. We really have to pray to the Lord to grant us the light of revelation that we might know ourselves and the salvation of God, in order that we may obtain the revival of the Holy Spirit.

To my readers who are expecting to be raptured, I

would say that we all must be watchful! A little thought
for the flesh is enmity with God; a little care for this life is
sufficient to make our hearts entangled. If we are not yet
ready, then let us not be at peace. Our brother Watchman
Nee says, "I tremble at the thought that the lamps of the
foolish virgins will not burn long enough." Readers, how
do you feel?

With her clear knowledge of the truth, rich experience of
life, absoluteness in following the Lord, and accuracy of discernment, she was able to give timely help, proper support,
and practical care to many needy ones. Through all the years,
Watchman Nee relied much upon her. She was a real
provision of the Lord.

Faithful to the End

Ruth Lee was imprisoned from 1956 until she rested in
the Lord at the age of about seventy-five. She kept her faith
to the end.

PEACE WANG

Peace Wang was born of non-Christian parents in 1899.
She was five years younger than Ruth Lee and four years
older than Watchman Nee. Her family was from the province
of Anhwei. Her original Chinese name was Wang Yih-sun.
After she became a Christian, she adopted the new name,
Wang Pei-chen, which means admiring and wearing the truth.

Saved and Called

Desiring that she could receive a modern education, her
parents sent her to a Christian girls' high school in Hangchow
in the province of Chekiang. It was there that she not only
contacted Christianity but also heard the gospel, believed in
the Lord Jesus, and received salvation. By that time her
father was a county mayor in the province of Chekiang. It was
a great shame to her parents that she had accepted a foreign
religion. Hence, she was very much opposed.

She was not only saved but also very much attracted by

the Lord, and she became zealous for the preaching of His gospel. This provoked her parents to be even more angry with her. Yet this was not all. Since she was so attracted by the Lord and fell in love with the Lord, she deeply felt that the Lord wanted her to give her life to serve Him in evangelistic work. This was extremely upsetting to her parents. They were greatly surprised at her announcement that she was leaving home and intended to travel for the preaching of the gospel. This was intolerable to them. They were determined not to let her leave. She prayed and fasted. Her stepmother, seeing how desperate she was and realizing that she was more than determined and that her mind could not be changed, interceded with her father and advised him to release her. Eventually, her father's anger calmed down, and he decided to let her make her own decision. The day came when she felt it was time to leave home and follow the Lord by faith. When she walked out the main gate of the house, her father and mother followed her, each standing at one of the two doorposts with tears in their eyes, saying, "My daughter! My daughter! You don't want your father and you don't want your mother; you only want your Jesus!" They all wept together. But even such parental affection did not influence her to change her mind. After leaving home she went to study at Nanking Girls' Seminary for a period of time.

Before she was saved, her father had engaged her to a young man of a well-to-do family, a recently returned student from Germany with a very promising future. In answering the Lord's call to give her life for the preaching of His gospel, she was desperate to terminate her engagement. Realizing her irreversible determination, her father was compelled to notify the young man of her decision. But the young man would not give her up until she herself had personally explained her situation to him. When this was done, he became sympathetic and released her from their engagement. Eventually, they all agreed that her cousin, the daughter of her father's brother, should be engaged to the young man in her place.

After finishing her studies in the Nanking Girls' Seminary, she began her evangelistic work. Her preaching was so

convincing and prevailing that many denominations invited
her to hold meetings. In the early years of her preaching,
she traveled through a number of provinces, and hundreds of
people were brought to the Lord through her preaching.

In April 1925 she was invited to my hometown of Chefoo to
preach in the Southern Baptist auditorium. I heard the
report and was intensely curious to witness such a young
lady evangelist, twenty-five years old, preaching the gospel.
We had never heard of such a thing before. Therefore, I
attended her meeting, and I can testify that from that day
to the present I have never seen preaching that was so
prevailing. She preached to a crowd of over one thousand,
not about sin or about hell, but concerning how Satan pos-
sesses and occupies people. She used the story of Pharaoh
possessing the children of Israel as the basis of her message.
I was immediately caught by the Lord.

Turning to the Lord's Recovery

While studying in the seminary in Nanking, she met Sister
Ruth Lee along with other sisters and also Watchman Nee.
Through her contact with them she received enlightenment
concerning the denominations negatively and the church
positively. Her fellowship with them caused her later to turn
to the Lord's recovery in an absolute way. By doing this, she
dropped her popular preaching which was highly esteemed
by hundreds of Christians in the denominations. To them it
was foolish to give up such a promising gospel work. To her,
however, it was obedience to the heavenly vision for which
she was willing to pay the price at any cost. Near the end of
1926, she and some other sisters moved to Shanghai where
they began to meet together.

A Great Asset

Following the establishment of the church in Shanghai,
she became a great help among the sisters. At the same
time she still did much evangelical work, preaching in schools
and visiting in other cities. She was excellent not only in
holding gospel meetings but also in contacting individuals for
salvation. When she stayed in Shanghai, she would visit new

contacts with the gospel. Very rarely was there one to whom she had spoken not eventually saved. While Ruth Lee was a great help to the sisters, Peace Wang's burden was to care for the gospel candidates.

She was a strict and frank person. Because of her love for the Lord, she disciplined herself very much. Hence, she had an excellent character. Her consecration to the Lord was more than absolute with a constant burning zeal. Her will was always submissive to the Lord's, her mind was constantly and instantly sober in understanding spiritual things, and her spirit was pure, strong, and always out front in contacting people. Hence, she reached a high point in spiritual things and had a great measure in spiritual life. By possessing all these qualities, she was equipped with a keen discernment in helping others.

Her whole being was for the Lord and His recovery. Nothing preoccupied, frustrated, or distracted her from the Lord's interest. She was always willing to take care of others' needs at the sacrifice of her own needs. She had a broadened heart to embrace the innumerable spiritually as well as physically needy ones. Thus, hundreds of believers, not only sisters but also brothers, received her warm, brooding care.

She possessed a prominent spirit with a loving heart, a sober mind, and a frank character. She was always bold to point out in tenderness and humility, the weak points, short-comings, defects, faults, and sometimes even sins of those with whom she spoke. Her word was strong, sometimes even sharp, but her tone was full of grace and anointing. Under such speaking, those to whom she ministered always received rich and appropriate help, not only in life but also in the practical matters of their daily living. Watchman Nee treasured her assistance in these aspects very much. The valuable help she imparted to her recipients will need eternity to reveal.

She was not only a great help to the church in Shanghai, but she visited the churches in other cities throughout China and the Southeast Asian countries as well. Early in the year following the establishment of the church in Chefoo, she came to visit us. Her visit greatly strengthened and helped us in the Lord's way. In 1943 I was sick, and the church in Chefoo was depressed due to my long illness. She arrived in the fall of that year to visit me and the church. That visit brought us timely help in our trial. On that same journey, she also visited the saints in Tsingtao and afforded them the supply they needed.

In her work of spreading the Lord's recovery, she was assigned a young sister apprentice to help me in starting the Lord's testimony in Tientsin. As a senior of ten years in the work, she sustained me in whatever needs I had in the Lord's work. Both the church in Tientsin and the church in Peiping were greatly and continually benefited by her presence. Peace Wang and I, along with others, traveled through northwest China and ministered in many places. In our trips she always strongly supported me, and those with her always received her help and care.

In the turmoil caused by the opposition of Mrs. Nee's aunt to her niece's marriage, Peace Wang was the only one who remained in Shanghai facing the difficult situation through the whole period of trouble. During those days she helped me care for the church there during Watchman's absence. Later, in the turmoil stirred up among the brothers and sisters in Shanghai in 1942, when Watchman was forced to discontinue his ministry, Peace Wang had a clear vision of the real situation from the Lord and stood firmly for the Lord's gift to His church, Watchman Nee. By then she was really a wall against the tide, withstanding all the misunderstanding and attacks. Her standing laid the foundation for the later recovery of Watchman's ministry.

After the church in Shanghai closed in 1942, she remained in Shanghai. This was done with the express purpose and expectation that both the church in Shanghai and Brother Nee's ministry would be restored. She was the unique seed for this two-fold purpose. Eventually, after the war, in 1946 the Lord used her with the help of Brother Yu Cheng-hwa to reopen the doors of the church in Shanghai. It was she in the summer of that year who earnestly invited me in writing to visit the restored church there. During my visit the church was greatly healed, and I was very much confirmed and strengthened. After the restoration of the church in Shanghai, she strongly exercised her spiritual function in taking care of the young believers. A number of young saints were raised up and edified through her function and under her care. All of this was a great step in bringing Watchman back to his ministry.

Through her earnest invitation, I was burdened at the end of 1946 to stay in Shanghai and work together with her for the rebuilding of the church and for the restoration of Watchman's ministry. She was an indescribable help to me in the ministry, so much so that a revival was brought in in 1947 and 1948. That was a further step in bringing Watchman Nee back to his ministry. Eventually, he resumed his ministry in Shanghai through that revival. From 1942 to 1948 she played a crucial role under the Lord's leading and anointing to maintain the lifeline of the Lord's recovery.

After he resumed his ministry, Watchman's first burden was to carry out his training on Kuling Mountain. In his second training there, in 1949, Peace Wang was of great assistance to him in caring for the sisters and young trainees.

After the revival reached Hong Kong in 1950, she came from Shanghai with rich blessing to visit the church there and the churches in Amoy and Foochow. Following this trip she returned to Shanghai. This was her last trip in the ministry.

I am deeply indebted to her for my salvation, growth in life, and ministry in the Lord's work. Next to Watchman Nee, she did the most to perfect me. Many among us remember her in the same way with heartfelt gratitude. She was a tremendous asset in the Lord's recovery.

Having Finished the Course

Sister Peace Wang was also imprisoned in 1956 and remained in prison until she went to be with the Lord whom she loved at the age of about seventy. Truly she finished her course in the race.

CHAPTER FIFTEEN

EXPERIENCING THE DISCIPLINE
OF THE HOLY SPIRIT

Like Jacob of old, Watchman Nee passed through many dealings in the Lord's hand. Following the long period of trial during which his ministry was discontinued, in our fellowship with him in Shanghai he frequently referred to the discipline of the Holy Spirit. He learned the following lesson by experience: While God's children are seeking after Him, whatever happens to them, whatever the source, whatever the nature of the dealing, and no matter how it happens, everything is arranged by the sovereign hand of God. This sovereign arrangement of our circumstances is the discipline of the Holy Spirit. The Spirit of God disciplines us by the things which happen to us.

Watchman Nee saw that what we are by nature means nothing; only what the Spirit constitutes within our being counts. Whatever we are by birth, whether good or bad, whether useful or not, is natural and altogether a hindrance to the Holy Spirit in constituting the divine life into our being. For this reason our natural strength, natural wisdom, natural cleverness, natural disposition, natural shortcomings, natural virtues, and natural attributes, plus our character and habits, must all be torn down in order that the Holy Spirit may form in us a new disposition, new character, new habits, new virtues, and new attributes. In order to accomplish this work of reconstitution, the Holy Spirit of God moves within us to enlighten, inspire, lead, and saturate us with the divine life. He also works in our environment to arrange every detail, person, matter, and thing in our situation to tear down what we are naturally. He may arrange to place a certain person in our home in order to tear down our natural quickness or slowness. He may arrange certain matters to abolish our natural cleverness or dullness. He may arrange another situation to tear down our natural wisdom or folly. He uses all kinds of persons, matters, and things to tear down all aspects of our natural being in order that He may conform us to the image of Christ.

Watchman saw in Romans 8 that, on the one hand, the Spirit of God works within us that we may realize our sonship, and that, on the other hand, all things work together for good in our environment that we may be conformed to the image of His firstborn Son. All persons and all situations related to us are arranged by the Spirit of God to match His work within us that we may be conformed to the image of the firstborn Son of God. The work of the Spirit within is to constitute a new being for us; whereas the work of the Spirit without is to tear down every natural aspect of our old being through our environment.

Watchman Nee stressed how vital this is. All things of our natural life must be torn down, that our being may be reconstituted by the Holy Spirit with the divine life. Through all the things that happened to him through the years, he learned that God's children need the discipline of the Holy Spirit. He learned to accept all kinds of circumstances without complaining, blaming, grudging, or criticizing. He considered everything a discipline of the Holy Spirit. Everything benefited him spiritually. He would not miss any opportunity to learn a lesson and gain profit. His frequent question to those who were suffering was, "What lesson have you learned? What profit have you gained?" He did not instruct any one of us to improve our character or correct our behavior; he helped all of us to learn the lesson of the Holy Spirit's discipline.

He continually reminded us that to improve character or correct behavior is simply to make the natural being better, whereas the discipline of the Holy Spirit tears down our natural being to constitute a renewed being.

I never saw or heard him condemn anything or anyone. He was always calm, peaceful, and willing to accept any kind of environment. Regardless of the situation, he gave the Holy Spirit every opportunity to tear down some aspect of his natural life and renew him with the divine life. He was always ready to cooperate with the indwelling Spirit to carry out His discipline through outward circumstances. For this reason, he was always at peace with others, at rest in the Lord, and growing in life.

Chapter Sixteen

EXPERIENCING THE BREAKING
OF THE OUTER MAN
AND THE RELEASE OF THE SPIRIT

In the early days of his Christian life, Watchman Nee learned how to bear the cross, to live a crucified life, and to live in the Lord's presence. The chapters in his book *The Normal Christian Life* were all lessons learned in those early years. Later, he learned the further spiritual lessons of the discipline of the Holy Spirit, the breaking of the outer man, and the release of the spirit. In fellowship with him after his many sufferings during the war, he stressed three main points: the discipline of the Holy Spirit, the breaking of the outer man, and the release of the spirit.

No doubt, during the long period of his suffering, he learned many lessons, but in his fellowship he indicated no other lessons. He not only talked about the breaking of the outer man and the release of the spirit, but these experiences were also his reality. In the late 1940s, when he resumed his ministry, what came out from him was an impression that this was a broken man, a man through whom the Spirit could be fully released.

He frequently shared that though the Holy Spirit dwells in our spirit, if our outer man is not broken, our spirit could never be released. The Holy Spirit dwelling in our spirit is confined and imprisoned by the outer man. For this reason the outer man must be broken that the inner man (the human spirit with the Holy Spirit) might be released. The scriptural basis for this reality is 2 Corinthians 4:16, "Though our outer man is decaying, yet our inner man is being renewed day by day."

Watchman Nee taught that when contacting others, preaching the gospel, ministering the Word, or testifying, we need the release of the spirit that the Spirit of life may come out of us to impart life to others. How much life can be imparted in testimonies and ministries depends on how much spirit can be released from within us. How much spirit can be released depends on how much the outer man has been broken. This is not simply a matter of tearing down some aspect of the natural being; this is a matter of breaking the outer man.

When contacting others, Watchman Nee did not exercise his natural insight to understand their situation. He always exercised his spirit to sense their real condition before the Lord. Whenever he was listening or speaking to others, his released spirit was foremost, not his broken outer man. The result was that what he spoke to others was not mere knowledge or instruction but life supply conveyed in his released spirit.

When he ministered the Word, what was crucial was the release of his spirit. What he cared for was not doctrine, but the release of his spirit.

To him the ministry of God's Word was a failure unless there was the release of the spirit. It was not difficult for Watchman Nee to release his spirit, for through years of suffering his outer man had been broken. However, it was difficult for those of us who were with him to release our spirit because our outer man still remained whole.

When he was with others or was ministering the Word, it was unnecessary for him to spend a long period of time to prepare his spirit to be released. In the opening word he could release his spirit with no time lapse. Since his outer man was broken, he could release his spirit anytime, unless he deliberately restricted it. It was not easy for others of us to release our spirit; but it was difficult for him to restrict his spirit because the shell of his outer man had been broken.

What we are speaking of here is not just a walk in the spirit that we may live a spiritual life; we are speaking of the release of the spirit that life may be released from within us to supply and nourish others. Watchman Nee's fellowship and ministry were rich in life. The secret was this: His outer man had been broken, and his spirit was easily released.

Watchman Nee strongly emphasized the breaking of the

outer man for the release of the spirit. He shared that the breaking of the outer man cannot be accomplished in a short time. All the situations and environments in our whole life are arranged by God to accomplish this one thing. This is the ultimate consummation of the Holy Spirit's discipline.

In the days after he resumed his ministry, he repeatedly stressed the breaking of the outer man. In his fellowship with us concerning the Lord's work, he pointed out that among the co-workers, the limitation of usefulness and fruitfulness in every case was due to the lack of this one thing: the breaking of the outer man. Through many years of suffering, he fully experienced this breaking and set a good example in this matter. Insofar as my personal knowledge of him is concerned, this was the final lesson he learned from the Lord.

CHAPTER SEVENTEEN

MATURED

The book of Genesis reveals that by the time Jacob reached the end of his life, he had matured to become Israel. We also see a matured life in Watchman Nee after his many experiences with the Lord and much suffering. His maturity was manifested in a number of ways.

He was one with the Lord because his whole being was saturated with the Lord. It was difficult to find a trace of anything natural in his being. He was always in the spirit, never frustrated by the flesh or restricted by the natural man.

He was always prepared to minister the Lord to others. It was unnecessary for him to prepare himself to minister; he was able to minister life to others constantly and instantly. Watchman Nee possessed a matured measure of life.

He was full of insight and able to discern the situation of others in a thorough way. He had the ability to isolate a person's problem and thoroughly diagnose his condition.

His heart was large, and he enjoyed bearing the burdens of others. The burdens of others were not a heavy weight to him; his care for them was like an ocean, without scarcity. He fully bore the burden of the Lord's recovery in building up the churches in China. Yet there was no indication that he was either striving or struggling to fulfill his commission.

In his dealings with others, sweetness, tenderness, and softness were spontaneous. He did not perform. The flavor of these virtues simply overflowed spontaneously from the fullness of his matured life.

It was his testimony that he was ready to be either raptured or martyred. As I write these words, on the desk before me are two paperweights made of stone. One bears the inscription of his word: "My future is to be either raptured or martyred."

CHAPTER EIGHTEEN

POURED OUT AS A DRINK OFFERING

In November of 1948 and February of 1949, Watchman Nee called two urgent conferences in Shanghai for the leading co-workers. In the last of these conferences, after much prayer and consideration, Watchman Nee made the decision to remain in Shanghai for the work of the Lord's recovery. On the one hand, he fully trusted in the Lord's sovereignty; on the other hand, he realized the risk and was prepared to be sacrificed for the Lord's testimony. Such willingness on his part was surely the supply of the Lord's grace. After he had made the decision to stay in Shanghai, he took immediate steps to carry out his second training in Kuling.

In January 1950, he visited Hong Kong with the intention of returning to the mainland after a brief stay. Brothers from different places advised him not to return and warned him of the risk. However, because of his burden for the churches, the co-workers, and the Lord's testimony on the mainland, without hesitation he determined to return. In this respect he was like the apostle Paul in Acts 20:24: "But I consider my life of no account as if precious to myself, in order that I may finish my course and the ministry which I have received from the Lord Jesus." He realized the risks, but his will was firmly set and his spirit courageous to finish his course and to fulfill the ministry which he had received of the Lord. At this same time he received a cable from Swatow that his mother had died. However, because of the urgent need among the churches and co-workers on the mainland, he went directly to Shanghai from Hong Kong in the middle of March and left his mother's funeral in the hands of his eldest sister.

This was a crucial time for the recovery in China. Upon returning to Shanghai, he labored to care for the churches and the co-workers and to edify many believers who had turned to the Lord's recovery from denominations and free groups. Anticipating what was soon to come, he also grasped the opportunity to publish the messages delivered in his two trainings at Kuling. It was his hope that these messages could be preserved for the future benefit of the churches.

In the spring of 1952, he was arrested and imprisoned; and in the summer of 1956, after a long trial, he was sentenced to fifteen years' imprisonment. He was, however, never released.

During his imprisonment, only his wife was allowed an occasional visit. She passed away on November 7, 1971. His wife's death was a great sorrow, and it cut him off from any contact with the outside. Not long after her death, on May 30, 1972, Watchman Nee also came to the end of his pilgrimage on this earth and rested with Christ, whom he served at the cost of his life.

His faith in the Lord never changed. He poured himself out as a drink offering upon the Lord's recovery for the care of the churches which were established through his ministry according to the vision and commission he received of the Lord. He fought a good fight, finished the course, and kept the faith.

During his imprisonment he was confined, but his ministry was not bound (2 Tim. 2:9). Under the Lord's sovereignty, his ministry has spread throughout the entire world as an anti-testimony to today's Christianity and a rich supply of life to all seeking Christians.

His unique burden was the churches as the house of God, God's tabernacle. Although his own earthly tabernacle has been dissolved, the churches, so much on his heart, are not only surviving but also continuing to grow vigorously and to spread widely on this earth. "Though he has died, he still speaks."

CHAPTER NINETEEN

WITNESSED

This chapter contains the testimonies of five persons who knew Watchman Nee personally. What they have written concerning him is drawn from their personal knowledge and firsthand experience extending over a period of years.

1. HIS BROTHER-IN-LAW

The first testimony is that of his brother-in-law, Samuel I. L. Chang, who was an elder in the church in Los Angeles.

His Relationship with Watchman Nee

Watchman Nee's grandmother and my grandmother were classmates in school. Their friendship began the relationship between our two families. Our fathers were also schoolmates, as were our sisters, and in due time he and I also attended the same school. Our relationship, however, was not merely the kind of friendship persons in the world have, but became the kind of relationship which exists between two Christian brothers. This relationship between us continued down through the years. It was through fellowship with Watchman Nee in 1927 that I was made clear concerning my own salvation. In 1934 he married my sister, but even though he became my brother-in-law, our relationship continued to be based not upon family ties but upon our relationship in Christ.

Assurance of Salvation through Watchman Nee

My spiritual relationship with Watchman Nee began when I received the assurance of salvation. He ministered Christ to me in the Spirit, bringing me into a genuine and living enjoyment of the assurance of salvation. He asked me simply, "Are you saved?" I replied, "I don't know." He asked again, "Why are you not saved?" Again I replied, "I don't know." Then he asked, "Do you believe John 3:16?" He then proceeded to break this verse down, clause by clause: "'God so loved the world that He gave His only begotten Son.'" He asked, "Do you believe this?" I replied, "Yes, I believe this." He asked, "Do you believe that 'every one who believes into Him would not perish, but have eternal life'?" I said, "Yes, I believe that also." He asked, "Are you saved?" I said, "I don't know." Then he said to me strongly, "But *God* said this. If you don't believe what He says, you make Him a liar!" These words lifted the veil from my heart and quickened my spirit. Immediately, I sensed the anointing within and fully believed that I was saved.

Ministered To by Watchman Nee

On a number of occasions when I had personal problems, I went to Watchman Nee for help. Not one time was I rebuked. He would simply ask, "What have you learned from the Lord?" He helped me realize that all things occur under God's hand and are working together for good to conform me to the image of His Son (Rom. 8:28-29).

On one occasion my wife entered the hospital for an operation. Following the operation, the enemy attacked her with accusations and caused her to think that she was about to die. This news was reported to Watchman Nee, and he and my sister went to visit her. He realized that she was under the accusation of the enemy and ministered to her from Revelation 12:11: "And they overcame him because of the blood of the Lamb and because of the word of their testimony, and they loved not their soul-life even unto death." Then he telephoned me and confessed that his failure to help keep me in the Lord's fellowship had given the enemy ground to attack my wife. For this failure he asked my forgiveness. He fully realized that the warfare was not simply a matter for my wife alone, but that the warfare also required her husband and the church. This is why he asked me to forgive him. He realized that in order to fight against the enemy I needed the church and that there had been neglect on his part in being one with me. I told him, however, that it was not his fault; the fault lay in my inadequate consecration and in my love for the world. That is what gave the enemy the ground. Immediately I repented to the Lord. The moment I repented, the enemy left my wife, and the Lord gave her peace. The next morning when Watchman Nee's mother came to pray with her, she was able to sing praises to the Lord and enjoy the Lord's sweet anointing. This incident shows that Watchman Nee knew the ways of God. Through his spiritual discernment, my family was helped and was brought back to a complete union with Christ in our daily living.

My Impression of Watchman Nee

Watchman Nee was a person who was thoroughly saturated with the Lord. He was a man who lived in the Lord's presence. His disposition, character, and behavior had been transformed through the years under the perfecting hand of Miss Margaret E. Barber. He could listen without interruption to the words or suggestions of others. He was a man whose inner being had been touched by the Lord, and one who had acquired much rich experience from being dealt with by the Lord. If it were not so, such a genius would have found it extremely difficult to maintain a relationship with a foolish, stupid young brother like me. Later on, when I worked closely with him, I observed that he could listen to any kind of person without giving the impression that he was superior. He was transformed to such a degree that he could be built up with anyone, no matter what their condition, without being frustrated by their shortcomings or childishness.

In observing Watchman Nee's way of working, I never saw him try to impose his authority. Rather, he would set an example himself. He would rise early in the morning and work regular hours. He never took things lightly or acted loosely. Neither was he lazy. He never assumed that he was the boss, nor did he require of others what he himself would not do. He worked with his own hands, teaching others to work together with tenderness, love, patience, and cooperation.

Today most of Christianity criticizes him for his ministry concerning the church. Yet, I can testify that his ministry regarding the church was not a doctrine, a theory, or an unworkable plan. Not only did he teach what God revealed to him concerning the church—he also put the revelation into practice. Although the practice of the church, as God revealed it to Watchman Nee, was not seen on a large scale during his lifetime, today it has been fully vindicated. It is workable. Thousands of believers today can testify that they are living in the full reality of the church life.

2. A CLASSMATE

Weigh Kwang-hsi, who passed away in 1988, was Watchman Nee's classmate. The following is his testimony which he wrote in 1973:

For several years Watchman Nee and I were classmates at Trinity College, a school founded by the Church of England in the city of Foochow. We were good friends and frequently studied and played together. During our junior and senior high school years, we were both nominal Christians. We both had some knowledge of the Bible, and we outwardly kept the Christian forms of baptism, holy communion, church attendance, Bible study, and prayer. But we had never accepted in our hearts the Christ who was crucified for our sins and who resurrected on the third day, and we did not know Him as our personal Savior. We both loved the world and pursued the vanities of the world.

Watchman Nee was pursuing scholastic attainment in the field of Chinese literature. He would frequently write articles for publication in the newspapers. The money he earned was spent on lottery tickets. He was also fond of the movies. I preferred sports and yearned for the fame and praise of men.

In our first college year, his life suddenly changed. He became a fervent Christian and ceased pursuing the world. He frequently testified to his classmates, exhorting them to believe in the Lord Jesus. Many schoolmates did believe in the Lord and began voluntarily to pray in the college chapel, even during weekdays. He would frequently study the Bible in class; however, this did not seem to affect his grades. He usually came out with the highest examination scores in every subject. The lives of many of the students were changed by accepting the Lord, and the dormitory director admitted that some mischievous students, who had previously violated school regulations, had accepted the Lord and experienced a great change in their lives. As a result, he found himself with fewer cases of violation of school rules by students.

Saved through Watchman Nee

Watchman Nee invited me to attend some gospel meetings, but I refused. My heart was set on becoming famous in the sports world. One day, however, he came to my room and preached the gospel to me alone, urging me to accept the Lord Jesus as my Savior. Though I attempted to argue with him concerning some religious problems, he would not argue; instead, he asked me several questions: "Have you sinned? Do you know if your sins are forgiven? Do you know if you are saved?" At the time I didn't understand why, but in my heart I felt sorrowful. Later I realized that this was the convicting work of the Holy Spirit. He preached the gospel to me, explaining that God loved me and gave His only begotten Son for me, and that if I would truly believe in Him, I would not perish but would have eternal life. When asked if I would believe in Christ, I said I would. We knelt together and prayed, with him praying first. Then I prayed, asking the Lord to forgive my sins and thanking Him for loving and saving me. When I rose up, my heart was filled with joy and peace. I experienced a great change in my life and brought forth the fruit of repentance. My name had been one of the names on his

prayer list, and the Lord answered his prayer. Praise the
Lord!

Recovered by Watchman Nee

In 1924 I transferred to Nanking University and came
under the influence of modernism. My faith was shaken.
At that time Watchman Nee was staying in a brother's home
in Nanking, recuperating from an illness. I frequently visited him for fellowship, and he helped me escape the
influence of modernism. After his health improved, I was
able to make arrangements for him to preach the gospel at
Nanking University. As a result of his preaching, two of my
classmates were saved.

Edified by Watchman Nee

In 1928, when I was about to leave the university, I
considered serving the Lord full-time. I did not want to be
a preacher on salary, but I did not know how to live by
faith, so I went to Watchman Nee for fellowship. At that
time he was quite lonely and greatly in need of co-workers
who would be of the same mind. When I raised this matter,
he did not encourage me in a careless manner to serve the
Lord. He was neither influenced by his need for co-workers
nor by the personal relationship between us. He simply
told me not to wait until the Jordan waters opened, but to
step into the water by faith—then the way would open
before me. He knew that I lacked this kind of faith. I was
waiting for the outward circumstances to change before
beginning to serve the Lord. (Fifty years ago in China it
was difficult to find anyone serving the Lord by faith like
Watchman Nee.) Hence, I laid aside the thought of serving
the Lord full-time and taught college for eight years.

In the spring of 1934, Watchman Nee held his third
overcomer conference in Shanghai. In the morning he
spoke on the centrality and universality of Christ. In the
afternoon he spoke on God's overcomers. Through his
messages in this conference, the Lord gave me revelation
which brought about a great turn in my spiritual life. As a
result, I stood up in the conference and for the first time

consecrated my entire life to the Lord. At that time I was still teaching school.

In 1935 in Chefoo, Brother Nee experienced anew the outpouring of the Holy Spirit. After this, he held a conference in Chuanchow, Fukien, and asked me to attend. There many were helped to experience the outpouring of the Holy Spirit, with the result that they had power and boldness to witness for the Lord. He also preached on the secret of the overcoming life, which is to let Christ live in our stead, according to Paul's testimony in Galatians 2:20. This conference brought in a great revival.

Confirmed and Assigned by Watchman Nee

In October 1936, Watchman Nee conducted a co-workers' conference in Kulangsu, Fukien. He cabled me and invited me to attend. By that time I had become clear concerning the Lord's call and was prepared to resign my teaching job to live by faith and serve the Lord. While I was seeking the Lord for His guidance, I received Brother Nee's invitation. I immediately realized that it was the Lord's will for me to attend the conference. I thank the Lord that at this conference I was given the rare opportunity of listening to Watchman Nee's testimony, which I was later able to publish as three articles. At the end of the conference, Brother Nee and the other co-workers assigned me to begin the work in Canton and later in Hong Kong. In 1937 Watchman Nee began the Lord's work in the southwest part of China in the city of K'un-ming in Yunnan province. After establishing the church there, he invited me to come and work in that locality. I picked up the burden and moved my family there. I worked there for three years, until my return to Hong Kong in 1940.

Following World War II, whenever Watchman Nee visited Canton or Hong Kong, I took the opportunity to seek his fellowship. I usually planned to ask him a number of questions, but after having some fellowship with him, it was unnecessary to ask the questions. In our fellowship I always received an abundant supply of life.

Trained by Watchman Nee

In 1948 I again had opportunity to attend a conference in the church in Shanghai. Brother Nee ministered on the matter of handing over ourselves with all we possess to the Lord. His words were full of impact and the power of the Holy Spirit, and the meetings were full of the Lord's presence. Many were revived and handed over themselves and their possessions, to be built together in serving the Lord. In the last meeting of the conference, because I was leaving for Foochow, Brother Nee, in the presence of all the assembled brothers and sisters, addressed me in the following words of farewell:

There is only one Christ, but due to different viewpoints and emphases of the workers, it seems that Christ has been divided into many Christs. If a worker cannot express to others the one Christ whom God desires to present, his work is a failure. Many today have had very intimate contact with the Lord, while others are merely pressing against Him (Mark 5:24). Perhaps some have indeed touched His back, held His hand, or torn His garments; yet they have no relationship whatever with Him in life. Among the many who thronged Jesus, the woman with an issue of blood was not the only one who was ill, but she was the only one healed in life (Matt. 9:20-22).

Some today indeed know the Christ of Bethsaida (Mark 8:22-26) or the Christ of Gadara (Mark 5:1-20) or the Christ of Emmaus (Luke 24:13-35). In their experience they have really seen the miracles and the wonders. They may even be able to perform the miracles themselves. Yet if there is no true inward revelation, none of these works will amount to any-thing. Some may be able to tell others with moving power of a Christ of Emmaus. They may be able to expound the Scriptures and may cause others to become truly fervent in their hearts; yet it is all to no avail. The real work is to impart a Christ of revelation to others. I speak these words not only to Brother

Weigh, but to all the co-workers and to all the brothers and sisters alike. If you and I cannot impart a Christ of revelation to others, our work is a failure.

Here we see that there are two basically different stands that a worker of the Lord can take: one emphasizes work, the expounding of the Scriptures, miracles, works of wonders, and answers to prayers, etc. The other presents before men a Christ of revelation.

In the same year, 1948, from the beginning of June to the end of September, Watchman Nee held a period of training on Kuling Mountain, Fukien, for the purpose of training co-workers from all over China. I attended that training. Every day we spent approximately seven hours listening to Brother Nee and receiving his ministry. I was greatly helped in my spiritual understanding and also in the principles of working for the Lord....

My Last Contact with Watchman Nee

In the early part of 1950, Watchman Nee came to Hong Kong. Soon Witness Lee also joined him. In the past it had been a rare occurrence for these two brothers to visit the same church at the same time. Their ministry issued in a great revival in the church in Hong Kong. Previously there had been about three hundred in the meetings. As a result of the revival the number increased to between two and three thousand. There was a special blessing upon the church in Hong Kong.

3. HIS TRAINEE

Chang Wu-chen, a leading co-worker on the island of Taiwan, was one of Watchman Nee's trainees. The following is his testimony regarding Watchman Nee:

Saved through Watchman Nee

I first met Watchman Nee in Chefoo, Shantung province, in the summer of 1935. I was then twenty-one years old. I was raised in a Christian family and studied in a

Christian school. Though my mother's father had been a
Free Methodist pastor, Christianity left me with a very poor
impression, and I became an atheist. God was merciful to
me, however, and caused me to meet Watchman Nee and
Witness Lee. It was through them that I received salvation.

My aunt, who was quite concerned for my salvation,
found occasion to introduce me to Watchman Nee in
Witness Lee's living room. He began to preach the gospel
to me, and we debated the matter of God's existence.
He gave many reasons to prove God's existence, but I
argued that since I could not see God, I could not believe in
Him. Then he asked, "Can you see everything with your
eyes? Do you deny the existence of something simply
because you cannot see it? For example, there are electrical
waves and air in this room. Can you deny their existence?
God is not physical; God is Spirit. You cannot contact God
with your eyes; you must use your spirit. If you seek
God with your spirit, you will find Him." Then I asked,
"How do I contact God with my spirit?" His reply was,
"Just speak to God from deep within, according to your
need and inner sense."

I went home and began to pray according to his instruction. Thank God! He answered my prayer and changed me
from within. The following Sunday I attended the meeting.
Witness Lee preached the gospel. His words were so
powerful that the Lord was able to conquer me, deliver me,
and clearly save me.

Helped through His Publications

After being saved, I secretly consecrated myself to the
Lord. The Lord was so dear and so precious to me that I
was willing to give up the world and serve Him the rest
of my life. Then for twelve years I did not see Watchman
Nee, but continued to receive much help through his spiritual publications.

Trained by Watchman Nee

I was a trainee in Watchman Nee's first training
on Kuling Mountain, Foochow, in 1948. I attended his

training for nearly four months and was greatly helped by him. On one occasion, after I gave a testimony, he made the following comments:

Brother Chang, you said that in spiritual matters you frequently felt flat and often felt dry. I hope that from now on you will disregard all these feelings. Whether or not you feel flat, disregard it. Simply commit yourself into the Lord's hand and believe that He is able to take care of you, and spontaneously He will bring you through. There are many problems we cannot overcome by ourselves. However, when we behold the Lord and draw near to the Lord, the problem disappears.

The following is a parable about a centipede. One day, as a centipede was about to walk, it examined its legs to consider which one should move first. Should the left leg move first or the right one? How about the eighth leg, or the tenth? The centipede was stuck there trying to make a decision. The problem of the mind became a problem of the practice. Eventually, the sun came up. Without thinking, the centipede ran out to see the sunrise without considering which leg should move first. It forgot about how to walk and simply walked. When the problem of the mind was gone, the problem of the practice also disappeared.

The more you try to deal with the inner dryness, depression, and flatness, the more you cannot overcome them. These things become an issue because you make them an issue. If you forget about them and let them go, they will disappear.

Sometimes a problem is conquered by fighting, and other times it is conquered by forgetting. Many things can be gotten over by the exercise of your strength. But at other times, simply by forgetting it, the problem is solved. Boast in your weakness and give up your striving and your methods; then His power will spread over you.

This is the secret: Ask God to give you a glimpse of His riches and His glory through reading the Bible, praying, attending a meeting, or having fellowship with the brothers. Spontaneously, you will forget about other things. The infilling comes by forgetting, and forgetting comes by touching the Lord. Once you touch the Lord, you will no longer look at yourself.

Following his comments on my testimony, I asked him the following question: "I was sick for a year with tuberculosis, even with blood in my mucus. One day God's word came, I received faith, and the sickness was healed. But occasionally I would vomit again and the symptom would reappear. Why does the symptom reappear, and how do I overcome it?"

Brother Nee gave the following answer:

Concerning the matter of healing, we must pay attention to three things: 1) Do not tempt God, 2) Do not accept the symptom, and 3) Believe that the grace is sufficient.

Timothy had a chronic stomach problem. Paul advised him to no longer drink water. In those days the Jews had water ponds beneath their houses to store rain water or water diverted from another source. Bacteria grew in the water and made it unsanitary. So Paul advised Timothy to use a little wine (1 Tim. 5:23). Wine has a warming effect and helps the blood circulation. Paul had the gift of healing, and he healed many sick ones, but he did not heal Timothy's sickness. Timothy himself was also gifted, yet he could not get his own stomach problem healed. God did not give a word. Timothy could not say, "It doesn't matter whether I drink water or wine." No! That would be tempting God. He should not drink the water out of a clay pond. To trust God and to tempt God may appear the same outwardly. The difference is in whether you have God's word or not. From all appearance, to rise up and walk with God's word is the same as to rise up and walk without God's word.

But to rise and walk without God's word is to tempt God. If I walk on the premise that God can heal me, I am tempting God. But if I have God's word, I do not need to worry about the law of sanitation. If I do not have God's word, I should not disobey the natural law. Look at the man with the withered hand. Because the Lord had spoken a word to him, he did not wait until the symptom changed to believe that he was healed. He could ignore the symptom. The Lord told him to stretch forth his hand, and he simply stretched forth his hand. The Lord's word is dependable; the symptom is not. The paralytic did not wait until he was stronger before picking up his bed and walking. The Lord told him to pick up his bed and walk; so he picked it up and walked. When you have the Lord's word, you do not need to check your pulse or see if your fever is gone. If one does not have God's word, he needs to abide by the law of sanitation. But if one has God's word, he can afford to be an extremist, fearing nothing.

Watchman Nee then gave this testimony of how he was healed:

I was sick. Then one day God sent His word to heal me. I only knew that I must take care of God's word and not my symptom. If God says I am healed, then His word has stopped the illness. If you continue to look at your sickness, God's word loses its effectiveness. I was neither delighted if my fever went down nor nervous if it went up. My eyes were not on my temperature but on God's word. Whether the temperature was high or low, whether the blood count was more or less, these were not the Lord. Only the Lord is the Lord. Learn to laugh at the temperature. It doesn't matter whether it is high or low. Learn to trust in God's word and not in the symptom. Only God's word is real; the symptom is false. When God says it is over, it is over. If you vomited blood, God must be testing your faith. Learn to trust in God's word

and not in the symptom, and the symptom will
change. At first, I could not believe that I was healed
either, because I did not have God's word. But one
day God's word came, yet my symptom was still very
serious. But I rose up and said, "Lord, rebuke the
symptom if it is false." One or two hours later the
illness was gone.

I had a lung problem, a kidney problem, a liver
problem, and a heart problem. In 1923 I had peritoni-
tis. I lay in bed for over a month. Breathing was
painful to me. My fever was high and I was in much
suffering. Brother Miao asked some saints to come
and pray for me. When he prayed I felt nothing. However, when a certain sister, Miss Barber, prayed,
"Lord, no one in the grave can praise Thee. If our
brother dies, he will not be able to praise Thee," my
heart was relieved, even though my fever was still
high and I was still in acute pain. When the day
dawned, I arose and walked to Lo-Hsing Pagoda to
edit an issue of *The Christian*. If you do not have God's
word, you must take care of your body. But if you
have God's word, you should ignore the symptom.
Treat the symptom as a temptation and a lie. Do not
stay with the symptom; stay away from it.

Some illnesses are healed immediately; others are
not. Once when sick, I asked the Lord to heal me. The
Lord said, "The healing will not take place quickly,
but My grace is sufficient for you." Then the Lord
showed me something. A boat sailing in the middle of
a stream was facing a big rock and could not get
through. The Lord asked me, "Shall I remove the rock
so you can get through, or shall I raise the water level
so that you can go over it?" At that moment I was
clear concerning the Lord's will, and I said, "Lord, I
do not ask to have the problem removed; I ask for an
increase of Your grace."

There is no illness in the world that a Christian
cannot overcome. If you have the Lord's word,
do not care for the symptom. Believe that God is

faithful. Be strengthened by contacting God's word, not by seeking removal of the symptom. Neither need you fear that the symptom will be an obstacle. Although the rock is not removed, the water level will be increased, not just some but greatly. This is our way.

In summary, these three things should be noted: 1) If you act without God's word, you tempt God; 2) If you have God's word, do not look at the symptom; 3) If God's word does not heal you immediately, then His grace will be sufficient for you. He never intended that we be sick and lack sufficient grace. Paul had an infirmity, yet he worked more than anyone else. Illness never stops the work. Learn to commit yourself to the true and faithful Lord.

A month before attending the Kuling training, I vomited a mouthful of blood and stayed in a Shanghai hospital. When the vomiting stopped, I went to Kuling. That was why I asked the question concerning the recurrence of a symptom after being healed. After receiving Brother Nee's help and guidance, the Lord showed me that in this universe only two things are real: God and His word. Everything else is false. Since I had God's word, I was healed, and since I was healed, there was no need to care for the symptom. Since God's word had come, any symptom was a lie. I thank God that from June 1948 until this very day in 1991, for forty-three years, I have not vomited blood again, not even a trace. The symptom has completely fled. Praise the Lord!

Impressed with Watchman Nee

Whenever Watchman Nee was asked a question, his answer was always practical, to the point, clear, full of anointing, and filled with light. His manner was very normal and open, and he was easy to approach. He had a great capacity and a broad heart. In spiritual matters, he climbed to the heights and touched the depths. Concerning God's principle and purpose, he was very rich in understanding and experience. He was frequently misunderstood and evil spoken of, but he never attempted to explain or vindicate himself. Once when asked why he would not make some effort to explain so as to avoid being misunderstood, he replied, "Brothers, if people trust us, there is no need to explain; if people do not trust us, there is no use in explaining." Not only would he not explain or vindicate when being backbitten; he would not reason or argue even when rebuked to his face.

He belittled the matter of riches. Substantial amounts of money passed through his hands. He was entrusted with large amounts to distribute in the Lord's work, and he also earned large sums in his business. Yet, while receiving with one hand, he would distribute with the other. On one occasion he said, "I believe that among the co-workers in China, I am the one who most frequently spends the last dollar." This was surely so. All those close to him knew that he was often empty-handed, keeping nothing for himself. But for the Lord's work and for the need of the church, he would give anything.

4. BY A CLOSE ASSOCIATE

The following is the testimony of a close associate of Watchman Nee, Dr. Chang Yu-lan, who was a leading brother in the church in Taipei, Taiwan:

Impression of Watchman Nee

Watchman Nee arrived in Chungking on March 6, 1945, and three days later attended a love feast to which he had been invited by the church in Chungking. He stayed in my home for ten days, and we continued to see each other for over a year. Later he moved to a place nearby called Little Lung-kan. Some of us would go to his home once or twice a week for fellowship. This continued for over six months. I would always have some questions prepared and would ask them one by one. His answers solved many problems. He always left a very sweet impression, yet one did not lose the sense of respect. His attitude was gentle and meek, and his words were full of anointing. In conversation with him, there was no sense of distance but a sense of being watered and supplied. Frequently seven or eight brothers and sisters would surround him, talking and asking questions for several hours, but he never showed tiredness. The impression left by his words and manner are unforgettable.

Concerning Spiritual Instruction

He told us about going to Margaret Barber weekly, during his student days, to be rebuked. At those times when there was nothing to rebuke, she would ask questions until some fault was found; then she would rebuke him. He said that through this means he received excellent spiritual instruction.

On one occasion Watchman Nee was rebuked by an employee. This employee pointed his finger and pounded his fist, rebuking Watchman Nee for almost four hours. At one point, some neighbors who felt the employee was being unfair, stepped in to intervene. But Watchman Nee sat calmly in his chair, holding a newspaper, without changing expression, as if nothing were happening. At times while he was being rebuked, he would nod his head. When I saw that, I could not understand it. Now I know that he was receiving it as a discipline from God's hand and was submitting himself to this circumstance God had allowed.

Frequently, Watchman Nee would suddenly lift up his eyes, look to heaven, and say, "He is God." The implication was that every circumstance was under God's sovereign arrangement and that he was willing to receive it as such and to obey.

Watchman Nee did not have the usual concept toward those who would inflict him with hurt. On one occasion he said, "The brothers who transgress are like little children who have fallen into a miry ditch. Their clothes and hair are defiled. But give them a bath, and they will be clean again. In the future all the brothers and sisters will be transparent precious stones in the New Jerusalem."

In Chungking the brothers asked him to participate in the Lord's table. However, he would not partake of the bread or the cup; he simply sat and prayed silently. His reason: "The problem in the church in Shanghai has not been resolved; therefore, I cannot break the bread here." I asked him when he would resume his ministry, and he replied, "There is no possibility."

Concerning the Lord's leading for the work, Watchman Nee was very keen in his discernment and quick in making decisions. In explaining why this was so, he said, "If I am wrong, the Lord will use the wall and the donkey to stop me, as He did with Balaam." This attitude indicates that Watchman Nee was one who always obeyed the discipline of the Holy Spirit.

Concerning the Christian Life

On one occasion Watchman Nee instructed some of us, saying, "Christians must escape the system of Christianity. It is more important to deal with the system than to deal with consecration. It is useless to consecrate inside the system." When asked whether it was permissible to play cards without betting money, he replied, "To the Christian there is no absolute right or wrong. It may be all right for one person to do a thing, but not all right for another person to do the same thing. What is right or wrong for a Christian depends upon the level of life he has attained; the level of life is reflected in how many things he cannot do."

Prayer and Fellowship with the Lord

Watchman Nee prayed in a slow way with one or two words coming slowly from his mouth. When I was in Chungking, I unconsciously picked up his way of prayer. By praying in such a way I sensed the presence of the Lord abiding with me. Every word was directed to the Lord, and the words kept springing up from within. Later, a leading brother rebuked me for that practice and told me that I should not copy another's way of prayer, so I stopped praying that way. However, even to this day, when I pray privately I still pray this way, pouring out to God one or two words at a time. By praying in this way, it is much easier to touch the anointing.

On how to maintain fellowship with the Lord, Watchman Nee used the following example: "Suppose a train is traveling from Szechuan to K'un-ming. It must pass through many tunnels. Sometimes it is traveling in darkness, sometimes in light. The experience of a Christian's fellowship with the Lord is the same. If one is in darkness, he must first confess his sin. If there is no sense of sin, he must exercise his will to continue on in the fellowship."

Maturity in Life

On the matter of maturing in life, Watchman Nee said this:

Time is needed for life to mature. Other than having a big head, young people cannot really be matured. Maturity is a matter of the enlargement of capacity. You must allow God to give you time to suffer beyond measure; then your capacity will be enlarged. Some could suffer the loss of five dollars, but could never suffer the loss of five thousand dollars. Some could forgive others two or three times, but the fifth time would make their hands tremble. One discovers by eating whether a fruit is raw or ripe. Raw fruit tastes sour and bitter and is tough and hard. Only ripe fruit tastes sweet and fragrant. Madame Guyon had the flavor of ripeness. She was a teacher to the elderly and a friend to children. The Christian life grows in a natural way. It is not a matter of being artificially ripened like the ripening of a banana with mild heat. The Son of Man came eating and drinking. With some people, their eating and drinking exposes their true condition. Life does not come as a result of spiritual cultivation. If you have the Spirit, there is no need of cultivation; if you do not have the Spirit, there is no way to cultivate. Lilies blossom and birds grow feathers quite spontaneously. There is no need for them to cultivate these features. Cultivation can only produce a "saint" according to the world's concept; it cannot produce a real Christian. It is sufficient to have the seal of the cross on the negative side. There is no need to strive to bear fruit. Striving only delays the growth of life; it cannot speed it up. It is important for us to receive God's arrangement in the circumstances. This arrangement is the discipline of the Holy Spirit. To escape God's arrangement just one time is to lose an opportunity to have our capacity enlarged. This will prolong the time required for life to mature in us and will even require us to make up this lesson in order to reach maturity. A believer can never be the same after passing through suffering. Either he will have his capacity enlarged or he will become more hardened. For this reason, when believers are passing through suffering, they must pay attention and they must realize that maturity in life is the sum total of receiving the discipline of the Holy Spirit. People may see a person who has matured in life, but they cannot see the accumulated discipline of the Holy Spirit which that person has received secretly day by day throughout the years.

A Few Spiritual Sayings

Watchman Nee once said, "The lower we put something, the safer it is. It is safest to put a cup on the floor." The implication was that the more the workers of the Lord humble themselves, the safer it is for them. On another occasion he said, "When the cross is not 'air-sealed,' it will be blown away." This means that when you are bearing the cross you should not tell the secret to others. As soon as you tell what you are passing through, the meaning of the cross is gone.

Another of his sayings went like this: "Some who fall, fall on the upper floor, while some who stand, stand on the ground floor. Those who stand on the ground floor should not laugh at those who fall on the upper floor."

Concerning admonishing someone, Brother Nee said, "There can be two results: 1) The person you admonish is restored, or 2) He is hardened. The way to tell whether your admonition was accurate or not is to observe the person you admonished. If by rejecting your admonition, such a one ends up in darkness, it proves your admonition was correct. But if after such a one rejects your fellowship, he still continues to have fellowship with the Lord, it proves your admonition was wrong."

One time he said to me, "If some beggars are sleeping under the eaves and you wake them up, treat them with won ton and then preach the gospel to them. Surely you will touch the anointing within." After coming to Taiwan, I met Watchman Nee's nephew, Soo-fu. He told me that when he was young he saw his uncle meet a group of coolies squatting around gambling. Watchman Nee also squatted beside them, talking and laughing. To all he really became all in order to gain some.

His Living

From observing Watchman Nee's way of life, I feel that he learned how to abound and how to be abased and that everywhere and in every way he learned the secret. When he first came to Chungking, he lived in a small apartment with only a bed and a table. When one went to visit him, the wooden stairs would sway and make creaking noises. Later, when he moved into his own factory buildings, it made no difference; his attitude was the same as before. Concerning eating, he sometimes ate only bread and water, and at other times he enjoyed an abundant love feast. To all such matters regarding his living he seemed indifferent.

---

5. THE TESTIMONY OF A WESTERN MISSIONARY

Elizabeth P. Rademacher was a missionary in Shanghai during World War II and now serves the Lord in the church in Huntington Beach, California, U.S.A. The following is her testimony regarding Watchman Nee:

Forty-eight years have elapsed since I last saw Watchman Nee. It was February 1943, and America was at war with Japan. Most foreigners living in the International Settlement in Shanghai, China, were under the jurisdiction of the Japanese. Just the evening before I was interned along with many other Americans (my co-workers were British), through our gate came Watchman Nee, unannounced, as was his custom when visiting us four Westerners. After sharing some refreshments and enjoying some sweet fellowship, he handed me a small unlabeled bottle of highly concentrated vitamins produced at CBC Laboratories with the instruction: "Take half a drop a day." What forethought and concern for a little sister about to be confined for an undetermined period of time!

When I first heard the name Watchman Nee in 1934, I knew nothing about him. I pictured an aged man with a flowing white beard! Little did I realize that he wasn't much older than I—probably at that time about thirty. Several years later I saw him for the first time at Hardoon Road, where, with an older missionary, I sometimes attended the Lord's table and special meetings.

The Spirit's Indwelling

At the beginning of 1938, Watchman Nee conducted a Bible study with the church in Shanghai on the Holy Spirit. Having had a Pentecostal background, I was somewhat confused and disillusioned. I desired to hear what he had to say, hoping to receive help on a number of puzzling questions. For example, why were there inconsistencies in the lives of so many who professedly had received the outpoured Spirit with manifestations? Where was the godly living? Why did I live a defeated life?

The word the Lord spoke to me through Watchman Nee made a revolutionary impact on my life. The evening

I heard him say that Jesus became the Spirit to dwell in us, light dawned. Before, the Lord had seemed so far removed from me; now He was real within. This solved my basic problem. I could now locate Him within my being. I saw further that the work of the Holy Spirit is twofold. There is the outward aspect with gifts and manifestations; but more important still, there is the inward aspect—the infilling that transforms lives.

He used a helpful illustration which made an indelible impression: If a heavily loaded vehicle is run without adequate air in the tires, it is possible that the car will be wrecked. This is an apt picture of one who experiences many outpourings of the Spirit without having a commensurate work of the Spirit within. I thanked God I had not become a wreck. Now I understood why so many I had been acquainted with in the past had wound up bringing disgrace to the Lord's name.

On another occasion he gave his testimony concerning the girl he had loved and given up for the Lord. He quoted Psalm 73:25: "Whom have I in heaven but thee? And there is none upon earth that I desire besides thee," and testified that this had become his reality. This testimony amazed me. I had never heard or met anyone who could honestly make such a statement.

The Kingdom

The Bible study ended, but the Lord wasn't through with me. The Sunday evening before Watchman Nee's departure for Hong Kong and England, six of us gathered around the fireplace in a missionary couple's home. We had met in such an informal way several times before. Usually a large number of Westerners were present, eating and fellowshipping together, listening eagerly to Brother Nee as he spoke in fluent English concerning the kingdom or as he answered questions relating to his messages on the Holy Spirit. Once there swept over me the deep inner sense: God is standing here speaking!

This occasion afforded him his last opportunity to share his burden before going abroad. He began, "I want to say something more about the kingdom." During the course of his speaking, he uttered these words: "The Lord needs heralds for the kingdom." At that moment something happened to me, and Watchman Nee, being aware of it, said, "Don't be afraid, Miss Peck." Simply by the power of the Lord's speaking, I was changed into another person. Praise the Lord for such a faithful, humble, and approachable servant of His.

Other Recollections

There are also other recollections of very practical and considerate expressions of loving concern: the day Watchman and Mrs. Nee dropped in with a silk wadded comforter for each of us missionaries; several invitations to their home for delicious dinners featuring Foochow delicacies; the conversation after a serious wrong decision on my part, and the comforting reply, "Sometimes even our mistakes are right."

During the period from 1940 to early 1943, there were changes in the church life. We began to meet in smaller groups in different areas of the city for the Lord's table and prayer meetings. Watchman Nee usually ministered on Sunday mornings, Wednesday evenings, and sometimes to the new believers on Friday nights, as well as during special conferences. I remember that he frequently referred to Margaret E. Barber, through whom he received so much help in his early Christian life. The ministry of the Word was life-giving, and many impressions were so deeply implanted as to be unforgettable. One example is his comment on Romans 12:1-2: "God's will is not for those who are unconsecrated. It is a question of what sort of person I am. Am I qualified to know His will? All good is not God's will, but God's will is always good." And this word to the new believers: "Salvation without consecration is like a railway with only one track. We need both to advance on the spiritual road." Also this word on John 14:6: "How many truths do you know that have emancipated you? The truth is Christ; so if truth is only 'truth' to you, it is ineffectual."

One message on the will of God left me overwhelmed. It portrayed the will of God from eternity in the past to eternity in the future. The essence of what he said was this: In the beginning there was only one will—God's undisputed will. Then Satan fell, and in the universe there was a second will—a rebellious will. Later God created man with a free will, able to choose to be one either with God or with Satan. In eternity future, after Satan has been cast into the lake of fire, there will again be only one will in the universe—but a will not the same as in the beginning, for God's will and man's will will be perfectly blended into one will.

Confidence in His Leading

Sometime in 1942 Watchman Nee's ministry ceased. Since we were not always aware of his movements or his engagements in other places, it did not seem strange at first. As the weeks passed, though I did not know that he had been asked not to minister at Hardoon Road, I began to sense an undercurrent. The day also came when the Westerners were asked not to attend the meetings. Whether or not this was due to the Japanese occupation and the fear that we might be accused of spying, I do not know. We were always delighted when Brother Nee would visit us unexpectedly in those days. Since at this time he was involved with the CBC Laboratories, we received a personally conducted tour through the company. No matter how others may have felt during that time of his "tentmaking," we had nothing but trust and confidence in his leading. How could we pass judgment on him? It was because of his faithfulness in following the Lord and proclaiming His Word that several of us had been brought into the glorious church life.

CHAPTER TWENTY

REVELATIONS RECEIVED BY WATCHMAN NEE

Watchman Nee fully believed in the scriptural, fundamental faith held by all true Christians. He believed in the verbal inspiration of the Bible and that the Bible is God's holy Word. He believed that God is triune—Father, Son, and Spirit—distinctly three, yet fully one, co-existing and coinhering each other from eternity to eternity. He believed that Jesus Christ is the Son of God, even God Himself, incarnated as a man with both the human and the divine life, that He died on the cross to accomplish redemption, that He rose bodily from the dead on the third day, that He ascended into heaven and was enthroned, crowned with glory, and made the Lord of all, and that He will return the second time to receive His followers, to save Israel, and to establish His millennial kingdom on the earth. He believed that every person who believes in Jesus Christ will be forgiven by God, washed by His redeeming blood, justified by faith, regenerated by the Holy Spirit, and saved by grace. Such a believer is a child of God and a member of the Body of Christ. He also believed that the destiny of every believer is to be an integral part of the church, which is the Body of Christ and the house of God.

In addition to these five basic aspects of the Christian faith, Watchman Nee was further enlightened to receive clear revelation from the Lord concerning fifty-three other scriptural teachings, which are crucial for fully understanding and practicing the Christian faith.

FROM 1920 TO 1932

1. The Assurance of Salvation

One of the first basic items which the Lord revealed to Watchman Nee was the believers' assurance of salvation.

Throughout all of China in those days, the scriptural teaching of the assurance of salvation was seldom taught by any Christian group. Watchman Nee, however, became exceedingly clear concerning this matter and preached the gospel to Christians to help them realize that they were saved. He was able to show from the written Word that the believer can be absolutely assured of his salvation. He would help the doubtful to take a Bible verse like John 3:16 and digest it until it became a definite word to them that they could never perish. He also pointed out to them that the Spirit of God dwells in them and witnesses with their spirit that they are God's children (Rom. 8:16). A further evidence of the assurance of salvation was given by Watchman Nee from 1 John 3:14: "We know that we have passed out of death into life because we love the brothers."

2. The Distinction between Grace and Law

Most Christians in those days did not have the assurance of salvation, because they did not know the distinction between grace and law. Watchman Nee received the Lord's clear revelation that salvation is by grace alone, not by works of law. If salvation were a matter of law, it would depend upon our own works. But salvation is of the Lord's grace, depending only upon what He is and what He has done for us.

3. The Difference between Salvation and Victory

Some Christians did not know the difference between salvation and victory. This was another cause of uncertainty regarding their salvation. At the moment we believe in the Lord Jesus Christ, our salvation is secured. Victory, however, is a matter of overcoming sin, the world, the flesh, the self, and all other negative things in our daily living. Our eternal destiny as children of God is forever secured by simple faith in Jesus Christ for our salvation. But victory is a matter of our daily life and is related to dispensational reward.

4. The Difference between Salvation and Reward

Any Christian who is not clear about the difference

between salvation and reward will have difficulty being assured of his salvation. This distinction was fully revealed to Watchman Nee. Salvation is by grace through faith (Eph. 2:8), whereas reward is the result of working according to the Lord's will (Matt. 16:27; 1 Cor. 3:14).

5. The Difference between the Kingdom of the Heavens and Eternal Life

Some Christians hesitated to say that they were saved, because the difference between having eternal life and entering into the kingdom of the heavens was not clear to them. When a person believes in the Lord Jesus for his salvation, he receives eternal life. But to enter into the kingdom of the heavens, one must live his daily life under heaven's rule. Such a living is an exercise in this church age and qualifies us to participate in the Lord's millennial rule in the kingdom age. Such participation is a reward for living a life under the heavenly rule and is not a matter of eternal salvation. Watchman Nee received a thorough and clear revelation concerning this matter.

6. The Kingdom Truths

Watchman Nee also saw the New Testament truth of the kingdom in its full scope. He saw that the New Testament distinguishes between the kingdom of the heavens and the kingdom of God. The kingdom of God includes the entire reign of God from eternity in the past to eternity in the future. But the kingdom of the heavens is a smaller sphere within the kingdom of God; it is the heavenly ruling among the believers in the present church age (Matt. 5:3, 10) and a reward in the coming kingdom age (Matt. 5:20; 7:21). All regenerated believers are in the kingdom of God (John 3:5), but only those who live a life under the heavenly rule will inherit the kingdom age as a reward. The kingdom of God is related to salvation, whereas the kingdom of the heavens is related to reward.

7. Rapture

Along with the revelation of the kingdom, the Lord also

gave Watchman Nee revelation concerning rapture. According to current fundamental theology, Christians are told that as long as they are saved, at the Lord's return they will all participate together in a general rapture with the whole church before the tribulation. But Watchman Nee came to see that not all believers will be raptured at the same time. Some believers will become matured overcomers before the tribulation; therefore, they will be raptured first. The majority of the believers, however, will mature later, so they will be raptured later. The kingdom is a matter of reward, and rapture is a matter of maturity. The rapture can be compared to a harvest. A crop is not harvested and taken into the barn when it is still green. It must first ripen into maturity. All Christians must ripen in life. When they are ripe, the Lord will harvest them and bring them into the heavenly barn. These two points must be kept clearly in mind: 1) the kingdom is a reward to the overcoming believers, and 2) rapture requires the maturity of the overcomers.

8. The Deviation of Christianity

Not long after they were saved, Watchman Nee and some other young believers who were still students began to realize, by studying the Bible, how abnormal Christianity is today. The Lord showed them that Christianity as it is practiced today has deviated in almost every point from the way God ordained in His holy Word.

9. The Church, the Ecclesia, the Body of Christ

The Lord gave Watchman Nee a clear revelation of His church. Brother Nee preached and taught that the church is not a building, an organization, or a Christian mission. The church, rather, is an organism. It is a living body. In another sense, it is the ecclesia, the gathering together of the called-out ones.

10. The Two Aspects of the Church

Watchman Nee saw that the church is both universal and local. In the entire universe there is only one church, the church of God (1 Cor. 10:32). This unique church is expressed in many localities on earth, and in each locality it is a local church. The universal church is composed of all the local churches, and the local churches are the practical expression of the universal church. In Matthew 16:18, the universal church is revealed, whereas in Matthew 18:17, we see the local church. Without the local churches, there is no way to participate in the universal church, and there is no way to have a practical church life. In the book of Acts, in the Epistles, and in Revelation, the church is expressed as local churches, i.e., the church in Jerusalem, the church in Antioch, the church in Ephesus, etc. The government of the church is not universal but local.

11. Denominationalism

At the same time he received revelation concerning the church, Watchman Nee also saw the evil of denominationalism. Denominations divide the Body of Christ into many organizations. This is condemned in the Scriptures (1 Cor. 1:11-13).

12. The Clergy System and Hierarchy

Watchman Nee also received light concerning the clergy-laity system. This system includes hierarchy, rank, and position in a form of Christianity which is reduced to human organization. The Roman Catholic Church has priests, bishops, archbishops, cardinals, and the pope. The Church of England has priests, bishops, archbishops, with the headship vested in the reigning sovereign. The Protestant churches have their pastors. This kind of clergy system is clearly contrary to the revelation of the New Testament and annuls the function of the members of the Body of Christ. Denominationalism cuts the Body of Christ into pieces, and the clergy destroys the function of all its members.

13. The Universal Priesthood

The universal priesthood was another truth revealed to Watchman Nee. He saw that the priesthood in the New Testament is different from that in the Old Testament. The priesthood in the Old Testament was eventually vested in

the children of Aaron, resulting in a clerical class different
from that of laymen. But the New Testament priesthood is
granted to all believers (Rev. 1:6; 1 Pet. 2:5, 9). In the New
Testament there are no clergy and no laymen; all are priests.

14. The Presbytery, the Proper Eldership

Watchman Nee received the clear revelation from the
Scriptures that the church should be governed by a presbytery
of elders. Every local church needs a group of experienced
brothers to take the lead and to exercise oversight over the
church's activities. In the Bible this group of men is called the
presbyters, the elders, the bishops, the overseers.

15. The Difference between Office and Gift

From the Bible, Watchman Nee saw that the offices of the
church are different from gifts. The church offices include
elders and deacons, who are local (Phil. 1:1); whereas gifts
include prophets, evangelists, and shepherds and teachers,
who are universal (Eph. 4:11).

16. Baptism and the Lord's Table

The Lord revealed to Watchman Nee that the proper mode
of water baptism is by immersion. The Lord also showed him
the scriptural way to practice the Lord's table. Baptism is the
believer's testimony that his old life has been terminated and
that he has been separated from the world to the Lord and
His Body. The Lord's table is a remembrance of the Lord
and a testimony concerning the oneness and the fellowship of
His Body.

17. Head Covering and the Laying On of Hands

Watchman Nee also saw the scriptural meaning of head
covering and the real practice of the laying on of hands. Head
covering is an expression of submission and obedience to the
headship of Christ in the church. The laying on of hands is
an act of identification, indicating that what is being done
is an impartation of something which is within the Body
to other members of the Body. By the laying on of hands,

spiritual gifts are imparted to the members, and fellowship is realized between the members of the Body of Christ.

18. Living by Faith in God

Watchman Nee saw that the real servant of God must live by faith in God and not be hired as the employee of a religious organization. The practice of living by faith was practically unknown in China in the early years of Watchman Nee's ministry. The Brethren assemblies do not hire the Lord's servants among them, but when the Brethren went to China, they thought it was impossible to teach the Chinese believers to live by faith in God. To live by faith was simply not in the Chinese Christian's concept; however, Watchman Nee both taught this way and practiced it himself.

19. Divine Healing

Watchman Nee not only believed in divine healing from the Scriptures; he experienced it himself. To him it was not merely an outward, miraculous gift, but an inward experience, producing the building up in life.

20. The Death and Resurrection of Christ

The Lord gave Watchman Nee specific revelation concerning the death and resurrection of Christ. He saw that Christ's death has two aspects: the objective aspect, which dealt with our sin, sins, the world, Satan, and the powers of darkness; and the subjective aspect, which dealt with our flesh, our self, and our old man. He also saw that in the death of Christ the old creation was terminated. This was the negative side of the cross. On the positive side, the divine life of Christ was released to germinate the new creation. In our Lord's resurrection, His divine life was released to regenerate the believers and make them members of the Body of Christ. From His resurrection the church came into existence, and also in His resurrection the Body of Christ is being built up. It is also in the power of His resurrection that believers are able to bear the cross and, in the fellowship of His sufferings, be conformed to His death (Phil. 3:10). While enjoying the resurrection life of Christ, the Lord's people are empowered to live a holy and heavenly life while they are walking on this earth. This resurrection is just the resurrected Christ Himself, and the Spirit of Christ is its reality.

21. The Ascension of Christ

Watchman Nee saw that Christ has ascended into the heavens far above all. Neither the gravity of the earth, the demons, the prince of the power of the air, nor all the powers of darkness could either frustrate or detain Him. These are all now under His feet. By His ascension He has been made Lord of all (Acts 2:36), and also by His ascension all His followers have been brought into the heavenly places (Eph. 2:6). His position, His ministry, and His life are now all heavenly. He is now engaged in the work of ministering the heavenly life and the very heavens themselves into His people to make them the heavenly people, living a heavenly life on earth.

22. The Coming of Christ

Watchman Nee acquired a clear and thorough view concerning the coming of Christ. He saw that the Lord's coming (Gk., *parousia*) has a secret aspect and an open aspect. To the watchful ones, who have been seeking Him and awaiting His return, He will come secretly as a thief (Matt. 24:43; Rev. 3:3) from the heavens to the air before the great tribulation. But to those engrossed in the world, He will come as a flash of lightning (Matt. 24:27, 30) from the air to the earth after the great tribulation. In His secret coming, believers will be raptured to the air; whereas, His open coming will bring judgment to the world on the earth.

23. The Indwelling of the Holy Spirit

The crucified, resurrected, and ascended Christ is now indwelling the spirits of His people as the Spirit of life, making Christ real to them. This indwelling Spirit of Christ is both the Holy Spirit and the Spirit of God. The main function of the divine Spirit is to impart the divine life into God's people, regenerating them, anointing them, sanctifying and transforming them by saturating them with the very element of God. Watchman Nee ministered on this matter extensively.

24. The Teaching of the Anointing

Along with the revelation he received concerning the Holy Spirit, Watchman Nee also received light concerning the teaching of the anointing. The anointing is the moving and working of the Holy Spirit within our spirit. The anointing teaches us everything from within (1 John 2:27). The law of life replaces the Old Testament law, and the teaching of the anointing replaces the Old Testament prophets. It is by the teaching of the anointing that we abide in the Lord.

25. The Outpouring of the Holy Spirit

Watchman Nee saw two aspects regarding the Holy Spirit: the indwelling of the Holy Spirit for life and the outpouring of the Holy Spirit for power. On the day the Lord rose from the dead, He breathed into the disciples the Holy Spirit (John 20:22). At that time the Holy Spirit entered into the disciples and indwelt them for the purpose of imparting life. But on the day of Pentecost, the Holy Spirit was poured out upon the disciples (Acts 2:4, 33). This pouring out of the Spirit was for the purpose of distributing power to the disciples. This second experience of the Spirit is what the Bible calls the baptism in the Holy Spirit. Most Christians do not see the difference between these two aspects of the Spirit. Watchman Nee, however, received a clear revelation concerning this distinction. Although he never spoke in tongues, he received repeated experiences of the outpouring of the Holy Spirit.

26. The Tripartite Man

In the early years of his Christian life, Watchman Nee came to see that man is composed of three parts: spirit, soul, and body (1 Thes. 5:23). He came to see that the soul is the personality of man; the body is the outward part of man for contacting the physical world; and the spirit is the inmost part of man for contacting the spiritual world. Since God is Spirit, we must worship and serve Him in our spirit (Rom.

1:9; John 4:24). Believers are regenerated by the Spirit of God in their spirit, the Spirit of God witnesses with their spirit (Rom. 8:16), the Lord Jesus is with their spirit (2 Tim. 4:22), and they are one spirit with the Lord (1 Cor. 6:17). The spirit must be divided from the soul (Heb. 4:12) so that believers can walk, live, and work in their spirit (Gal. 5:16, 25) and be spiritual men (1 Cor. 2:14-15).

27. Sanctification by Faith

Some time prior to 1925, Watchman Nee came to see the matter of sanctification by faith. He received light concerning the holiness teaching of John Wesley and said that what Wesley taught was not really holiness but sinless perfection. Through his study he came to realize that the Brethren surpassed Wesley in their vision of holiness. Yet while their teaching on holiness was accurate, it was too objective and consisted merely of a sort of positional change. The Brethren taught that gold in the world was common, while gold built into the temple was sanctified. As a further example, the Brethren taught that sheep and cattle in flocks and herds were common, but when offered upon the altar, they were sanctified (Matt. 23:17, 19). In addition, the Brethren illustrated sanctification by pointing out that food in the market is common, but food on the table of Christians becomes sanctified with prayer. Watchman Nee pointed out that all these examples refer to an outward change of position, but none involves an inward dispositional change. He taught that sanctification is not merely a positional change, but that it must also be dispositional (Rom. 6:19, 22).

28. Christ as Life

To His believing ones Christ is life (Col. 3:4), and this life is the Spirit of life (Rom. 8:2) in their spirit. Whatever the believer does must be done out of this inner life. Every believer should live by this divine life within (Gal. 2:20).

29. The Law of the Spirit of Life

The divine life that believers receive from the Lord is in the Holy Spirit. The Holy Spirit is called the Spirit of life

(Rom. 8:2). This divine life has its own law and characteristics, and its function is to regulate and supply us with
God's divine element. This is not the mere outward letter of
the law but the law of life (Heb. 8:10) enforced by the Spirit
of God within us. Watchman Nee received a full revelation
concerning this inner law. It is by this inner law, called the
law of life, that we are freed from the law of sin and death
and are able to live a righteous and holy life.

30. The Law of Sin and Death

Watchman Nee saw from the Scriptures that to sin and die
is a law (Rom. 8:2). This law is in the members of our body
(Rom. 7:23) and is derived from the evil life of Satan. Every
fallen man is under its power. But the law of the Spirit of
life is more powerful than the law of sin and death and is able
to free us from it.

31. A Better Covenant

The new covenant which the Lord Jesus enacted for us
with His blood is better than the old covenant (Heb. 7:22; 8:6).
The old covenant is according to the Old Testament law, with
a priesthood according to the law of a fleshy commandment;
whereas, the new covenant is according to the law of life, with
a priesthood according to the power of an indestructible life
(Heb. 8:10; 7:16).

32. The Overcoming Life of Christ

Because Christ has overcome Satan and every negative
thing in the universe, His life is an overcoming life. If we live
by Christ, His life overcomes every negative thing for us.

33. The Calling of the Overcomers

Watchman Nee received revelation concerning the calling
of the overcomers. Because the whole church has become defeated, failing to meet the Lord's purpose, the Lord has come
in to call some of His believers to be overcomers. This is
clearly revealed in the seven epistles in Revelation 2 and 3.
Because the whole church has missed the mark, the Lord

has sounded His call to those who love Him to overcome the degraded church.

34. Spiritual Warfare

By 1925 Watchman Nee had seen the matter of spiritual warfare. He saw that for the accomplishment of God's divine purpose in this universe, there is a consummate battle shaping up between God and His enemy, Satan. This battle involves all of God's children. If they take sides with Satan, they are rebelling against God; if they take sides with God, they are fighting against Satan. All the overcoming believers must realize that they are on the battlefield; they are fighting for God's divine purpose. To fight in this spiritual warfare requires the believer to see his heavenly position. Ephesians 2 makes it clear that we are seated in the heavenly places, and Ephesians 6 indicates that we are fighting against the powers in the heavenlies. The believers must keep their heavenly position so that they can defeat God's enemies in the heavenly places. If the believers' position is on the earth, they are under the enemy, and they lose the position to overcome.

FROM 1933 TO 1937

35. The Boundary of the Local Church

In the years 1933 and 1934, Watchman Nee saw that the boundary of the local church is the boundary of the city where the church is. He pointed out that within the boundary of a city there should not be more than one church. This spontaneously eliminates division.

36. The Centrality and Universality of Christ

In 1933 and 1934, Watchman Nee also saw the centrality and universality of Christ in God's eternal purpose. He saw that both in the universe and in the Christian life Christ should have the preeminence (Col. 1:18); he also saw that Christ is all and in all in the new man, which is the church (Col. 3:10-11).

37. The Ground of the Local Church

In 1937 Watchman Nee began to see the ground of the local church. This is a further step beyond the boundary of locality and indicates that believers should not be divided by anything. The ground of the church is the ground of oneness. Wherever we go and wherever we are, we should be one with the believers in that place. A city should have only one church. The church is not the church in a home, the church in a factory, the church on a campus, the church on a certain street, or the church with any other kind of designation. The local church is a church in the city. If there is more than one church in a locality, the believers in that locality will be divided.

38. Migration

Watchman Nee saw clearly from the book of Acts that there were two ways to spread the gospel: one by the sending out of the apostles, and the other by the migration of the believers (Acts 8:4). Under his ministry both methods were employed to spread the gospel.

FROM 1938 TO 1942

39. The Practicality of the Church Life

In 1939 Watchman Nee received further light regarding the church, this time concerning the practicality of the church life. He received clear light from the New Testament about how elders should carry out their eldership practically and how deacons and deaconesses should serve the saints and the church. He also helped all the members of the church to participate in the affairs of the church.

40. The Reality of the Church

Along with the practical aspect of the church, Watchman Nee saw the reality of the church. He stressed that the content of the church must be Christ living in and being lived out through all the members. Anything that is not Christ is not the church. Practically speaking, the church is Christ.

Christ, therefore, is the reality of the church, and the church should be the expression of Christ.

41. The Oneness of the Church

The genuine oneness of the church is the oneness of the Spirit (Eph. 4:3). Real oneness is not the oneness of doctrines, opinions, or certain practices; real oneness is the Spirit Himself. Even though we may be one in doctrine and in the way we do things, if we are not in the Spirit, we do not have genuine oneness.

42. Seeing the Body

In the years 1939 to 1942, Watchman Nee was consistently burdened concerning the revelation of the Body of Christ. He was burdened to help Christians see the Body, not in a doctrinal way but in a practical way. He continually stressed that seeing the Body makes it impossible to be individualistic. Once one sees the Body, he behaves and acts in a corporate way.

43. The Authority of the Holy Spirit in the Body

Watchman Nee saw that since the Body of Christ is an organism, the Holy Spirit must have authority over everything in every part. All the activity of the Body must be under the authority and direction of the Holy Spirit.

44. The Reality of the Holy Spirit

The Holy Spirit is the reality of all spiritual things. The term *spiritual things* is vain and empty unless the Holy Spirit Himself is the content and reality of every spiritual thing. The Holy Spirit is the reality of the Christians' life and also the reality of their living. Whatever they are and do must have the Holy Spirit as the reality.

45. The Authority of the Church

For the practice of the practical church life, Watchman Nee saw the necessity of authority. The authority that Christ as the Head imparts to certain members of His Body is called deputy authority. The local churches must be under this kind of deputy authority in a marvelous order. This authority is crucial for the building up of the local church. By this means the church becomes a vertical vessel. For this, submission is necessary.

46. The Building of the Church

The Lord has revealed through Watchman Nee that believers must be practically built up with others in the local churches under the authority of the church. This kind of building is a test to genuine spirituality. If one cannot be built up with others in a local church, his spirituality is questionable.

47. Coordination in the Church Life

Another revelation received by Watchman Nee, which is closely related to authority and building, was the revelation concerning coordination in the church. All the members in the local church need not only to be built up with others but also to coordinate with others. The service of the church cannot be carried out individually. All the members must serve in a coordinated way.

48. The Body and the Spiritual Warfare

In the early years of his ministry, Watchman Nee saw the spiritual warfare as a personal matter. However, from 1939 on, he saw that it was not just a personal matter, but a matter of the Body. The warrior in Ephesians 6 is not an individual believer but the Body. Watchman Nee stressed strongly that if believers are individualistic, it will be difficult for them to fight against the powers in the heavenlies. To fight the enemy we need the Body. We need to be not only in the heavenlies but also in the Body.

FROM 1942 TO 1948

49. The Discipline of the Holy Spirit

The period from 1942 to 1948 was a period of longsuffering for Watchman Nee. During this time he learned to see the need of the Holy Spirit's discipline for the reconstitution of

our being and for the breaking of the outer man. He saw
that God sovereignly arranges our environment to work good
for us through the discipline of the Holy Spirit. The Holy
Spirit arranges our environment and disciplines us through
our environment in order to reconstitute us within with the
divine element.

50. The Breaking of the Outer Man and the Release of the Spirit

While he was undergoing his longsuffering from 1942 to
1948, Watchman Nee saw the breaking of the outer man and
the release of the human spirit. The Spirit of Christ dwells in
our spirit. If our outer man is not broken, our spirit with the
Spirit of Christ is confined in the shell of our outer man. For
this reason, there is a crucial need for our outer man to be
broken in order that our spirit with the Spirit of Christ may
be released to impart life to others. The discipline of the Holy
Spirit is both to tear down some aspects of our natural life
and to break our outer man.

51. Using the Spirit

Along with the light he received concerning the release of
the spirit, Watchman Nee also saw that the believer must
learn how to use his human spirit. In ministering the Word,
in preaching the gospel, in contacting people, and even in
matters of daily living, believers must use their spirit first,
not their mind, emotion, or knowledge. The spirit must
always be ahead of these. By our spirit we can touch another's
spirit. Only by his spirit can the believer convey the Spirit
of life and impart life into others.

FROM 1948 TO 1950

52. The Region of the Work

In 1948 Watchman Nee received revelation that while the
church is local, the work is regional. The church is a matter of
locality, but the work is a matter of region or district. The
churches under Peter's work were in respective localities, but
Peter's work was in a district which comprised all these

localities. It was the same with Paul's work and the churches raised up through his work.

53. Handing Over All Things

In order for the work to accomplish its purpose and for the local churches to be built up practically, Watchman Nee saw the necessity for all the believers in the Lord's recovery to hand over not only themselves but all their possessions to the work. By this means the believers are delivered from being selfish and individualistic. This also helps believers to submit to the Lord's authority. It even affords the Lord an opportunity to use their possessions for His purpose and to grant them more physical blessings.

This is not all. Watchman Nee received much light from the Scriptures on many other matters concerning gospel truth and practical matters, such as the Lord's Day, marriage, clothing, dealing with money, etc. This is referred to in chapter twenty-seven.

CHAPTER TWENTY-ONE

THE SUFFERINGS OF WATCHMAN NEE

Watchman Nee endured much suffering for the sake of his ministry. He was absolute in following the Lord and faithful in fulfilling his commission. Because of his faithfulness and absoluteness, he was continually mistreated and underwent many hardships. Because he continually fought the battle for the Lord's recovery, he was continually under attack from the enemy. At the same time, he was also under God's sovereign hand. The sovereign arrangements of God in his environment were also a source of trouble and a means by which God dealt with him. For these two reasons, he lived a life of suffering. For the most part his sufferings came from the following sources:

I. POVERTY

In the early years of Watchman Nee's ministry, the economic situation in China was very difficult. Still, he was enlightened to the extent that he was able to fulfill the Lord's calling by serving Him entirely by faith. The light he received made it impossible for him to work as an employee for anyone: not for a mission, denomination, so-called church, or individual. Because of what he saw, he was exercised to live purely and singly by faith in God. In those days, this was not an easy way. In that kind of financial situation, he came to learn what poverty was. In the early days of his ministry in Shanghai, there were times when he had nothing to eat but a little bread.

II. ILL HEALTH

Brother Nee also suffered frequent ill health. He began his ministry before 1923 and was not married until 1934. There was a period of eleven years when he had no wife to help him. During those years he lived by himself. It was during this period that he became afflicted with tuberculosis of the lungs and suffered for several years from this disease.

He was also afflicted with a stomach illness and with a heart ailment called angina pectoris. He was never cured of the heart disease. He told me that a number of times before a conference meeting he was forced to lie on his bed until the time arrived to minister. Only then would he rise up. Immediately after speaking, he would return to bed.

Because of his ill health, Watchman learned how to be greatly dependent upon the Lord. He learned how to live by resurrection life in order to meet his physical needs. Many times he ministered not by physical strength but by resurrection life.

The following excerpts from his open letters in *The Christian* and in *The Present Testimony* give a picture of his ill health and the spiritual lessons he learned through it. The following letter is from the December 1927 issue of *The Christian*, Volume 2, Number 12:

When this issue reaches you, it will be the end of the year. Looking over the past year, we really thank Him for the way He has blessed us, led us, taught us, supplied us, urged us, healed us, rebuked us, chastened us, and disciplined us. Praise the Lord, Oh my heart! Again considering ourselves in this past year as being so defiled, defeated, head-strong (willful), rebellious, ungracious, unrighteous, lacking, and wrongful, we feel thoroughly discontented with ourselves. How we wish that these dark spots were not part of the history of our life. But wishing is wishing; still we are defeated. What a pity! Nevertheless, knowing our condition only convinces us more that our flesh is incurable and causes us to loudly sing praises to the Lord, for in such defeat He is still so gracious to us. O Lord! How can we forget Your grace?

It seems that my ill health during this past year was known far and wide. In three localities it was even rumored that my earthly tabernacle had been destroyed. For this reason there were increased prayers for me more than ever before. I greatly appreciate those who care for my physical welfare. In the past days my natural strength has been much weakened. Even light activity causes my body to feel its burden. But praise the Lord that this year was still filled with many days of work. Instead of resting and getting rusty, why not labor and trust? The strength of promise in time of need is never decreased. For this fact I cannot but praise the Lord.

The scarcity of fruit, the emptiness of life, the staleness of the spirit, and the weakness of the body are each enough to make me feel ashamed. Actually, I deserve nothing but to be ashamed. That all things work together for good to them that love God is true and trustworthy. In my situation these words again have become so real.

The following excerpt is from the twelfth issue of *The Present Testimony*, published in December 1929:

I believe that from other sources as well as through this magazine you all know that I have been ill. Indeed, since 1926, my body has daily grown weaker. I have been ill time after time, and in addition, I have suffered from lack of rest due to the many responsibilities which are still upon me. My health has been increasingly deteriorating. The writing of *The Spiritual Man* exhausted my strength, and since completing its writing, I have suffered continual illness even up till now....

Of course, what I have experienced during my illness is most profitable. From the very beginning I prayed that I would gain from this illness what I needed, for I am not willing to be ill for nothing. As I look back over the past year, I can gratefully say that God's treatment is just right; not one single day could be omitted. Many of these experiences cannot be made public, but I fully believe that they are for my personal enrichment and for your gain as well.

Now, through God's unlimited and inexhaustible grace and through your ceaseless prayers, once again I have returned from the gate of death. I look to the Lord that in a time convenient to Him He would bring me to complete recovery. At present I rest and at the same time work. I now present myself once more to God to accomplish His will and to serve His saints.

From the nineteenth issue of *The Present Testimony,* published in January—February 1931, the following excerpt is taken:

My illness during the last two or three years has surely been used by God to test the compassions of many saints. My weakness has become the opportunity for many to love the Lord. When I consider your love and kindness toward me, how grateful I am! When I hear of the many brothers and sisters scattered in different places who, though they have not met me, yet because of our relationship in the Lord, have wept bitterly before Him for my health, I feel that what you have bestowed upon me is so deep while that which I have given you is so shallow. Because of this I cannot help feeling that if I had more life, energy, and time, how much I would like to spend it on the saints.

Though my sickness has been accumulating over many years, it was worsened by writing *The Spiritual Man.* Thank God, now I am recovering. I am again able to write a few letters, prepare a few articles, lead several Bible study sessions, and attend a few meetings. There are still many other things I could wish to do but cannot do. Still I am thankful to God for what I can do. Those who know the human body say that I have been close to death several times, but thank God He has been keeping me up to this day. I hope that in the days of my sojourning on this earth I may be able to serve Him and you faithfully.

The following excerpt is taken from the twenty-fifth issue of *The Present Testimony,* of May—June 1932:

In the last few months, due to heart disease and other

physical illness, my earthly tent is again in danger of collapsing at any moment. Many times I tarry at the fork of the road, not knowing what way to take. Humanly speaking, in many experiences I do not know whether to cry or laugh. But thank the Lord, for the Lord's sake nothing is too difficult and no price is too great. In the eyes of those who trust and obey, a dark, cloudy situation is still a bright and clear sky. Those lines are true: "If there's less of earth-joy, give, Lord, more of heaven. Let the spirit praise Thee, though the heart be riven."

III. DENOMINATIONS

Opposition from the denominations was a third source of Watchman Nee's suffering. He was an anti-testimony against them, and because of this it caused him much suffering.

A. Despised

The denominations thoroughly despised Watchman Nee, and this caused him a great deal of suffering. He began writing the three volumes of *The Spiritual Man* at the age of twenty-three. One top theologian in China reacted by saying, "Watchman Nee is just a clever young man who has excelled in reading English books. He has gathered all these things from the books and translated them into Chinese." Sometimes being despised cuts more deeply than being criticized. At that time Hebrews 13:13 was very real and applicable to Watchman and to others as well: "Let us therefore go forth unto Him outside the camp, bearing His reproach." Watchman and those with him fully followed this word to bear the reproach of Christ outside the camp of organized Christianity. That reproach was actually the experience of the cross.

B. Criticized

Along with being despised, Watchman was also severely criticized by the denominations. Even though they despised him, Watchman Nee was accomplishing something; when this became evident, they began to publicly criticize him. In his paper, *The Christian,* published from 1925 through 1927, he strongly exposed the deviation of the denominations from the pure truths of the Scriptures. They could do nothing but criticize him. They put out many writings criticizing his ministry.

C. Opposition

On the heels of the criticism came the opposition. Such a ministry to God's people as Watchman Nee's stirred up the opposition of the denominations, and they rose up to oppose him. They opposed him secretly and openly. Some preachers opposed him from their pulpit, publicly warning their congregations against him.

The following excerpts from his open letters in *The Present Testimony* unveil his attitude toward the opposition. In the twelfth issue, published December 1929, he wrote:

Beloved brothers, the time of the Lord's coming back is fast approaching. We must be faithful. In the days ahead we may suffer more misunderstanding and more severe opposition; but since we have been destined for this we should remain faithful....Brothers, please continue to remember me in your prayers so that in all my afflictions I may be able to stand fast, faithfully bearing a good testimony for the Lord.

Just a few more miles beloved;
And our feet shall ache no more;
No more sin, and no more sorrow;
Hush thee, Jesus went before;
And I hear Him sweetly whispering,
"Faint not, fear not, still press on;
For it may be ere tomorrow;
The long journey will be done."

In the twenty-sixth issue of July—August 1932, he wrote:

This issue was completed in the midst of much suffering. I know that Satan and his evil spirits are very busy, for he is aware that the message of *The Present Testimony* is harmful to him. Therefore, both the message and the one who preaches it are the objects of his attack. For this reason I beg all the brothers in the Lord to supply me with more prayers.

The various temptations, oppressions, misunderstandings, and hardships which come can weaken even the physically strongest one, to say nothing of someone like me whose earthly tabernacle is often being shaken. It is difficult to become a martyr, but it is also difficult to become an apostate. It is difficult to be faithful, but even more difficult to lose chastity. To restrain our lips is indeed painful, but to vindicate ourselves does not bring joy either. An evil name brings sorrow, but a good name does not necessarily bring gladness. We care only to work faithfully, keeping the first love and maintaining a single eye while waiting for the Lord's return. Did not the Lord tell us from the outset that we must bear the cross and encounter sufferings on this earth?

What follows is from the twenty-ninth issue, published in January—February 1933:

This surely is a time of temptations; everything is confusing, cold, and harsh. In this hour it is indeed difficult for Christians to stand. But have we not known this for some time from the beginning already? What else can we say?

We walk in solitude and bewilderment; we must either put down our weapons or be raptured. O Lord, which do You think is best?

This is the first issue of this year. We cannot say that there is greater hope, greater courage, or greater interest than last year. On the contrary, there will probably be greater hardships; still we need to go on as usual.

Opposition came not only from local Christians but also from missionaries. Most of the missionaries opposed Watchman

Nee because of his anti-testimony. Since they had sacrificed their countries, their homes, and their careers, and had come to a pagan country to help people be saved and to build their mission churches, they deeply resented his ministry. In the midst of that situation, this young man, a young national who had never been outside of China, rose up and published arguments which attacked the very foundations of their work and the denominational churches they had built. He taught that all denominations were unscriptural and that only one kind of church is scriptural: the church in the locality. He expressed appreciation to the missionaries for bringing the gospel to China, but he strongly protested their bringing the denominations with them and building up their mission churches in division. He said that all the denominational names such as Presbyterian, Baptist, Methodist, Anglican, etc., must be dropped. He put this message in print and spread it all over China. He was strongly convinced that his view was scriptural, and he paid a high price to maintain it.

After he offered a prayer in 1938 in the Keswick Convention that deeply touched the attendants, the chairman, who was also the chairman of the China Inland Mission, talked with Brother Nee. Brother Nee grasped the opportunity, feeling that it was the proper time to fellowship with a leader of one of the best missions that had gone to China. Throughout their fellowship, the chairman of the CIM agreed with him. He told Brother Nee that what the Lord had commissioned him to do in China was exactly the burden of Mr. Hudson Taylor, the founder of the CIM, and that their missionaries in China were wrong in opposing him. Eventually, the chairman of the mission went to China and called the missionaries of the CIM together in Shanghai and told them that they were wrong in opposing the work of Watchman Nee. He told them that what Watchman Nee was doing was exactly what they should be doing. He advised them never to do anything from that day forth to oppose him. But after he left and returned to London, they still kept opposing him.

D. Attack

The denominations opposed him, attacked him, and did

their best to destroy his ministry. The following illustration is one example. When Mrs. Nee's aunt was opposing her marriage to Watchman, some denominational Christians collaborated with her to attack him and did their best to damage his ministry. They hated him and launched a full-scale assault against him.

E. Rumors

One of the methods his opposers used to attack him was by spreading rumors against him. This is the "evil report" mentioned by Paul in 2 Corinthians 6:8. Rumors are the most subtle and damaging kind of attack. A rumor is nothing but a lie. Some opposers defamed Watchman by spreading rumors and evil reports. While Watchman was single and living in Shanghai, his mother came to stay with him for a period of time. Some spread the rumor that he was living with a woman. What an evil rumor that was!

By 1934 Watchman Nee's ministry was completely rejected by the denominations. He presented his ministry to them; what he received in return was their despising, their criticism, their opposition, their attacks, and their spreading of rumors. He was fully rejected!

When the Lord was on earth, the Judaizers also despised Him, criticized Him, opposed Him, attacked Him, and spread rumors about Him. The same thing was done to the apostles. These are the basic weapons Satan uses against God's economy. He attacked Watchman Nee with the same weapons.

F. Misunderstanding and Misrepresentation

Watchman Nee was also misunderstood and misrepresented. Watchman illustrated this misrepresentation by saying, "The Watchman Nee portrayed by them I would also condemn." Watchman Nee was often presented through the filter of inaccurate information coupled with a suspicious imagination on the part of those who misunderstood him. For this reason people who presented him in this way gave a completely wrong impression concerning him. This also caused him to suffer.

IV. BROTHERS AND SISTERS

Another source of Brother Nee's sufferings was the brothers and sisters. These sufferings were of a more serious nature than those from the denominations. Sufferings from the denominations came from without, while sufferings from the brothers and sisters came from within. Sufferings coming from within the inner circle afflicted him more than any other kind.

A. Excommunication

Two years after the church life began to be practiced in Watchman's home town in 1922, he was excommunicated by his co-workers. He was excommunicated because he stood for the truth of the Lord's recovery and protested against the leading co-worker's being ordained by a denominational missionary. Considering his dissent too pronounced, they excommunicated him. Excommunication is a very serious matter, and in this case it was done while he was away on a ministry trip. Most of the believers who met with them sided with him, but the Lord would not allow him to do anything to vindicate himself. That was really a suffering to the natural man.

B. Dissension

From the time that Watchman began his work, he was in fellowship with an older sister. She loved the Lord, sought the Lord, and was quite gifted of the Lord. Having gained the respect of Christians from several directions, she began to travel and preach. She became one who continually dissented from Watchman Nee. In January 1934, while he was conducting the third overcomer conference in Shanghai, this sister was in the meetings. When Watchman spoke, she would often shake her head. This was a suffering to him, and this was not the only case. Through the years, in the work and in the churches, this kind of dissension happened to him a number of times.

C. Immaturity and Incompetency

Among those who worked with Watchman Nee and bore

the responsibility with him in the church life, no one approached him in maturity and competency; all the others were immature and incompetent. Fifty years ago in China, Watchman was unique and extraordinary in his knowledge of things. He went forward much further than all the rest. He saw many things the brothers did not see, and their immaturity and incompetency caused him a great deal of suffering.

D. Stubbornness

The stubbornness of the brothers also caused him to suffer. One day a learned young man came into the meeting of the church in Shanghai and was saved. He intended to go to the United States for further study. However, before leaving China, he desired to be baptized.

Watchman was very clear concerning him and agreed that he should be baptized. But an older co-worker disagreed. His reason was that this young man was too new. He had come to the meetings only once or twice, and he was about to leave for the United States. Such a person should not be baptized. He based his reason upon Watchman's own teaching that nothing should be done in the church life without fellowship, and his fellowship was that this brother should not be baptized. He held stubbornly to this point concerning fellowship and used it to insist that the young man should not be baptized. His concern was that the young man might not be saved. Watchman told him that if to baptize the young man was a mistake, he would bear the full responsibility before the Lord. But still the co-worker stubbornly refused.

In 1933 Watchman began to realize that for the sisters not to pray in the prayer meetings of the church was a great loss. He became convinced that it was proper for the sisters to pray in the meetings. However, the leading ones in the church at that time stubbornly kept the old way. That too grieved him.

E. Ambition

Brother Nee also suffered from the brothers' ambition for position. Among the first three brothers to come into the

church in Shanghai in the very beginning, one was very
ambitious to be a leader. Due to his ambition he caused a
great deal of trouble. Eventually, in 1948, after being in the
church for twenty years, he left. He began a meeting in his
home with a traveling preacher. That traveling preacher later
wrote a long article against Watchman Nee. This also caused
him to suffer.

That was just one case. A number of Chinese preachers
throughout the past fifty years passed through the church
life. They came to the meetings expecting to be placed in
some position. But Watchman always made it clear that the
church was not an organization and that no positions were
available. When asked concerning position he would say,
"Who would give me a position? There is no position. The
church is an organism." Some came and met with the church
for a time, expecting to receive some post in the work.
Eventually, however, when they discovered that they could
not obtain what they were after, they left and became
opponents.

F. Rebellion and Attack

Rebellion of the brothers and sisters was another source
of suffering to Watchman Nee. A brother co-worker committed immorality. Watchman assisted the church in that
co-worker's locality to excommunicate him. He in turn rebel-
liously attacked Brother Nee. During World War II, after the
Japanese army occupied Shanghai, that co-worker sent mail
to Watchman of such a nature that if the contents had been
disclosed or discovered by the censors it would have caused
much trouble. What an evil attack that was!

Through the years a number became rebellious and
attacked him. The most serious case centered around his
involvement in business and involved the saints in Shanghai
in 1942. Most of the brothers and sisters, including the
co-workers and elders, rebelled against him and attacked
him. This was the greatest cause of suffering to him and
forced him to discontinue his ministry for six years. That
was a severe and long suffering.

Through all these sufferings, however, he learned the

lessons. These sufferings not only assisted him in trusting the Lord; they also worked for him in dealing with his flesh, his self, his soul, and his natural life. In my own personal knowledge of him, the final experience he learned through his sufferings, when his ministry was terminated for six years, was that of the breaking of the outer man. He never passed on mere teachings and doctrines; his messages contained the reality he acquired through the experience of suffering. The experience he acquired through suffering served as a great help to all of us and became a rich heritage to all the churches in the Lord's recovery. This rich heritage was acquired by him at a high price.

His sufferings also helped him to receive revelations from the Lord. Often through a certain kind of suffering, he received a certain kind of revelation. His sufferings often became the Lord's revelation. He was purified, dealt with, torn down, and constituted by the Holy Spirit with the divine life through his sufferings. Through such experience of suffering, he was equipped and positioned to receive the Lord's revelation.

V. OTHERS

A. False Condemnation and Imprisonment

Watchman Nee was arrested in March 1952. He was judged, falsely condemned, and sentenced to fifteen years imprisonment in 1956. He died in confinement on May 30, 1972. There is no way to know what he experienced of the Lord during this long imprisonment. The following eight letters were written at the end of his confinement in his own handwriting and are the only means through which we can see a small glimpse of his suffering, feeling, and expectation during his confinement.

Letter One

April 22, 1972

Eldest Sister Pin-cheng,

I received your letter of April 7, and found that you had

not received my letter, in which I notified you that the things you sent me every time have been received. All the things you mentioned in your letter I have received. I am very grateful to you.

You know my physical condition is chronic, an illness of the organ itself. When it is activated I suffer much, but even when it is latent, it is still present with me. The difference is whether or not it is activated. Summer is here, and although more exposure to the sun can alter a little the color of my skin, it cannot change the illness. However, I maintain my joy, so please do not worry. I hope you will also take care of yourself and be filled with joy in your heart.

I wish you well.

Shu-tsu

Watchman wrote this letter to his sister-in-law, who was his wife's oldest sister and whom he addressed in the letter as "eldest sister."

This sister lived in Peking and was away from Mrs. Nee for about twenty years. In 1971 Mrs. Nee fell from a stool and broke two ribs. Because of this fall, Mrs. Nee's high blood pressure increased, and this caused her death. Due to this great loss, the eldest sister felt it necessary after Mrs. Nee's death to stay and take care of Watchman and to send him the things he needed. "The things you sent me every time" refers to this.

"When it [the 'chronic ailment'] is activated I suffer much" and "it ['more exposure to the sun'] cannot change the illness" indicate that he was still suffering from his illness.

"However, I maintain my joy" indicates that he was practicing the word of the apostle Paul in Philippians 4:4: "Rejoice in the Lord always." "Be filled with joy in your heart" indicates that he not only rejoiced in the Lord Himself, but also encouraged his sister-in-law to be filled with the joy of the Lord. Both of these words show us that while he was suffering his imprisonment, he trusted in the Lord and had much fellowship with the Lord. He was like the apostle, who, while suffering imprisonment, rejoiced in the Lord and encouraged his readers to also rejoice in the Lord (Phil. 2:17-18). In his letter he did not quote anything from the Scriptures, indicating that he had no freedom to do so. This letter was dated April 22, 1972, thirty-eight days before he passed away. He signed this letter with his name, Shu-tsu, which was commonly used among his relatives.

Letter Two

May 6, 1972

Eldest Sister Pin-cheng,

Tomorrow (May 7) it will be half a year since the death of Sister Hwei. Too many changes have transpired during the past half a year. In reminiscing over the former days, and in perusing and caressing the articles left behind by her, I could not help but grieve and ache in my heart. For over twenty years, I have not been able to take care of her once. This will be a lifelong regret to me. It was all because of me; I owe her so much and have given her so many hardships. My sickness is chronic and has frequent setbacks. As far as my living goes, I try as much as possible to make things simple, so that I would not bother others. In my sickness, I really miss my own relatives and long to be with them. However, I submit to the arrangement placed on my environment. For the past ten days or so, I could not help but have unceasing deep feelings for Sister Hwei.

How is your health? You are always in my remembrance. As an older person, you should take more care of yourself. Are you still thinking about coming to the south? I do not know what to say. I can only wish you well.

Shu-tsu

In this letter "Sister Hwei" refers to Watchman's wife, Charity, whose Chinese name is Pin-hwei.

Letter Three

May 16, 1972

Eldest Sister Pin-cheng,

Both your letter dated the 6th from Peking and the one dated the 11th from Shanghai have been received. This time when you come, I hope that you can stay longer and have more rest. In my sickness, I do long to be in contact more with my own relatives. Here the mountains are beautiful and the water clear. One thing special about this place is that the children are especially handsome, more so than all the ones I saw in Shanghai. I hope that you can find some rest here.

Sister Hwei's ashes are indeed a problem. When you come, we will discuss this.

I do not have much need. Just bring me an electric flashlight.

I wish you well.

Shu-tsu

Letter Four

May 22, 1972

Eldest Sister Pin-cheng,

I have talked with the supervisor concerning the question of my leaving the farm here. He said, "You cannot go to Peking or Shanghai. You can only go to a small place, a village. As long as the verification papers come, the government will deal with the matter according to the set policy. There is no need to discuss this with me."

Therefore, please find for me someone among my relatives whose name I can come under. You can explain to them that I can take care of my living. I hope that they can receive me and that they can ask the commune administration there to issue a certificate saying that I can stay there and that they will accept me.

I hope that someone can be found among my relatives. Ma Hsing-tao is one who may be willing to do it. Please discuss it with him, or with some others.

On Saturday night, I had another relapse. For a few hours, my heart was quivering. Later I took some Diacin and was able to be sustained. On Sunday, I slept the whole day. In my sickness, I deeply long to return to my own relatives and be with them, as a falling leaf returning to its roots. I have lost contact with all of them for over twenty years. Therefore, I can only ask you to help me.

When you come, bring with you one catty of Tai-Chang shredded beef and one catty of dried beef. Because of my angina pectoris, the doctor has told me not to eat egg yolk, fat, or any internal organs, for fear that the illness will worsen. So I can only eat some lean meat. If I do not eat anything, I will not have the supply of amino acid in the protein. This is a problem to me.

I wish you well.

Shu-tsu

In this letter, Watchman Nee referred to his sickness more than once. Diacin is a trade name of Niacin, a nicotinic acid. Angina pectoris, the chronic illness which he had, is a disease which causes chest pain due to a lack of blood supply to the heart muscles.

"Ma Hsing-tao" is Watchman's nephew-in-law, the husband of his niece who was the daughter of his cousin. During his imprisonment, this nephew-in-law and his wife took care of Mrs. Nee, who had poor health. Both he and his wife were brother and sister in the Lord. Eventually, his wife died, leaving this nephew-in-law to take care of Mrs. Nee alone.

On the same day that the above letter was written, Watchman wrote another letter to this relative (see Letter Five).

Letter Five

May 22, 1972

Nephew-in-law Hsing-tao,

I believe your aunt, while she was alive, must have talked to you about my situation.

You know that my eldest sister is supplying my needs; therefore, my living is no problem. I am old and with much illness, longing very much to be with my relatives. As a falling leaf returning to its root, so I seek a final resting place. I earnestly hope that you could take the responsibility to accomplish this matter for me. In every respect I am depending on you.

Because of the death of your aunt six and a half months ago, all my five internal organs hurt, and it is difficult for me to pass through the days. I hope that you would make every effort to mail the certificate here. When your aunt was alive, she many times mentioned Hwei-yi and her children. I wonder how the children are now? I miss them.

I heard that going to Chekiang may cause a problem with the food coupons. I believe since I eat very little, there will be a solution; so it does not matter.

For more than twenty years we have not corresponded with each other. You are often in my remembrance.

I wish you well.

Shu-tsu

This letter was written by Watchman to his nephew-in-law.

"Your aunt" refers to Mrs. Nee. "Must have talked to you about my situation," according to the context of the whole letter, apparently refers to Watchman's health and matters involving his release from prison. "My eldest sister" refers to his eldest sister, Mrs. Chen, who lived in Hong Kong. During his imprisonment it was she who sent financial supply to Shanghai for Watchman Nee and his wife. It was because of this that his "living is no problem."

"Longing very much to be with my relatives" indicates that he was expecting to be released from prison and to stay with his nephew-in-law. At that time he considered himself "as a fallen leaf returning to its root," seeking "a final resting place" for the remaining years of his life. "To accomplish this matter for me" indicates that he had requested his nephew-in-law to prepare a resting place for him. "In every respect" concerning this matter he was depending upon that relative.

"Because of the death of your aunt six and a half months ago, all my five internal organs hurt, and it is difficult for me to pass through the days." This shows the deep sorrow he experienced regarding his wife's death and the hardship he suffered from it.

"Make every effort to mail the certificate" may indicate that Watchman desired this relative to send him a certificate certifying their relationship so he could be released from prison.

"Going to Chekiang" indicates that this relative's home was in Chekiang where Watchman intended to go and rest during his remaining years.

"May cause a problem with the food coupons" indicates the possibility of a problem for him to buy food stuff in Chekiang since he would be a stranger there.

This letter was dated May 22, 1972, only eight days before his departure.

Letter Six

May 25, 1972

Eldest Sister Pin-cheng,

Tomorrow, I will be reassigned from Feng-Shu-Ling to Shan-Shia-Pu Farm. When you come, do not buy your ticket for Feng-Shu-Ling. Instead buy your ticket for Shan-Shia-Pu. It is a little further away from Feng-Shu-Ling, at the next station. I have sent you one letter before this one. I do not know if you have received it. I hope to see you soon.

I wish you well.

Shu-tsu

This letter to his sister-in-law shows that on May 26, he was to be transferred from the farm in Feng-Shu-Ling to another more remote farm in Shan-Shia-Pu, one station away.

Letter Seven

May 26, 1972

Hsing-tao,

While in Feng-Shu-Ling I wrote you a letter, hoping you could obtain a certificate for me from the commune administration, which would clearly indicate your desire to receive me and guarantee my living. (You know my eldest sister is supplying my daily needs.) Your attitude should be firm and clear.

[Series of long dashes supplied by Watchman Nee here.]

Today I was transferred from Feng-Shu-Ling to the Convalescent Group at Pai-Yun-Shan. I hope you will try your best to do this and give me a reply. The certificate should be sent directly to Group No. 14, Pai-Yun-Shan Farm. In the salutation it should be the commune administration writing to Pai-Mao-Ling Farm, Kwang-Te County, Anhwei province. But when you mail it, you should address it to Group No. 14, Pai-Yun-Shan Farm, Kwang-Te County, Anhwei province.

I hope very much to go back to my relatives. Please make an effort.

I wish you well,

Shu-tsu

This is the second letter written by Watchman to the same nephew-in-law. It was dated May 26, 1972, only four days before his death.

"While in Feng-Shu-Ling I wrote you a letter" indicates that the earlier letter was written in Feng-Shu-Ling.

"Address it to Group No. 14, Pai-Yun-Shan Farm, Kwang-Te County, Anhwei province" indicates that Watchman died in the Pai-Yun-Shan Farm, Kwang-Te County, Anhwei province. Pai-Yun-Shan Farm is probably the same as Shan-Shia-Pu mentioned in letter six.

"I hope very much to go back to my relatives" indicates how he desired to be released and go to his relatives. But he died four days later.

In all of the above letters, there is no mention of the name of the Lord or of God. This indicates that he did not have the freedom to do so.

Letter Eight

May 30, 1972

Eldest Sister Pin-cheng,

I have been reassigned to Shan-Shia-Pu Group No. 14. It is ten [Chinese] miles away from the station and is separated from it by a mountain. It is very inconvenient for you to come. You do not need to come anymore.

In my sickness, I still remain joyful at heart. Please do not worry. I am still doing my best to not allow myself to be grieved by my own illness.

Pin-hwei's ashes will be left to your care. I am trusting in you for everything. I give my consent to everything.

This letter is short, yet my feelings run deep. I can only wish you well.

Shu-tsu

This was the last letter of Watchman Nee. It shows that the farm in which he died was quite remote, being ten Chinese miles from the station and separated from the station by a mountain. The fact that he had changed his mind and no longer wanted his sister-in-law to visit him and the fact that he had left the care of his wife's ashes to his sister-in-law, seem to indicate that he had sensed his imminent death. He died the same day.

B. Death and Humiliation

There is no way to trace the cause of Watchman's death. However, at his departure not one relative, brother, or sister was with him. Humanly speaking, what a miserable and humiliating way to die. There was no proper notification of his death and no funeral. He was cremated on June 1, 1972. Only the eldest sister of Mrs. Nee was informed of his death and cremation on June 1, 1972. It was she who picked up the ashes and gave them to Watchman's nephew-in-law. He in turn buried the ashes with those of Mrs. Nee in his home town of Kwanchao in the county of Haining, Chekiang province.

The following is an account by Brother Nee's grandniece, who accompanied Mrs. Nee's eldest sister at the time when Brother Nee's ashes were picked up:

In June 1972, we got a notice from the labor farm that my granduncle had passed away. My eldest grandaunt and I rushed to the labor farm. But when we got there, we learned that he had already been cremated. We could only see his ashes....Before his departure, he left a piece of paper under his pillow, which had several lines of big words written in a shaking hand. He wanted to testify to the truth which he had even until his death, with his lifelong experience. That truth is—**"Christ is the Son of God who died for the redemption of sinners and resurrected after three days. This is the greatest truth in the universe. I die because of my belief in Christ. Watchman Nee."** When the officer of the labor farm showed us this paper, I prayed that the Lord would let me quickly remember it by heart....

My granduncle had passed away. He was faithful until death. With a crown stained with blood, he went to be with the Lord. Although God did not fulfill his last wish, to come out alive to join his wife, the Lord prepared something even better—they were reunited before the Lord.

Such is the way that Watchman Nee ended his time on this earth. In May 1989, after a period of seventeen years, his ashes and the ashes of Mrs. Nee were both transferred by his two nephews from Chekiang to a public cemetery in Shiangshan in the city of Soochow of Kiangsu province. They were both buried in "The Christian Cemetery" beside Watchman's brother Nee Hwai-tsu and the latter's wife.

Watchman Nee was a man of suffering. Along his pathway of following the Lamb, he suffered. Today as a result of his suffering, we have such a rich heritage in the Lord's recovery. The following two stanzas are the conclusion to Hymn #635 in our hymnal, which is on the suffering of the grapevine. These words, which he helped me arrange into singable verse in Hong Kong in 1950, summarized his entire life.

> Not by gain our life is measured,
>> But by what we've lost 'tis scored;
> 'Tis not how much wine is drunken,
>> But how much has been outpoured.
> For the strength of love e'er standeth
>> In the sacrifice we bear;
> He who has the greatest suff'ring
>> Ever has the most to share.
>
> He who treats himself severely
>> Is the best for God to gain;
> He who hurts himself most dearly
>> Most can comfort those in pain.
> He who suffering never beareth
>> Is but empty "sounding brass";
> He who self-life never spareth
>> Has the joys which all surpass.

Watchman Nee realized that life is measured not by gain but by loss and that the one who has suffered the most has the most to share with others. For this reason, he never spared himself, but bore the cross and the fellowship of Christ's suffering, being conformed to His death, in order to live Christ out that others might be nourished and enriched with Him.

CHAPTER TWENTY-TWO

THE MINISTRY OF WATCHMAN NEE

We have seen the revelations Watchman Nee received from the Lord and the sufferings he underwent. After seeing something of his revelations and sufferings, we come to his ministry.

MINISTRY ISSUING FROM
REVELATION PLUS SUFFERING

Ministry is the issue of revelation plus suffering. Without revelation one cannot have ministry because he has nothing to minister. But though one may have revelation, if he lacks suffering, he still has no ministry. He may have some sort of teaching or gift, but this is not ministry. There is a difference between teaching and ministry. Ministry is something higher and deeper. Gift is superficial and costs little, while ministry is weighty and costly. If you have received revelation from God, He will put you into suffering in order that you may have ministry.

From the writings of the apostle Paul, we can see that before he endured suffering, he received revelation. When he received the revelation, he did not immediately go out to pass it on as teaching or knowledge. To do so would not have been ministry; it would have been a sort of teaching or an exercise of gift. But after receiving the revelation, the Lord put him into some suffering. Hence, in all his Epistles we have this sequence: first, the revelation; second, the sufferings; and third, the ministry which came out of the first two. To receive revelation is one thing; to have that revelation wrought into our being is something else.

In the process of producing a porcelain vase, a pattern for a picture is painted onto the vase. The vase is then put into an oven, and the painting is burned onto it. By passing through the oven, the painting and the vase become one.

Receiving a revelation is similar to having a picture painted upon us; but this painting must be burned into us to make the painting one with us. When the painting is burned into the vase, no one can erase it; neither can the vase be separated from the painting. If the vase is broken, the painting is broken, for they are one. It is the same with us. The only way for us to be burned is by suffering. No real minister of God can avoid suffering.

The measure of life, the amount of reality, and the riches of Christ we are able to minister to others depend entirely upon two elements: how much revelation we have received and how much suffering we have undergone regarding that which has been revealed to us. When suffering is added to revelation, we have ministry.

Paul said, "Therefore having this ministry..." (2 Cor. 4:1). He did not say that he had a certain teaching or a gift, but a ministry. Again he said, "I Paul became a minister" (Col. 1:23). He did not say that he was made a speaker or a teacher, but a minister. We are not referring to today's "minister." The word "minister" has been spoiled and misused in today's Christianity. A minister is a person who has a real ministry, a ministry which issues from these two things—revelation plus suffering.

THE DIFFERENCE BETWEEN GIFT AND MINISTRY

We may illustrate the difference between gift and ministry by the example of Balaam's donkey. One day the donkey of the Gentile prophet suddenly spoke with human language (Num. 22:28-30). Could that be called ministry? Certainly not! That was a gift. A ministry is the expression of what we are, while a gift is merely a performance. When you behold a man speaking, walking, and gesturing, you do not imagine that he is a horse or some other kind of animal. Since he is a man, whatever he does is just the expression of that man; that is his ministry.

Consider monkeys for example. Sometimes their trainers can entice them to perform like men, but that is entirely a gift or performance. In today's Christianity there is much acting. Much of it is performance. If the apostle Paul were to visit us for one month, we would exclaim, "He is really what he ministers!" What he has seen has been wrought into his being; hence, what he ministers is what he is. The person is the message. Today we have those who are eloquent and learned, those who have degrees after their names, those who dress in a certain way, stand upon a platform, and with a certain tone deliver a sermon. That is merely a performance; it is not the ministry. The apostle Paul was different, and Watchman Nee was also different.

I was with Watchman Nee for years. He talked about the cross, and in him I saw the cross. He was a person of the cross. The sufferings he received from all directions were just the working of the cross, and the revelation he received concerning the cross was wrought into him. What he did in years past was not merely to teach or exercise a gift. I can testify from the depths of my being that what he did was a ministry; what he did was what he was.

For the building up of the churches, gifts are not as necessary as ministry. What Watchman Nee had was not merely a gift, but a ministry. He had seen something of God and these things were burned into him. Even his presence ministered life to people. His presence always meant a great deal in a meeting. If he was there, the meeting was rich; if he was absent, the meeting was not so rich. His presence, even his silent presence, made a difference. He had a real ministry. It was not his knowledge, his doctrine, nor his gift, but something of God wrought into his being so that his very presence in the meeting made a difference. Sometimes when the troubled saints brought their problems into his presence, there was no need for him to say a word; their problems were solved. In his presence they received the light they needed. His presence became their enlightenment, for God's light had been wrought into his being. They saw light in his light. How much we need such a ministry in the church today!

Throughout the years that I was with Watchman Nee, I noticed how he continually belittled gifts. What he stressed over and over again was the need for ministry.

There are two Epistles in the Bible written by the apostle Paul to the Corinthians. The main topic in the first Epistle

is "gifts," and it is mentioned negatively. In the second Epistle
the main word is "ministry," and it is mentioned in a positive
way. In the first Epistle Paul depreciated the gifts, and in the
second Epistle he uplifted the ministry. In the second Epistle
it is difficult to find the word "gift," but in the first Epistle it
appears many times.

WATCHMAN NEE'S MINISTRY—
CHRIST AND THE CHURCH

Out of Watchman Nee's revelations inwrought by his
sufferings, a ministry came forth. His ministry was clearly of
two aspects: first, of Christ and, second, of the church. His
ministry was full, proper, and adequately balanced. I have
never known anyone so thoroughly and adequately balanced
in the aspects of Christ and the church as Watchman Nee. He
saw a clear vision of Christ, and he also received a full revelation of the church. In his spoken ministry and in his
publications as well, he was always properly balanced in
these two aspects. Many in the United States are aware that
he put out book after book concerning Christ as life and
Christ as everything. But many may not realize that he also
published book after book on the matter of the church.

Concerning the church he covered two main points in his
ministry: the content of the church and the practice of the
church, or in other words, the reality of the church and
the practicality of the church. The content and the reality of
the church are Christ Himself. Watchman saw the vision that
Christ is not merely for the believers individually but even
more for the church corporately. His vision was unlike those
who are today considered to be spiritual people; they hold
that Christ is mostly for Christians as individuals while
caring little for the church. They even fear to speak about
the church, for they realize that whenever the matter of the
church is raised, a problem is created, and they would rather
steer clear of all problems. Watchman Nee's vision of Christ
was that Christ is for individual believers to enjoy in order
to be built up in the church. Eventually, the Christ whom
we experience becomes the reality and the content of the
church. Watchman also saw that this reality of the church is

also practical and that we need the practicality of the church. Hence, he ministered both the reality and the practicality of the church. The reality of the church is the content, and the practicality of the church is its expression.

Christ is not just for individual Christians but for the corporate Body. And the Christ we enjoy as Christians individually is entirely for the building up of the corporate Body. For this reason Christ is both the content of the church and the reality of the church. The church's reality is simply Christ realized by many individual Christians in a corporate way. To match this reality, we need the church practice. If we stay at home and hold Christ as the reality, there will be no church. Even though we might hold the reality individually, we would be short of the practicality. Christians need to come together and to be built together; each one needs to come out of his little cell and into one big cell, under one roof, to practice the church life. Then we not only have the reality, but also the practicality of the church. These were the two main points of Watchman Nee's ministry.

Watchman's ministry regarding Christ as our life was fully accepted; but his ministry regarding the church was frequently rejected. Today it is the same. Many have received help from his ministry regarding Christ as life, but those same people would not take his ministry regarding the church. Many bookstores carry his books on Christ as life, but purposely will not carry his books on the church. Some publishers publish his books on Christ as life with great appreciation for his ministry in this aspect, yet they condemn his ministry on the church. Publishers and booksellers have even done their best to hide his ministry on the church. We fully agree that his books concerning Christ should be published, for they are marvelous. But it is altogether unfair and dishonest to hide his books on the church.

A rumor was even spread after World War II that Watchman Nee changed his concept concerning the practicality of the church life and the ground of the church. This is absolutely not true. His book *Further Talks on the Church Life* documents and shows beyond a shadow of a doubt that after 1948, rather than changing his concept concerning the

church, he ministered even more strongly than before
concerning his original vision. In one of these messages, given
shortly before his imprisonment, he said that what he saw
in 1937 concerning the church was absolutely right. He rather
confirmed what he had seen before; he did not change at all.
He was faithful to the Lord's vision and commission concerning Christ and the church. During his whole life, his ministry
was for Christ and the church—not for Christ only, but for
Christ *and* the church.

CHAPTER TWENTY-THREE

THE GENERAL MEANS
OF WATCHMAN NEE'S MINISTRY

Watchman Nee used eight different means to carry out the ministry wrought into him by the Lord. Five were general and three were specific. The five general means were preaching the gospel, teaching the Bible, traveling, contacting people, and corresponding with people. The three specific means were holding conferences, conducting trainings, and issuing publications.

I. PREACHING THE GOSPEL

The first means Watchman Nee adopted to carry out his ministry was preaching the gospel. This means was primary in the early years of his ministry. He preached to both crowds and individuals; he preached in homes and on the streets; he preached in cities and in villages. He also preached at home and abroad. In addition to speaking, he used tracts and pamphlets to preach the gospel. Although he was not considered an evangelist primarily, he did much evangelistic work and brought hundreds of solid fruit to the Lord for the building of His churches.

II. TEACHING THE BIBLE

Watchman Nee also used Bible teaching to carry out his ministry. Before 1928 he conducted a thorough study of the book of Revelation in Shanghai with a small number of believers. At the end of 1931 he conducted a one-month Bible study on church truth with the saints in Shanghai. After 1931 he conducted an intermittent study of the Gospel of Matthew with the church in Shanghai over a period of years. In or around 1932 he held a Bible study on tribulation and rapture truth with the saints in Shanghai. This study was published in a booklet entitled *Tribulation and Rapture*. In

February 1934 following his third overcomer conference, he conducted a study with the church in Shanghai and a number of co-workers from different localities on the boundary of the local churches. These messages were published in a book entitled *The Assembly Life.* In May 1935 at the request of a few co-workers (fewer than ten), he conducted a thorough study on the Song of Songs at West Lake, Hangchow. These messages were also published in a book entitled *The Song of Songs.* In May 1937 he held a study with the church in Shanghai on gospel questions and how to enter into the kingdom. In October of the same year, he held another study with the church in Shanghai on the difference between the local churches and the work. In February 1938 he studied the truth of the Holy Spirit with the church in Shanghai. This study included the Comforter's work within the believers, the work of the Holy Spirit as poured out upon the believers, and the need for the believers' life to be filled with the Holy Spirit. In February 1938 he conducted several Bible study meetings with the church in Hong Kong. In 1945 he conducted a study on the orthodoxy of the church with the church in Chungking. This study was published in a book entitled *The Orthodoxy of the Church.* By means of such Bible studies, many saints were enlightened and the churches established.

III. TRAVELING

Traveling was the third means Watchman used to carry out his ministry. Although he had no desire to be popular, under the leading of the Lord, he traveled through a number of provinces in China. Wherever he went, sinners were saved, believers were edified in life, and either the church was strengthened or the way was paved for a church to be established.

A. Domestic

In 1922 he visited Shanghai, testifying in the Christian and Missionary Alliance Auditorium at North Szechuan Road.

In 1924 he preached in Hangchow. From there he went to Nanking to assist in the work of the *Spiritual Light.*

In 1925 he held revival meetings with the denominations in Changchow, south Fukien.

In March 1926 he visited Amoy, Kulangsu, Changchow, and Tung-An, in south Fukien for approximately two months.

In the summer of the same year, he held revival meetings in the province of Anhwei.

In the second half of 1926, he visited south Fukien again and established gatherings for the Lord's recovery in Amoy, Tung-An, and nearby places.

In the late fall of 1926, he was invited by Cheng Chi-kwei and Ruth Lee to visit Nanking for the second time. He stayed in the home of Brother Cheng and helped him translate Scofield's Bible Correspondence Course and preached at Nanking University.

In the beginning of 1927, he took up residence in the town of Tsao-Chiao, Wusih, Kiangsu, where he wrote the first volume of *The Spiritual Man.*

In March 1927 he visited Shanghai, attending the gatherings there with the saints in the Lord's recovery. He later settled in Shanghai.

In the summer of 1928 and in July of 1930, he went to Kuling, Kiangsi, for rest.

In January 1931 he visited Swatow and Chieh-Yang, Kwangtung, returning to Shanghai at the end of the same month.

In the same year he visited Peking.

At the end of March 1932, he visited Tsinan, the capital of Shantung province. While in Tsinan he spoke to over eighty students at Chi-Loo University who were on a mountain retreat in Taishan. Following this he worked at the university for eleven days. This visit paved the way for the church in Tsinan to later come into existence.

In June of 1932, he was invited by the Chinese Independent Church in Chefoo, where he spoke to denominational believers for one week. That visit facilitated the raising up of the church in Chefoo.

In July of the same year, he was invited to speak to the students and the church members at the Southern Baptist Seminary in Hwang-Hsien, a city close to Chefoo.

In April of 1933, Watchman visited the saints in the Lord's recovery at Tsinan, the capital of Shantung. From there he continued on to Chefoo to visit the church and spoke both to the saints in the Lord's recovery and to those in the denominations.

In the winter of the same year, he again visited Tsinan to visit the church and strengthen the saints there.

In October 1934 he held his fourth overcomer conference in Hangchow.

In the spring of 1935, he traveled with Samuel Chang, his brother George, and a third brother through the provinces of Chekiang, Kiangsi, and Hunan to visit the provinces of Kwangsi, Kweichow, and Yunnan to look over the situation as it related to the furtherance of the Lord's recovery.

In August of the same year, he visited Chefoo from Shanghai and held a special conference with the church there.

In October, again of the same year, he visited Kulangsu in south Fukien, holding a conference with the co-workers.

In January 1936 he traveled from Shanghai to Peking to visit the church there. From Peking he went on to Tientsin to strengthen the new work there by holding special gospel preaching meetings.

In May of the same year, he was invited to speak to the provincial officials in Kaifeng, Honan. From there he returned to Shanghai.

In November of 1937, he visited Hankow and conducted a retreat for the co-workers from the coastal provinces. At this conference he released his messages on the *Rethinking the Work,* which has been republished as *The Normal Christian Church Life.*

In December of 1937, he went to Hong Kong, polished messages for the *Rethinking the Work,* and returned to Shanghai in January of 1938.

In February he left Shanghai for Hong Kong again and held Bible study meetings there.

In 1941 he visited Hong Kong.

In March of 1945, he went to Chungking to live for a period of time during World War II. While he was there, a number of seeking saints contacted him. Meetings were held with them on the seven epistles in Revelation 2 and 3, which was the study that formed *The Orthodoxy of the Church.* In February or March of 1949, he visited Taipei, had fellowship with the leading brothers for ten days, and imparted much help to them in the matters of spiritual knowledge and experience of life.

In January of 1950, he visited Hong Kong from Shanghai for a period of two and a half months. He conducted church meetings in the evenings and met with the co-workers and leading ones in the church in Hong Kong in the mornings for a considerable period of time. In the first part of his visit, his ministry brought a revival to the church there. Due to this revival, many of the saints in Hong Kong handed over their possessions.

B. Abroad

In addition to his domestic traveling, he also visited a number of foreign countries.

In November 1924 he visited Sitiawan in Malaysia. He visited the same place the following year and established the first church in Southeast Asia. He returned to China from Malaysia in May 1925.

In March 1931 he worked in Japan for one week.

Late in June 1933, he traveled through France and stayed in London, England, for a period of time. He visited the Brethren assemblies and also met with T. Austin-Sparks and those who met with him at Honor Oak, London. In London he also visited D. M. Panton and George Cutting who told Watchman, "Without Him I cannot live, and without me He cannot live." The Brethren brought him to America to visit the assemblies in Vancouver, Canada, and New York City. In New York he spoke in English to over two thousand Brethren believers. He returned to China in August of the same year. Through that visit the real condition of the Brethren assemblies became clear to him.

In July 1937 he visited Manila in the Philippines and conducted meetings there morning and evening. While in the Philippines, he held a mountain retreat in Baguio. There he spoke to over one hundred believers on the overcoming life of Christ, the outpouring of the Holy Spirit, and the truths concerning the church and fellowship.

In September of the same year, he traveled from Manila to visit Singapore, Sitiawan, and Penang in Malaysia.

In February 1938 he traveled from Shanghai to Hong Kong, Singapore, and Penang, holding meetings with the churches in these places respectively.

In April Watchman traveled through India, arriving in London in May to meet with T. Austin-Sparks.

On July 22 he attended the Keswick Convention with Brother Sparks. In the morning a missionary meeting was held. The chairman of the meeting, Mr. W. H. Aldis, knowing Watchman was present at the meeting, asked him to offer prayer. He hesitated at first, but after checking with Sparks and being encouraged by him, he offered the following prayer: "The Lord reigneth. He is reigning, and He is Lord of all. Nothing can touch His authority. It is the spiritual forces that are out to destroy the interests of the Lord in China and Japan. We do not pray for Japan. We do not pray for China. But we pray for the interests of Thy Son in China and Japan. We do not blame any man. They are only tools in the hand of the enemy of the Lord. Lord, we stand in Thy will. Lord, shatter the kingdom of darkness. Lord, the persecution of Thy church is persecuting Thee."[1] This prayer was offered in the presence of a Japanese Christian at the time the great havoc of the invading Japanese army was increasing. The whole congregation was both captivated and deeply impressed by this prayer.

In October of the same year, he was invited to visit Denmark. He also visited Norway, Germany, and Switzerland. He returned to London by way of Paris. While staying in London, his book *Rethinking the Work* was translated into English. The work of translation was done with the help of some sisters, and the book was published by Austin-Sparks' bookroom under the title *Concerning Our Missions*. This book was published with the hope of being able to minister to the Lord's people in the Western world on the practicality of the

---

[1] From *The Keswick Convention,* 1938, p. 246.

church life. At that time his ministry on Christ as life was fully accepted in northern Europe. However, the atmosphere at that time was not conducive to the release of his ministry on the practicality of the church life. It was for this reason that he was burdened to leave with them his main publications on this matter.

He left England in May of 1939, returning to Shanghai in July by way of India and Singapore.

His visits to the foreign countries left those who met him with a deep impression that he was commissioned by the Lord. These contacts paved the way for the future furtherance of the Lord's recovery outside of China.

IV. CONTACTING PEOPLE

Watchman Nee also fulfilled his ministry by personally contacting people. He used this means mostly in dealing with special cases. He was rich in life and keen in discernment, always affording timely help to those who came to him. Through his personal fellowship, many wanderers were brought back to the Lord, many distracted believers were brought back on track, many defeated saints were recovered to the Lord's victory, many needy persons received the supply of life, and many seeking ones were enlightened to turn to the Lord's recovery. His spirit was always strong and able to discern the real situation of those who came to him. Thus, he was able to give them proper instruction either in the spiritual life or in practical matters.

V. CORRESPONDING WITH PEOPLE

The last of the several general means Watchman Nee used to fulfill his ministry was correspondence with others. Contacting and fellowshipping with people by letter is the same, in principle, as contacting them personally. Letters containing questions and personal needs frequently came to him from believers in many places. If time had allowed, he could have given his full time to this matter alone. He possessed the adequate knowledge and bountiful life supply to answer the questions of his correspondents and supply their need.

What follows is an excerpt from his open letter in the fourth issue of *The Present Testimony*, published in July 1928. This letter reveals how much he engaged in letter writing to carry out his ministry:

In the last four months I have devoted my entire being to the writing of *The Spiritual Man*. Because of this, I have been unable to reply to many incoming letters which have piled up. I wish the brothers and sisters who have written me will realize that my delay does not mean I do not have a heart for you. Every letter has been carefully read. I am most sympathetic toward your problems. However, because of the time limitation, I have been unable to reply immediately. I wish all those who correspond with me will bear this in mind.

The following is another excerpt from his open letter in the thirteenth issue of *The Present Testimony*, published in March 1930:

Regarding many who have written asking questions on the Bible, frankly speaking, I cannot reply. If I were to answer each question, I would need to open a Bible correspondence course. However, if there are problems concerning spiritual life, I might be able to allot a little time for them.

CHAPTER TWENTY-FOUR

THE SPECIFIC MEANS
OF WATCHMAN NEE'S MINISTRY

(1)

The five general means of Watchman Nee's ministry mentioned in the previous chapter are common to all Christian workers. But since Watchman was burdened and commissioned with a specific ministry for the Lord's present testimony in this age, he adopted three further specific means for the carrying out of his particular ministry.

I. HOLDING CONFERENCES

The first specific means Watchman employed in his ministry was the holding of conferences. The regular meetings of the church were not sufficient for the release of the special messages he received from the Lord for the present day. A larger audience composed of those genuinely seeking the Lord and His interest and consecutive meetings held within a designated time span were needed for the release of his specific burdens. For these reasons he held many special conferences. The main conferences were called overcomer conferences, while the rest were simply called special conferences.

· The following excerpt from his open letter in the twenty-second issue of *The Present Testimony,* published in September—December 1931, explains the purpose of his conferences:

In our conferences our intention is only to speak forth the message of the victory of Christ, not to speak of other matters. The preaching of this message is our particular responsibility....In reality, unless a person knows God in the aspects of trusting and obeying Him, it is of little use to speak to him concerning other matters. We can mention many other matters to those who are faithful, but if we share them with those who are yet unwilling to serve God faithfully, it will only give rise to disputes....Our Bible study meetings, on the other hand, are of a different nature: They are conducted for those who are willing to serve God faithfully and are seeking to have a clearer understanding of Bible truths. For this reason, we are free in these meetings to bring up those things which we would be reluctant to bring up in conferences. We hope that in our future conferences, neither the speaker nor the listeners will bring up, either publicly or privately, any matters outside the victory of Christ, in order that we might have God's full blessing....This does not mean that other matters are not important; but it does mean that when men sincerely desire to receive the victory of Christ and to believe and obey the Lord, He will spontaneously direct their attention to these other external matters, and they will automatically obey....At this stage, if certain things are not clear to some, we would be most willing to help them in the Bible study meetings. We deeply sense that what the church of God urgently needs and what she absolutely must experience today is the victory of Christ—the facts and principles which He declared through His death and resurrection. In this matter we need to be faithful and steadfast, and we need to preach it wholeheartedly.

The following is his second personal testimony, given in Kulangsu, October 20, 1936 concerning the overcomer conferences:

God has shown me that in every local church a group of overcomers should be raised up (as those mentioned in Revelation 2 and 3) to be the Lord's witnesses. For this reason, every year an overcomer conference has been held to faithfully deliver the messages that God has given me.

Watchman's first overcomer conference was held in Shanghai in February 1928. His messages were on the eternal purpose of God and the victory of Christ. He unveiled the mystery that a spiritual warfare has taken place: God had a plan to accomplish, but His enemy Satan, the power of darkness, opposed it. However, Christ defeated Satan in His death on the cross and won a full victory. Now God's need is for believers in Christ to share His victory and fight against the power of darkness by executing what Christ has accomplished. The number attending the first conference was fifty, at the most. Twenty or thirty were from outside Shanghai, mostly from the northern province of Kiangsu and the county of Ping-Yang in Chekiang province. The audience was small, but the impact and the result were great.

The second overcomer conference was held in Shanghai from October 8-18, 1931. The announcement of the conference in the *The Present Testimony*, published in May 1931 reads:

> The purpose of this conference is to unite all the believers in every place who are of the same mind that they might wait before God and receive the message which comes from Him. Our past experience tells us that we must all receive deeper edification. For this reason we must lay much emphasis on the testimony of "the victory of Christ," which the Lord has committed to us. May those who intercede before the Lord pray in one accord for this conference that we may genuinely have the power which is purely of the Holy Spirit with no mixture of soulish power whatsoever.

Watchman's burden in this conference was the covenant of God and the wisdom of God. He unveiled the real meaning and content of the new covenant God enacted for us through the redemption of Christ. God first dealt with His people by His Word. First, He promised His people in His Word that He would do certain things for them according to His plan; then, His Word became His promise. When His promise was accomplished in Christ, it became the fact. When He bequeathed the fact to His chosen ones, a covenant was established. This covenant is the new covenant, which is better

than the old one. It was established through the blood of
Christ and supported by the ministry of His indestructible
life. These messages were first delivered in this second
overcomer conference, then published in *The Present Testimony* from 1932 to 1934, and later printed as the first half of
a book entitled *What Is the New Covenant?*

In November of 1932 he held a special conference with the
church in Shanghai. At that time eight brothers and sisters
came to have fellowship with us from the Brethren assemblies in England, the United States, and Australia.

In January 1934 he held his third overcomer conference in
Shanghai. The following excerpt is taken from his announcement of this conference. The announcement appeared as part
of his open letter in the thirty-second issue of *The Present Testimony* of October—December 1933 and tells us the nature of
that conference:

We have previously held two conferences of the same
nature, one in February of 1928 and one in October of 1931.
The conference held in November of last year was of a
different nature, and for that reason we consider the
upcoming conference to be the third overcomer conference.

I want all the brothers to understand the nature of this
type of conference; no attention will be paid to the less significant matters of the Bible. What we want to see in the
Holy Spirit is Christ and Him crucified. Matters such as
prophecy, church organization, Scripture exposition,
types, baptism, laying on of hands, speaking in tongues,
miracles, and a hundred other questions have their proper
place. As Christians we should not deny them their proper
place. However, these are neither the center of the Scriptures nor the center of the life of the Holy Spirit. God has
only one center, which is Christ—Christ and Him crucified. Our annual conferences of this nature are to bring us
back to this center. Therefore, we are reluctant to mention
any minor matters in these conferences. Rather, we would
emphasize only the central point which God Himself
stressed....

In our conference this time, as before, we wish to stress the central message. After much prayer I feel the theme which the Lord has given me for this conference is "God's overcomers." Everything in the conference will focus on this center....

Finally, in this conference, our hope is to meet Christ, to receive light and revelation from heaven, and to be filled with the life that is unknown to ordinary people. We do not intend to pay attention to the many minor, outward matters. "To know Him" (Phil. 3:10)—this is what we seek.

The number of attendants at the third overcomer conference was about three hundred, with over one hundred from different provinces throughout the country. There were two lines of messages. One line was the centrality and universality of Christ. This line disclosed how Christ is the center and the circumference in the universe and in the Christian life. He must have the preeminence in everything. The second line was God's overcomers. This line revealed how God called His overcomers in every age to replace His defeated people for the fulfillment of His purpose. The extract of these messages was published in the thirty-fourth issue of *The Present Testimony* of March—April 1934.

In October of the same year, his fourth overcomer conference was held in Hangchow. The attendants were generally the same ones who came to his third conference in Shanghai. His messages again were along two lines. The first line was the life of Abraham, showing how Abraham was an overcomer to fulfill God's purpose. The second line was the spiritual warfare, showing how to fight the enemy for the fulfillment of God's eternal purpose.

In his third visit to Chefoo in August of 1935, he held a special conference with the church there on the overcoming life of Christ. At that time the saints were greatly helped to experience the outpouring of the Holy Spirit. Through this conference a revival was brought in, which spread to Shanghai and other cities. After the revival broke out in Chefoo, Watchman returned in September to Shanghai and held a conference with the church on the outpouring of the Holy Spirit.

In October, following the conference in Shanghai, he also held a conference with the co-workers in Kulangsu in south Fukien on the same subject.

In January of 1937 he called an urgent conference in Shanghai for all the co-workers throughout the country. His burden was to share with his co-workers the new vision he had received from the Lord concerning the work and the local churches.

In the following November he held a conference in Hankow with his co-workers to release the same messages more adequately on his new revelation regarding the work and the local churches. Although the messages were the same as those given in Shanghai, the content was deeper and the revelation clearer. These messages were printed in a book entitled *Rethinking the Work (The Normal Christian Church Life).*

After his return from his trip to Europe, he called a special eleven-day conference in August of 1939. In this conference he released his messages on the principles of the Body.

In the years from 1940 to 1942, he held many special meetings. During this period he was both carrying out a training of the co-workers and at the same time helping the church in Shanghai to be built up practically. The crucial point he stressed in all these meetings was the need to see the Body. He also delivered a number of messages on the deeper things of the spiritual life. The messages contained in his book *The God of Abraham, Isaac, and Jacob* were delivered at that time.

In April and May of 1948, a special conference was held in Shanghai not only for the local saints but also for about eighty seeking saints from other cities throughout the country. In this special conference he spoke mostly concerning the work. His burden was to learn from the lessons of the past how best to go on in the future. It was in this special conference that he resumed his ministry. This conference resulted in all the brothers and sisters handing over all their possessions to the work. Brother Nee took the lead in this matter. This resulted in a revival, which in turn resulted in about eighty seeking brothers and sisters attending Watchman's first prolonged period of training in Kuling Mountain, Foochow.

In 1950 during the months of January and February, he held a long special conference with the church in Hong Kong. He spoke on overcoming wealth and how to hand over all our possessions for the furtherance of the Lord's work. At the same time he stressed that the believers who have been baptized in the Spirit into one Body should be built up in the church that the church might be a corporate means for the Lord to spread His gospel. A number of brothers and sisters were led to hand over all their possessions to the work, which in turn revived the whole church. Through this visit, the foundation was laid for the church in Hong Kong to receive much blessing in the years to come, both in life and in numbers.

II. CONDUCTING TRAININGS

Watchman conducted trainings as the second specific means of fulfilling his ministry. Let us read his own word concerning this matter, given in his second testimony in Kulangsu, October 20, 1936:

If the return of the Lord should be delayed, it will be necessary to raise up a number of young people to continue the testimony and the work for the following generations. Many co-workers have already prayed concerning this matter with the hope of providing a suitable place for the purpose of training young people. My thought is not to establish a seminary or a Bible institute, but to have young people staying together to live the Body life and practice the spiritual life. In such a place they would receive training for the purpose of edification, by learning to read the Scripture, to pray, and to build up a good character. On the negative side, there would be training for the purpose of learning how to deal with sin, the world, the flesh, and the natural life. At a suitable time, the young people would return to their respective churches in various places to be tempered together with other saints to serve the Lord in the church.

I have purchased over ten acres[1] of land at Chenru, in the suburbs of Shanghai. Planning for building on that site is in progress, and before long, young people will be able to go there for training.

A. The Initial Stage

Watchman's trainings were initiated in 1933. In the initial stages he began with a few young brothers, who stayed upstairs in the meeting hall in Shanghai. At that stage the training was informal. The trainees lived together, studied the Bible, and spent some time with him individually for spiritual help. On occasion he would spend time with us in the evening when there was no church meeting. Such informal training lasted for a period of two years.

B. The Training in Shanghai

In 1936 Watchman began to build a training facility in Chenru, in the suburbs of Shanghai. Just before the building work was completed, the war between Japan and China broke out, and the building was destroyed. After that he had no opportunity to carry out his burden until 1940.

After returning to Shanghai from his trip to Europe, he determined to stay in Shanghai all the time to release his messages on the Body of Christ and to help in the practical building up of the church. At that time he rented a place in Yu-hwa village in Shanghai in which to conduct his first training. Since his burden at that time was mostly on the Body of Christ, his training was focused on that theme. In the training he would frequently ask us to give our testimony on how we had seen the Body. Following each testimony, he would frequently declare, "No, you have not seen the Body." Then he would proceed to prove by the very words the trainee had used that the trainee had not seen the Body. To some who testified, he pointed out that the Body to them was just a doctrine or theory, not a vision.

---

[1] Chinese acres: one acre equals a little more than six thousand square feet—Editor.

He also trained us in the matter of consecration. Every morning he asked one of the trainees to give a testimony regarding his or her consecration. After each testimony he would diagnose it like a medical doctor, judge it with the thorough discernment of a judge, and frequently operate mercilessly on us as a surgeon. Only a few passed his keen and stern examination regarding their consecration. All, however, received practical help in life. The training lasted about two years, and quite a few from other cities remained in Shanghai for a longer period to be trained. The number of trainees was approximately seventy or eighty.

C. Trainings in Kuling Mountain

During Watchman's silent years, he took the opportunity to purchase many houses on a mountain which was called Kuling, close to Foochow, where many missionaries had their summer retreat. During World War II most of the missionaries left the country and gladly sold their houses at very low prices. Watchman bought more than fifteen of their houses with the intention of preparing them for his trainings.

Then, following the revival which came to Shanghai in 1948 when his ministry was recovered, about eighty brothers and sisters went with him to Kuling Mountain and occupied those houses for a four-month training period, from June to October 1948. The following is a testimony of Chang Wu-cheng, one of his trainees:

At the opening of the training Brother Nee first gave some explanations. "First, this training is not a seminary. Our purpose is not to pass on some scriptural knowledge or methods of work to the trainees, but to help those who are already following the Lord and walking on this way to go further. My ministry is somewhat different from that of Brother Witness Lee. He can cause those who have no heart for the Lord to have a heart for the Lord, those who are incapable to become capable, and those who are not going on to go on. I admit that I do not have what he has.

For twenty years I have only been able to help those who had something already to have something more, and to help those who are seeking, to receive help. Whether this training is a success or failure all depends upon what kind of people you are. If you are preoccupied and self-satisfied, you will not receive help. But if you really want to go on, I can help you go on further, and if you have some light, I can help you receive more light. My ministry is not to revive you or to change you, but to lead you if you are already on the way. My ministry is not to pull out those who are sitting at home and force them to walk.

"Second, this training will cover four parts: 1) how to be a minister of God's Word, 2) how to help new believers, 3) things to pay attention to and the solution to problems, 4) how to administer the church affairs."

The content of the training was very rich. Brother Nee gave messages for six hours a day, five days a week. Some of the details are as follows:

I. How to be a minister of God's Word. A minister of the Word is one who serves men with God's Word.
  A. You must know how to use your spirit. To be a minister of the Word, the basic requirement is that you learn how to use your spirit; otherwise, what you do will be from the soul, the emotion, and the mind.
  B. You must touch authority. A worker must touch authority. He must not only submit to direct authority but also to deputy authority. Only one who touches authority and learns to obey can be the authority and can minister God's Word.
  C. You must know people. You must know whether the spiritual condition of the brothers and sisters is proper or abnormal before you can help them. To know people, you must not simply listen to their words, but learn to touch their spirit. This requires that you yourself receive God's serious dealing and let God dig deep and touch you thoroughly. If you have never been dealt with and

if you are unclear and foolish, you can never know others. So you must live in God's light.

D. Learn how to study God's Word.

   1. Spend time. Especially the young people must spend time to study the Word.

   2. You must be the right person. What kind of person you are determines what kind of Bible you read. You should not be sloppy, subjective, hardened, or curious.

E. Learn how to deliver God's Word. You must not preach yourself, but the Word. With some, what comes out of their speaking is not God's Word, but man's thinking, concept, and opinion. Not only must your spiritual condition be right, even your words must be right. Otherwise, people will not touch God or receive light and supply.

F. You must have revelation and a burden. One who serves the Lord must receive revelation from God and discharge that burden. Only thus can you give people the real supply.

II. How to help new believers:

A. The past must be torn down. After a new believer has been saved, he still carries on his back all the things of his former life. He mixes the Lord's life with all his past. In evaluating himself, he is still righteous and proud; he still covets vainglory; he still has a peculiar temper and cannot get along with others. All these things must be done away, and he must become like a little child in order that he might begin to be a new man.

B. Christians have a standard. There is a standard for the Christian in his living, concept, and opinion. If he does not know this standard, it will be very easy for him to boast in himself, be satisfied with himself, and trust in himself. What he thinks is wrong may not be wrong, and what he thinks is right may not be right. Only those who know this standard know what things they should not do and what words they should not speak. Only those who know the standard are able to discover what is right and what is wrong. The kind of edification that new beginners need is that which helps them tear down what should be torn down and add what should be added. Only by this means can they be expected to become Christians with a Christian standard.

C. Practice:

1. Who is a new beginner?

   a. After a sinner believes in the Lord and is baptized, he is a new beginner. Regardless of his age, education, position, or experience in the world, he needs to receive the new beginners' edification.

   b. Those who have believed in the Lord for years but have never been edified should also participate.

2. The way:

   a. By speaking. When you speak, you should speak loudly and clearly, pick up the main points, and stay with the subject. Do not use a topic as a platform to speak what you want to speak; do not speak as though giving a sermon.

   b. Ask questions. You should encourage the asking of questions (1 Cor. 14:35). However, questions should be in line with the subject and should not go beyond.

   c. Answer. The answer must be clear. If the question is too far off, you must bring it back in line. When you answer, you must not try to save face by not paying attention to the truth. If you know, you must say that you know; if you do not know, you must say that you do not know.

   d. Speak according to the order of the fifty subjects for the new beginners' edification. Cover fifty subjects every year.

   e. Get into the matter of the daily living. Do not

just speak. You must check to see if they have carried out what you said. You must keep on pushing and checking until the word has been implemented into their living and until it is clear that they really mean business.

D. Concerning those who take the lead:

1. Have a proper attitude. The position of those who take the lead must be that of messengers delivering God's Word, not of teachers coming to teach. They must be like low ones speaking to low ones, not like high ones teaching low ones.

2. Touch the fresh spirit. The fifty subjects already mentioned will be repeated every year, so those who deliver the messages must touch the fresh spirit. If your spirit becomes old, what you say will be merely a doctrine, like repeating a prayer book.

3. Ask for the Lord's blessing. A Christian's life depends upon the Lord's blessing. If you do not have the Lord's blessing, even though what you say is nicely arranged and in order, you still cannot work it out well. It is not a matter of whether Christians walk on the right path; it is a matter of whether they walk on the path of the Lord's blessing.

III. Things to pay attention to and the solution to problems:

A. Things to pay attention to:

1. Take care of your body. Someone asked an elderly brother what was the most useful age of a man's life. After considering for a moment, he said, "The period between the ages of seventy and eighty." Some were sent to the grave before they reached their most useful age. When this happens, it is a loss to the church. You should not damage your own body. You should exercise self-control regarding your daily living, including your eating and drinking.

2. Exercise your character. The Lord's servant

needs a good character. A loose, lazy, or low
character can damage and destroy one's work,
even if he is gifted.

B. Solution to problems. Every day during the training there was a meeting in which the trainees took
turns testifying and asking questions. After each
testimony Brother Nee would give a thorough
judgment and correction according to each person's condition and need. On the one hand, he
pointed out where the real problem was, and on
the other hand, he laid out before each one the
way of blessing. His words of judgment and
direction were very much to the point, full of light,
and sometimes stern and solemn. When he was
finished, those who were judged prayed, and most
of them repented and confessed with tears and
weeping.

IV. How to administer the church affairs. Brother Nee
gave much fellowship on this matter. What he said can
be summarized in seven points:

A. The offices in the church. The two offices are the
deacons and the elders (overseers).

B. How to serve. Service should be the service of the
whole Body and not a one-man show. The church
is the Body of Christ, and all the saved ones, as
the members, must function. There are two aspects
to the church service: the priestly service on
the spiritual side, and the Levitical service on the
business side.

C. How to meet. The church should have the following kinds of meetings: gospel meetings, new
beginners' meetings, prayer meetings, the Lord's
table meeting, the meeting referred to in 1 Corinthians 14, sisters' meetings, and children's meetings.
The local church need not maintain a message meeting on the Lord's Day. And it should definitely not
establish the system of pastors. At any rate, the
church should not follow after "the customs of the

nations" (denominations). We must throw away the tradition and take the way of recovery.

D. The relationship between the local church, the work, and the apostles.

1. The highest authority of the local church is the eldership. Elders are set up by apostles. The removal of elders is also up to the apostles; so the elders should listen to the apostles.

2. The apostles are responsible for the work, and the elders are responsible for the church. But within the region of the work, the apostles can also be elders.

3. When there is a problem between the churches, the apostles and elders should come together before the Lord to seek His mind, have fellowship, and resolve the matter, according to Acts 15. But at the same time we must not just practice the scriptural way; we must have the Spirit of the Scriptures.

E. The matter of coordination among the workers. The workers must coordinate. To have coordination you must:

1. Know authority. In God's work there is the master builder who takes the lead among the apostles. For this reason you must learn to submit.

2. Seek fellowship. Without fellowship there is no coordination. In order to practice fellowship, the co-workers must learn to:
   a. Open up their hearts to each other.
   b. Forsake individualism and be in one accord as one man.
   c. Bear one another's burdens.
   d. Actively seek fellowship.

3. Only in the authority and in the fellowship can there be the real practice of arrangement, sending out, staying, and commitment.

F. Who is a co-worker and who is an apostle:

1. Apostle. The apostleship is not a gift but an office. From the gifted ones God chooses some

who are vessels fit for His use and sends them
to work and establish the church for Him. For
example, in Acts 13 Paul and Barnabas were
prophets and teachers according to their gifts.
But once sent out by the Holy Spirit, they were
called "apostles" in Acts 14:4. An apostle is not
required either to have an occupation or to forsake it if he has one. Paul's occupation was that
of an apostle, not a tentmaker. He simply
worked as a tentmaker so that he could be an
apostle.

2. Co-worker. The scope of the co-workers is larger
than that of the apostles. All the brothers and
sisters must make their occupations a secondary
thing for the purpose of serving God. All of
those who are for the Lord are our co-workers.

G. The matter of finances:

1. Concerning the distribution of money in a local
church, there are the following categories:
a. Regular expenses.
b. Care of the poor.
c. Care of the need of the responsible brothers.
d. The need of other local churches.
e. The supply to individual workers.
f. The supply to the entire region of the work.

2. The financial relationship among the co-workers:
a. The one who takes the lead should supply
the co-workers.
b. The co-workers should be supplied according to individual need, not according to gift.
c. All must learn to live by faith, to trust in
God instead of in some human source, and
not to be responsible for anyone else. All
must learn to receive by faith and to give by
faith.

Following the training in October, the trainees returned to
their respective places throughout China, taking with them

the help they had received. Wherever they went, they spread the revival. The result was a tremendous spiritual explosion. Hundreds of sinners were captured for the Lord's kingdom, many believers were set on fire for the Lord's recovery, and the churches were increased and built up more than ever before.

This was Watchman's first training in Kuling Mountain. His burden was to conduct this kind of training at least once a year on an ongoing basis. The situation then required him to postpone the time of the second training from February to August 1949. The content of this training was the same as that of the first, with some improvements. The trainees were a different group of believers. In the midst of the training, he moved it from Kuling Mountain to his home at Customs Lane within the city of Foochow.

After the second training was completed, due to the political change, he had no more opportunity to continue his training. Although his training plan was terminated, what he released during his two trainings at Kuling were printed and have become a great help to many who are seeking to follow the Lord in the Lord's recovery. The issue of those trainings is invaluable to us today.

CHAPTER TWENTY-FIVE

THE SPECIFIC MEANS
OF WATCHMAN NEE'S MINISTRY

(2)

III. ISSUING PUBLICATIONS

The third specific means Watchman Nee employed for his ministry was that of issuing publications.

A. Gospel Tracts

Early in 1922 Watchman began to print gospel tracts for his preaching work. In his open letter in the thirteenth issue of *The Present Testimony,* published in March 1930, he said, "In these two years hundreds of thousands of gospel tracts have already been distributed. We constantly hear of their effect in saving people."

In his open letter in the nineteenth issue of the same magazine, published in January—February 1931, he said, "The gospel tracts we have printed have been greatly blessed by the Lord. In the past two or three years we have sent out more than five million tracts, and this year we have printed one and a half million tracts."

B. *The Present Testimony*

At the end of 1922 Watchman was burdened to publish a magazine entitled *The Present Testimony*. In Chinese it is called *Fu-shing,* which means "revival." The first issue of fourteen hundred copies was published in January 1923 in Foochow. Its theme was specifically the deep things of God and was composed of messages on life with the Lord Jesus as the center, especially emphasizing His life, His crucifixion, His resurrection, His intercession, His Body, His coming back, and His kingdom. These messages were especially designed for the cultivation of the spiritual life and made no attempt to engage in intellectual debate.

This magazine continued until 1925, when Watchman had the burden to publish *The Christian*. The publication of *The Present Testimony* was resumed in January 1928 in Shanghai. The following excerpts taken from his second testimony, given at Kulangsu on October 20, 1936, and his open letters reveal the purpose of the magazine and the reason for resuming its publication:

Before I became ill, I not only visited various places to conduct special meetings, but I also had a great ambition to compose a good comprehensive commentary. I intended to devote much energy, time, and money in writing a large commentary consisting of about a hundred volumes. After completing *The Spiritual Man,* which I began in Nanking when I became ill, I realized that the task of expounding the Scriptures was not for me. However, since that time I have frequently met with temptation in this respect. After my illness, God revealed to me that the central point of the messages He gave me was not for expounding the Scriptures, preaching the ordinary gospel, paying attention to prophecies, or anything outward, but for laying stress on the living Word of life. For this reason I felt I should resume publishing *The Present Testimony* to assist God's children in spiritual life and warfare.

We continue with a portion of his open letter from the twenty-fourth issue of *The Christian,* published in December 1927:

The Bible contains numerous teachings which ordinary believers cannot fully understand. Moreover, the testimony of the Lord is so incomparably great that we cannot receive and preach it completely. During the time of my waiting and praying, God committed to me the testimony which He wishes me personally to bear. I consider the book *The Spiritual Man* to be an outline of the special testimony which the Lord has committed to me. In the past years, day by day the hand of the Lord has become heavier upon me, forcing me to realize that He desires me to bear a special testimony for His Son, the Lord Jesus Christ. There are many who have ordinary testimonies, but the Lord wants me to bear a special testimony for Him. Therefore, I am ready to give up the work of expounding the Scriptures, which thing I would like to do most, in order that I might bear the specific testimony which God has freshly committed to me. The wonderful thing about it is that the Lord is also leading all the brothers and sisters who are meeting and having fellowship in Shanghai in the same way. Hence, by means of the coming issues of *The Present Testimony,* according to what we have received from God, we shall specifically explain "the deep things of God" to the Body of Christ. We wholeheartedly desire to bear this unique testimony which the Lord has committed to us. We also fully realize that the Lord will raise up many other believers besides us to bear this testimony together. The more we walk on the spiritual path, the more we realize the importance of the message of the cross. Believers today have failed because they have not allowed the cross to work deeply and destroy all the works of the flesh. There is still a mixture of the new and the old creation in the lives of believers, because the old creation has not yet been replaced by God. Such mixture always results in loss to the new creation. Correctness in outward behavior, excellence in church organization, increase in Bible knowledge, and exertion in God's work are all insufficient to guarantee against a mixture of the flesh within. On the contrary, the flesh can act freely in all these things and promote them with all its might. For this reason, the work of the cross annihilating the old creation is indispensable. Without the cross standing between the new and the old creations, a person's spiritual life is false, shallow, and superficial. Since a believer's life is always related to both "self" and the Lord, the cross must destroy the self so that the Lord can have His legitimate place. The time of the millennium will be the right time for the Lord to overcome Satan.

Therefore, by the grace of the Lord, we would remind the church of God that the Body of Christ must rise up to work with Him to bring in the kingdom. Our desire is that the enemy might soon be put to shame and that Christ might soon be glorified.

In his open letter published in the first issue of *The Present Testimony* of January—April 1928, he said:

We publish this little magazine because we have received the commission from God to help His children specifically in matters relating to spiritual life and warfare. In every age there is a unique truth especially needed for that period. For those of us living in these last days, there must also be some specific truth which we especially need. By means of *The Present Testimony*, we intend to bear testimony to the truth needed in this present age.

The following words are taken from the open letter in the nineteenth issue of *The Present Testimony* of January—February 1931:

Some may think that the content of *The Present Testimony* is too deep and too specialized. However, many readers have written to us saying that while other magazines are greatly used by the Lord, *The Present Testimony* provides what the others do not. For this reason we are convinced that the command which we have received of the Lord is right. By the grace of the Lord, *The Present Testimony* will therefore continue to speak forth the deep things of God this year and in the years to come, the Lord willing.

Publication of *The Present Testimony* was suspended following the thirty-sixth issue of July—August 1934 and was replaced by *The Testimony* in 1948. However, publication of *The Present Testimony* was resumed in January 1951.

C. *The Christian*

In order to lay a foundation for understanding his deeper periodical, *The Present Testimony,* Watchman issued another periodical called *The Christian.* In the *Narration of the Past* delivered on the Lord's Day, December 4, 1932, at a meeting in Shanghai, he referred to his burden concerning this paper:

Publication of *The Christian* began in January 1923. It was published at irregular intervals and was discontinued in 1925. While I was staying in Lo-Hsing Pagoda, I felt the need to issue a regular publication which would give more emphasis to the truths of salvation and the church and deal as well with prophecies and types. I intended this magazine (called *The Christian*) to be temporary in nature. In 1925 two issues were published; in 1926 ten issues were published; and in 1927, because of continuous demand, another twelve issues were published.

The announcement in the combined thirteenth and fourteenth issues concerning *The Christian* was as follows:

PURPOSE: To proclaim the salvation of the cross, to cultivate the Christian's spirituality, to warn of the danger of modernism, and to declare all of God's will.

CONTENT: *The Christian* contains messages, short articles, stories, signs of the times, studies, expositions of the Bible, and questions and answers (anyone desiring to ask questions about the Scriptures may do so). Every other month we issue a "Scripture-expounding" special, devoted exclusively to expounding the Bible. The current topic is the book of Revelation.

Each issue of this monthly periodical was approximately eighty pages in length. In those issues he expounded the first three chapters of Revelation, spending much time on the seven epistles. It was through these messages on the seven epistles that denominationalism was fully exposed and the proper church revealed. By reading these papers, many young people throughout the whole of China had their eyes opened. I was one of them. It was thus that I came to see the evils of the denominations and also to see the church. We still have twenty-three of the original twenty-four issues of *The Christian*. They were filled not only with much revelation but also with much inspiration. They were marvelous. It is almost unbelievable that that young man of just twenty-two years of age could expound the Scriptures in such a way. In those issues he expounded not only the first twelve chapters of Revelation, but also the first two chapters of Genesis. He spoke of the first, second, and third days and applied them all very much to Christ. He said clearly that the land rising out of the water on the third day was a type of Christ coming forth from the dead. Christ was the good land resurrected on the third day to produce all kinds of life. What a marvelous revelation!

The following five excerpts, four of which are taken from the editor's word in *The Christian,* and one from *Notes on Scriptural Messages,* reveal his burden and purpose in publishing *The Christian.*

From the fifth issue of *The Christian* published in March 1926:

From now on, the Lord willing, each issue of *The Christian* will contain a column on "The Signs of the Times" that our readers might better understand the situation in the last days and know how the prophecies of the Bible are being fulfilled step by step. May the Lord use this column to inspire His children to watch and pray and get themselves ready. Knowing that the Lord is coming soon should not make one lazy, but rather cause him to forsake the world. Those who are aware of the Lord's soon return, yet still love the world, are in a very pitiful spiritual condition.

The purpose of *The Christian* is not to preach any person, any man's ideals, or any "ism." Its mission is to preach the Lord Jesus and Him crucified. We thank the

Lord that this paper has aroused many people's sympathy and prayers. Our intention in these pages is to preach the message of the Lord to people far and near. I deeply believe that if the Lord's servants clearly preach the gospel of the vicarious death of the cross and depend on the mighty power of the Holy Spirit in order that sinners might become regenerated, they will by no means be fruitless. Unfortunately, what is preached today is not the gospel of God, the gospel of the *grace* of God. Rather, the message of the cross as revealed by God is replaced with man's ideals and rules for improvement. No wonder sinners are not affected. Others preach the salvation of God by their own intelligence and wisdom and do not have the Holy Spirit working with them by power. Hence, even though they preach, in the end they cannot save men's souls. I pray humbly that the Lord may have mercy on us and cause us not to rely on our own ability or strength but rather on God's Spirit to speak forth the gospel of the Lord.

The following is taken from the combined thirteenth and fourteenth issues of *The Christian* published in January—February 1927:

When we first began publication of *The Christian*, our original intention was to try it for only one year. While, on the one hand, there are not many spiritual publications today, on the other hand, there are enough to make us wonder whether there was sufficient need for us to publish *The Christian*. Yet, since its inception, readers everywhere have indicated that it does meet a great need in the church today and has its unique place. Their subscriptions, recommendations, and encouragement have been continually pouring in. We thank God that He has made *The Christian* so acceptable to His children. We intend therefore to continue the work for another year....

When we published our first issue of *The Christian*, we

included a statement stating our goal, standard, and affiliation. We would now like to reprint what we said then:

> GOAL: In this little monthly publication, our desire is to supply spiritual milk to the young believers and solid food to the older ones. We especially stress the salvation of the cross. But we are even more concerned with the spiritual condition of the believers. We ask God to strengthen us that we could preach all of God's will. As to the errors of modernism, we will strive to warn God's children of its dangers.
>
> STANDARD: The Bible is our only standard. We are not afraid to preach the pure Word of the Bible, even if men oppose; but if it is not the Word of the Bible, we could never agree even if everyone approved....

The contents of *The Christian* this year will continue as before. Besides "The Signs of the Times," "Stories," and "Questions and Answers," all of which were included last year, we have also prepared three articles on "The Shortcut to Hell" for this year's gospel messages (the first of which is published in this issue). Other articles which also proclaim the gospel of the grace of God will be published in succession. All our readers may feel free to pass on the gospel messages to others (whether or not you mention the name of this magazine). There is a certain pastor who regularly reads the gospel messages of this paper to his congregation on Sundays. He feels that even though they cannot hear our preaching personally, he still can use this direct method to meet the need. The Lord has greatly blessed what he has done.

This year there will be many messages especially dealing with faith in the "Spiritual Instructions" column. The articles on prayer by Mr. Meek will still be published. We also hope to print some practical articles written by other children of God. In the first half of this year, we intend to publish "The Practice of Faith," "The Deeds of Faith," "Important or Not," "The Condescension of Jesus," "Bribing the Conscience," and others. "An Hour's Conversation with Mr. George Müller" has been translated by Mr. Wang

Tze and will be published in the "Testimonies" column. The Lord willing, Mr. Wang will translate other articles for us. "An Unspoken Message" in the "Stories" column is the most touching one. We also hope to publish some testimonies of high school and college students this year. Please pay attention to them.

We have translated "The Origin of the Bible" and hope to publish it soon.

Concerning the exposition of the Bible, we will continue "Meditations on Genesis." However, each article will be a separate entity. The sixth and seventh articles have been completed. One is "The Story of Creation and the Basic Truth of Dispensations," and the other is "The Story of Creation and the Seven Great Characters of Genesis." Those who enjoy reading this column will receive much spiritual food.

After twenty-four issues of *The Christian* had been published, Watchman was burdened to resume the publications of *The Present Testimony*. *The Christian*, therefore, was discontinued in January 1928. After six and a half years, in July 1934, publication was again resumed. The following statements explain the reason and purpose for discontinuing *The Christian*. This excerpt is from Watchman's open letter in the twenty-fourth issue of *The Christian* published in December 1927:

After a long period of waiting and praying, I am now clear about the Lord's will concerning *The Christian* for next year. When I first began publication of this paper, I knew it would not be of a permanent nature. At first I intended to publish it only on a trial basis for one year. Following the first year, I continued its publication for another year. Now two full years have passed. When I began, a few friends asked, "What is your purpose in publishing *The Christian*? What do you plan to do with *The Present Testimony* which you published before?" My answer was, "The goal of *The Christian* is to lead believers to read *The Present Testimony*. Whenever I feel the time has come, I will stop publishing *The Christian*." This was what I said to my friends then. Now the time has come, and *The Christian* will be discontinued.

This whole year I have been continually before God, contemplating and praying over the future of this paper. Day by day I have become clearer that the message of this paper is now adequate. God is now leading me on to bear another special testimony. As this instrument has been used in the hand of God, and as He now desires to put it aside, who am I that I should say no? Some friends who learned of my decision felt sorry that *The Christian* was being discontinued. Also, humanly speaking, it seems that since this paper is enjoying such a wide circulation, that it is a shame to discontinue it. According to my natural thought, I also am reluctant to discontinue *The Christian*, for I am most delighted with such a work. But God has stepped on the brake, and I must obey with rejoicing. In that day you will know that I was obeying God in this matter.

I feel deeply that the various testimonies we have printed in *The Christian*, especially those concerning the outward behavior of believers, are sufficient. If we continue our tiring reiteration, it will make *The Christian* a paper specializing in "leaving the denominations," "baptism by immersion," etc. I thank God that He gave the co-workers and me the same feeling concerning this matter....

Does this mean that we will cease printing such writings concerning our testimony? The Lord is leading the believers meeting in Shanghai to publish *The Present Testimony*. Henceforth, *The Present Testimony* will be a written testimony of the believers who meet and have fellowship in Shanghai.

The following statement was Watchman's announcement concerning his publications, issued in the June 1934 edition of *Notes on Scriptural Messages*:

In the winter of 1927, having become clear concerning God's will that I was especially called to bear testimony on the spiritual side of the truth (which excludes everything that might cause dispute regarding prophecy, the church, and Bible interpretation), I discontinued *The Christian* and reissued *The Present Testimony.* This does not mean that the work of *The Christian* is unimportant; on the contrary, it has a significant place. But I feel that what the Lord has committed to *me* are truths more in keeping with the nature of *The Present Testimony* of these few years. Teachings which are in keeping with the nature of *The Christian* are also greatly needed, but what the Lord has not committed to me, I must wait for someone else to do.

In 1930, after seeing so many young believers (spiritually speaking) without help, I published a simpler and easier paper entitled *Notes on Scriptural Messages.* It was my hope that God's children might receive benefit and be linked up with the truths which have the nature of *The Present Testimony.* Meanwhile, I was continually expecting in my heart, and I frequently mentioned to the co-workers, that it would be best if God would raise up someone else to do this in-between work.

Last year during the time of my weakness, I received a special dealing from God and felt deeply at that time that if I continued in this way, I could not adequately accomplish the things God had committed to me. There was also the danger of making void my obedience of 1927 if I continued to be careless. As a result I had the thought then of discontinuing *Notes on Scriptural Messages.*

This matter was brought up to the brothers this year in a conference, and it was pointed out that since so many brothers have been raised up, they should begin to take up the burden for many things. The unanimous decision of the brothers then was to resume the publication of *The Christian* and to allow me to discontinue the *Notes on Scriptural Messages.*

This does not mean that I will no longer bear the responsibility for the content of *The Christian.* I will be happy to follow after the brothers and publish in *The Christian* the manuscripts which I have accumulated from the past. But as for me, from now on I will only bear the spiritual testimony.

Notes on Scriptural Messages will cease with this issue, and *The Christian* will resume with the next issue. May God receive the glory in our new arrangement!

The following announcement by Witness Lee appeared in the first issue of *The Christian*, newly published in July 1934:

The discontinuation of *Notes on Scriptural Messages* and the resumption of *The Christian* were announced by Brother Watchman Nee in the fiftieth issue of *Notes on Scriptural Messages*. At this time we wish to add a few words here on the reissuing of *The Christian*.

Since 1928 when Brother Nee suspended *The Christian* and resumed *The Present Testimony*, even though truths of the nature of *The Present Testimony* have helped many of God's children in their spiritual life, it seems that teachings of the nature of *The Christian* have become hidden to God's children. We realize that the principles of the spiritual life are truly of foremost importance, but the light on the pathway cannot be lacking either. While we should certainly pay attention to the spiritual life, scriptural knowledge should by no means be ignored. Today a believer's inner life needs edification, and his outward behavior also needs cultivation. Even though *Notes on Scriptural Messages* can be of considerable help in this aspect to the children of God, it still is not the same as the former publication, *The Christian*. Hence, we felt the need to reissue *The Christian*.

Though the resumption of *The Christian* was decided by the brothers after the conference in January of this year, it was not until today that, by the grace of God, the first issue has come out. While we confess the delay to be our fault, we also believe that it was God's ordering.

After its resumption, the nature and content of *The*

Christian will be largely the same as before. The differences are that the former "Messages" column is now changed to "Notes on Scriptural Messages" and the former "Scripture Expositions" to "Bible Studies." These changes are only in style; the function will be the same as before. The reason "Scripture Expositions" is being changed to "Bible Studies" is because we intend to publish, in succession, notes of Bible studies which Brother Nee conducted with the brothers and sisters in Shanghai during the last few years. By this means the truth-seeking brothers and sisters in every locality will receive help. "Messages" is being changed to "Notes on Scriptural Messages" in order to keep *Notes on Scriptural Messages* continuing so that the help God's children have been receiving will not be interrupted. Hence, although the *Notes on Scriptural Messages* ceased to be an independent publication, its essential existence has not been abolished. We simply incorporated it as a column into *The Christian*. Thus, on one hand *The Christian* resumes publication, and on the other hand, *Notes on Scriptural Messages* is also preserved. On the one hand, we want to restore the former testimony of *The Christian*, and on the other hand, we want to carry on the present help of *Notes on Scriptural Messages*.

Our hope is that God will use this little testimony to lead His children to draw near to His living Word, Christ, and to His written Word, the Bible. In this way they will be able to see how to go on today and obey Christ that He might have a larger and fuller place in their lives and work. It is our hope that they will also be helped to see the heavenly pattern—Christ—and turn their attention to His central work—the church—in order that Christ might be exalted and the Body of Christ, the church, be built up. It is also our desire that God would use this paper to declare His will and release His truths that the spiritual life of His children could be nurtured and their problems resolved. Although this responsibility is great and we are poor and weak, we do not look to ourselves nor to anything of ourselves. Rather, we look to Him, to His sufficient grace, and to His overshadowing strength.

Today with the church in such a confused, dark, desolate, and apostate condition, to speak the will of God
straightforwardly and not to shun His truths will inevitably
bring upon us the enemy's attack and men's opposition. But
since this earth is one that has rejected the Lord, should not
attack and opposition also be the portion of those who
follow Him? In the work of serving the Lord, we seek nothing but His pleasure and satisfaction in heaven. We dare
not compare ourselves with the apostle Paul, but we desire
to follow his faithfulness and say with him, "For am I now
trying to win the assent of men or of God? Or am I seeking
to please men? If I were still trying to please men, I would
not be a slave of Christ."

Finally, dear brothers, because of the greatness of this
responsibility, the attacks of the enemy, and our own weaknesses, we do need you to pray for us with the same heart,
in the same mind, and under the same yoke. May God
bless you all!

The following is the announcement in the same issue of
the magazine concerning the resumed publication of *The
Christian:*

THEME: To speak forth God's will and to cultivate a
    Christian's spiritual life.
CONTENT: Notes on the Scriptural Messages, Twelve
    Baskets Full, Stories, Testimonies, Questions and
    Answers, and Bible Studies.

The Christian continued until 1940. It was then suspended until it was replaced by *The Way* in 1948.

CHAPTER TWENTY-SIX

THE SPECIFIC MEANS
OF WATCHMAN NEE'S MINISTRY

(3)

III. ISSUING PUBLICATIONS

D. *Notes on Scriptural Messages*

After Watchman Nee discontinued *The Christian* and resumed *The Present Testimony* in 1928, the need for messages for young believers still remained. To fulfill this need he published his third paper, entitled *Notes on Scriptural Messages*. The following announcement appeared on the back cover of the collected volume for December 1933:

---

1) This paper was first issued in April 1930. By the end of 1933, forty-four issues have been published. The Lord willing, we hope to publish one issue per month.

2) This paper is somewhat elementary. At times it covers the gospel, at other times the work and person of the Lord, and at still other times messages for edifying young believers.

The messages published in this paper, of which some titles are listed in chapter twenty-seven under the subtitle, "Books for the Edification of New Believers" (second group), were mainly for the edification of young believers.

This paper was eventually merged with *The Christian*, resumed in 1934, and became the first column of that paper.[1]

---

[1]Concerning this matter see chapter twenty-five, regarding the announcement by Watchman Nee in the *Notes on Scriptural Messages* of June 1934 and the announcement by Witness Lee in the first resumed issue of *The Christian* of 1934.

E. *Collection of Newsletters*

For fellowship between the churches and communication between the saints in different localities, Watchman was burdened at the end of 1933 to publish *Collection of Newsletters*. The following open letter, addressed to the brothers and published as the first issue of this paper, explains its origin:

November 30, 1933

To the brothers who call on the Lord
out of a pure heart:

The Lord is gracious to us, and for this we thank Him. In this end time He has given us light and enabled us to know that it is His pleasure to manifest through us in this world the characteristics which befit His church in order that He might obtain something for Himself. We also thank Him for bending our hearts and producing in us the willingness to obey Him and please Him. Except for this, we are incapable of generating even one good thought.

In the past few years we have been enabled to see that in order to please Him and manifest the characteristics of the church, we must not meet divisively; but rather, we must meet in His name. (This is a very small matter, but we still thank the Lord for it.) Hence, there are many brothers meeting in the name of the Lord in different localities. (We know of over a hundred of these places.) This is surely a joyful and comforting matter. However, although the assemblies in the Bible all had their own local administration, they still maintained fellowship with each other. There are many assemblies now; yet some of them do not even know that other local assemblies exist. This being the case, they surely could not be aware of what is happening in other places. This cannot be considered as fellowship.

We believe God's will is that we should be local in administration and yet at the same time be open to correction from others. Local administration enables us to bear our own responsibility, while fellowship enables us to receive help and correction from others. This is why in 1 Thessalonians there are such words as "imitators" and "pattern" (1:6, 7; 2:14). Unless we are open to correction from others, we may be wrong without realizing it, and others may advance while we do not know how to follow.

Many brothers have written letters to individuals among us giving news of their respective localities. Also brothers have written asking us for information about certain localities. We feel that such intercommunicating of news is both fitting and urgent, but we have lacked adequate time to write such letters.

When we published the first issue of *Notes on Scriptural Messages*, we intended to include news from various localities. Later, however, we realized that the majority of the readers of *Notes on Scriptural Messages* were not walking with us, and for this reason we felt that publishing the news in that paper would inevitably give rise to misunderstanding. For this reason we discontinued that practice. However, the need for intercommunication of news has by no means disappeared. Rather, it has been increasing daily.

After receiving a little light from God to see the Body of Christ, we feel deeply that for an individual to act alone is regrettable and that for an assembly to move independently is terrible. If we are accurate in our perception, the greatest shortage among today's believers is that they do not know what the Body life is. It seems that they have been detached from the others who are faithfully following the Lord. The individualism of believers today is almost universally prevalent, and the work of the cross, the life of resurrection, and the power of the Holy Spirit are being used almost exclusively for the development of *individual* holiness, for *individual* spirituality, and to help achieve *individual* victory. To be an individual is truly important, but to be only an individual and not to know how to be a brother among the brothers or a sister among the sisters is simply another form of the most hateful "self." How we wish that from now on the children of God would learn to forget about the self and to be the servants and slaves of the brothers.

To this end we desire to issue a little publication entitled *Collection of Newsletters*. It is not our intention to make this publication available to all believers, but rather it is for those who meet with us and walk with us in every locality. We will not send it to those who do not stand on the position of the church as required by the Lord.

The contents of this publication will be exclusively news and prayer requests from the various localities. The source of the news will be mainly from correspondence we have received. One source will be mail which we have received directly from the brothers, and another source will be letters which were written to a third party and then forwarded to us.

Concerning the nature of this publication, we need to give a word of explanation. We know that the common practice is to publish news so that men might 1) obtain the glory and 2) use the news as a basis for advertisement to make material gain. Because of this, there will no doubt be some spiritual brothers among us who, desiring to avoid this kind of thing, would rather not have their news published. We must remember, however, that the fellowship of the brothers is important. Your move and the activities of the assembly in your place are the concern of all the brothers. You should not deprive your brothers of the encouragement which they might receive from you and the privilege of making supplications for your work simply because you prefer your activities to remain hidden. No doubt, on your part you are humble, but what about the brothers who will not receive your help? The Body life is a life of caring for the brothers. It is, no doubt, wrong to seek prominence in the religious world, but to purposely hide yourself among the brothers (not the outsiders) is not being humble but shrinking back. To do such a thing does not mean that you are free from self-consideration; on the contrary, it means that you are always looking at yourself. This is not spiritual living, but an activity purposely performed by the flesh. May God deliver us, on the one hand, from the evils of today's religious world and, on the other hand, from excessive self-consciousness of the soul and from "deliberate humility." Please keep in mind the examples in the Bible. On the one hand, the Bible says the following: "Your faith is proclaimed throughout the whole world" (Rom. 1:8); "For from you the word of the Lord has sounded out; not only in Macedonia and in Achaia, but in every place, your faith toward God has gone out" (1 Thes. 1:8); and "We have heard of your faith..." (Col. 1:4). But, on the other hand, it also says, "And when they arrived and gathered the church together, they declared the things that God had done with them and that He had opened a door of faith to the Gentiles" (Acts 14:27) and "They declared the things that God had done with them" (Acts 15:4).

What is needed today are not spiritual giants who cultivate themselves seclusively and who are self-conceited, but we need brothers who care for others and know how to be members together with others. We do not need hiding brothers; we need helpful brothers.

It is altogether a matter of your intention. May we, on the one hand, not purposely try to shrink back, and, on the other hand, not intentionally try to show off. Let us not seek glory from men, but in all things let us seek to glorify God and to build up the brothers.

Please pay your attention to the following points:

1) Please do your best to send us news regarding the situation of the work, difficulties encountered, results accomplished, requests for prayers, and other information.

2) In principle, all reports should be accurate, clear, and edifying. There is no limitation as to length and style.

3) If some individuals should send you letters mentioning news of the assembly in a certain locality, please forward the letters to us in order that the brothers in different localities might know more about the Lord's work.

4) We would also like to publish announcements regarding the assemblies and the work.

5) The responsible brothers in each locality are cautioned against passing on this publication to those who do not meet with us. It is better not to give this publication to any but those who are walking with us.

6) All mail should be addressed to the Editor, *Collection of Newsletters*, Box 323, Shanghai.

We now put this matter in the hand of God and before the brothers. May this be acceptable to you as it is to God. May the grace of God be with your spirit.

Peace be with you.

> Your brother,
> a bondslave of Christ,
>
> Watchman Nee

This paper continued for only two and a half years until July 1935. A letter by Watchman Nee published in the twelfth issue of *Collection of Newsletters,* July 1935, tells us the reason for its being discontinued. It reads as follows:

June 19, 1935

To the brothers who are of
the same mind in all localities:

Our intention when first publishing *Collection of Newsletters* was that through this little publication the brothers in all the localities might be able to share their news with each other and that the assemblies in various places might be able to fellowship with one another. We had also hoped to obtain more news concerning the personal spiritual experiences of the brothers and sisters so that all the saints in different localities could be mutually edified in their spiritual life. Our work is spiritual, and our emphasis is life. This has already been pointed out in "The Origin" in the first issue and in "A Letter about This Publication and the Co-workers" in the ninth issue. It was also pointed out in "Some Words from the Responsible Brothers" in the tenth issue.

However, although this was our intention and hope, the letters which we received from the saints have for the most part not paid attention to this matter. And even we ourselves have not held firm to our purpose in the way we have edited the material. Articles in the past have mostly dealt with outward matters such as baptism, leaving the denominations, etc. Thus, it seems that this paper has become a special publication on leaving the denominations.

It is now clear to us that since this is the case, we have not only failed to achieve the objective of this publication, but have also fallen short of our testimony. Brothers, we have deviated from the Lord's heart in this matter. We can therefore only seek the grace of God and hope for a change.

We have pointed out before that "our work is spiritual, and our emphasis is life. We are clear that God wants us to manifest the life of Christ in the local churches. Hence, the reality of our work is the life of Christ, and the outward expression of our work is the local church. In this present time, when the outward church is desolate, we do not have the slightest intention to start a new 'movement,' 'group,' 'organization,' or 'denomination.' We dare not even call ourselves the churches in the various places. We stand only on the *position* of the local church.

"What is our center? Is our work to preach Christ as Lord or to preach leaving the denominations? I am really fearful that in every locality there are brothers who, being limited in understanding and spiritual experience before God, only have a little knowledge about outward matters such as baptism, head covering, and denominations, and exhaust their efforts to publicize these matters. By doing so, they cause outsiders to misunderstand us, thinking that we only emphasize these outward things and that we do not exalt Jesus Christ as Lord. We know that if anyone follows the Lord, he will certainly take care of these outward matters. But it does not mean that anyone who practices these outward things is necessarily following the Lord completely. We must emphasize again and again for the sake of the ignorant brothers among us that although we believe in these outward matters, our testimony, that which makes us different from others, is not in these outward things." (See issue nine and ten of this publication.)

We have, therefore, decided that after this issue we shall no longer publish this paper. We hope our decision will seem good to the brothers. Hereafter may we pay more

attention to the inward testimony than to the outward matters. This is not to say that we are neglecting the outward
matters but that we should not over-emphasize them. We
admit they have their place, but they are neither our center
nor our testimony. We can only ask God's forgiveness and
the brothers' forbearance for the past failure. May the Lord
cause us to pay attention to what is important to Him. The
Lord bless you all.

Peace be with you in the Lord.

Your brother,

Watchman Nee

F. *The Open Door*

Because of the Japanese invasion in July 1937, many
saints and co-workers in the Lord's recovery were forced to
move to the interior of China from the coastal provinces.
Watchman was burdened to publish *The Open Door*, not as
an official publication, but as part of his personal ministry
to serve the scattered saints. The open letter published in
the first issue in September 1937 unveiled to us his purpose
in publishing this paper:

An Open Letter

September 19, 1937

To all the brothers who are partakers
of the gracious calling:

For years I have felt the need of a publication which
could be used to communicate news of the work in all of
the localities. A local newsletter belongs to a particular
locality and serves a particular church. But we need a
paper for the intercommunication of news which will
serve all the localities, that is, one which will serve the
work. The name, *The Open Door*, was chosen much earlier,
and I had hoped that others would be raised up by the Lord
to bear its responsibility. This was my hope because, on the
one hand, there is the need, and, on the other hand, my

special stand makes it impossible for me to undertake the task myself. If this had been undertaken by someone else, it would have been merely personal and done by someone who was gifted to do it. But if I were to do it, it would become official and would be based on my position. Therefore, in order to avoid this, I dared not move for years.

I never believed that this newspaper would be issued under this kind of circumstance, at this time, and in this place. Now I must do what I did not wish to do. However, please keep in mind always, brothers, that this is a personal ministry and not the instrument of an organization. If any co-worker or church in any locality is unwilling to see their news appear in this publication, please say so in order that none might be offended in this matter. But I do wish that I could receive news from all the localities so that those who are concerned for you could make intercession.

The original intention of my recent trip was to go on to England and America. I did not know why, but I kept being delayed on the way. After spending ten weeks in Southeast Asia, I still had not entered the Indian Ocean. While at Penang, I felt the Lord wanted me to return to take care of some work before proceeding on to England.

The emphasis of *The Open Door* is the gospel work in all the localities. It seems that now is the time that the door for preaching the Word is open the widest, and we pray that God would cause us to make use of this opportunity. In this publication we will print:

1) Articles concerning the principles of the work.

2) News of gospel preaching in all the localities.

3) The addresses of the workers (the apostles) on the move.

4) The addresses of the meeting halls of the local churches in order that the brothers who are escaping the war might know where to meet.

5) The whereabouts of the brothers (the disciples) in the Lord at every place in order that comfort might be given those who are concerned for them.

We are now temporarily publishing at Gospel Court, Lane 1, Hsiao-Dong-Jia, Hankow. In the future we may move to Ch'ang-sha, though this is difficult to predict. Our correspondence address remains at Hankow until further notice.

There is still one further matter. Because the itinerary of the co-workers in the various places is continually changing, it presents a problem to those who wish to write them. We wish to serve the brothers in this matter. Anyone wishing us to forward their mail may send it to the above address, and it will be taken care of accordingly.

This publication is not for sale. We trust in God for the supply of its need.

Peace be unto you.

Your brother,

Watchman Nee

This paper, after its nineteenth issue in September 1939, was suspended until it was replaced by *The Ministers* in 1948. It was eventually resumed in June 1950.

G. *The Glad Tidings*

Besides the papers which have already been mentioned, a paper on the gospel was also published. The following announcement concerning this paper appeared in the seventh issue of *Collection of Newsletters* in June 1934 and reveals its purpose and contents:

After the third overcomer conference this past January, the co-workers from the various localities had a meeting in Shanghai. In that meeting most of the co-workers expressed the hope that a written testimony could be issued solely for the preaching of the gospel.

Recently, several co-workers in Shanghai also increasingly felt the burden to publish such a written testimony. We have, therefore, decided to publish a paper entitled *The Glad Tidings* beginning in July of this year. This publication will be solely for the preaching of the gospel to sinners.

The contents of this paper will include three columns: messages, stories, and testimonies. The messages will be simple gospel messages, the stories will be salvation stories of believers from the past, and the testimonies will be salvation testimonies of today's believers.

This author was asked to bear the burden to write the messages and to edit the paper. The first issue of *The Glad Tidings* was published in July 1934. The gospel message for the third issue, entitled "There is a God" was one of Watchman Nee's spoken messages. This paper had only three issues and was discontinued in 1936.

H. The Replacement Periodicals

Immediately following the 1948 conference in Shanghai, when Watchman resumed his ministry and the brothers handed over their possessions to the work, he made arrangements with us to put out four papers to replace those which had been temporarily suspended.

1) *The Testimony* was to replace *The Present Testimony.* The subject of this paper was to be specifically the messages of life. The content of it was to be the light received and the lessons learned before God and help for the children of the Lord to have the real growth in life.

2) *The Way* was to replace *The Christian.* The subject matter of *The Way* was to be the biblical truth showing the spiritual way. The content of this paper was to be the way of the gospel, the way of life, the way of Bible study, and the people of the way.

3) *The Ministers* was to replace *The Open Door.* The nature of *The Ministers* was to help the churches and the serving ones in the matter of knowing the way to serve and to solve the problems in the ministry. Watchman wrote a few words for the publication of this paper in the first issue of July 1948:

For many years there have been many rumors but little news from the various localities. Many localities have been out of touch with the others. There is a real need for fellowship among the ministers. For this reason, we are publishing *The Ministers* with the hope that the brothers will understand what we as ministers really are. We hope also to help each other solve the problems related to the ministers. Finally, we hope that through this, the brothers will find out some of the things that are happening among the ministers. In these end times everything is solemn. These days are more urgent than we think. May the Lord have mercy upon us.

4) *The Gospel* was to replace *The Glad Tidings.* The subject matter of *The Gospel* was the proclamation of the gospel of God, and the content was to be gospel messages, testimonies of salvation, and gospel stories.

Following the political change in June 1950, *The Open Door* was resumed with the twentieth issue containing the following announcement:

The Open Door
(*The Ministers* is now combined into this paper)

NATURE: To show the way to serve, to help the serving ones and the churches in the different localities to go on, and to solve the problems of the ministry....

ANNOUNCEMENTS: From this year we hope to *resume* the publication of *The Christian* and *The Present Testimony.* Hence, *The Way* will be *merged* with *The Christian,* and *The Testimony* will be *merged* with *The Present Testimony.*

This paper continued to be published for three more issues until 1951 and automatically ceased with the arrest of Watchman Nee.

The Present Testimony was resumed in January 1951 with the thirty-seventh issue and continued for two more issues until April 1951. It also was automatically discontinued with Watchman's arrest.

The Christian was never resumed.

CHAPTER TWENTY-SEVEN

THE SPECIFIC MEANS
OF WATCHMAN NEE'S MINISTRY

(4)

III. ISSUING PUBLICATIONS

I. Books

In addition to publishing periodicals, Watchman Nee also published many books for the carrying out of his ministry. Some of these books were messages published in his periodicals and reprinted in book form. They could be classified as follows:

1. Books on the Gospel

Although gospel preaching was not the central feature of his ministry, Watchman Nee published twenty-one booklets on the gospel.

1) *There Is God*
2) *God Is Willing*
3) *The Passover*
4) *The Suffering of the Cross*
5) *The Paths to Hell (1)*
6) *The Paths to Hell (2)*
7) *The Paths to Hell (3)*
8) *Judgment*
9) *The Robber Saved* (Luke 23:39-43)
10) *The Salvation of the Adulterous Woman* (John 4:1-15, 28-29)
11) *Why Good Men Go to Hell*
12) *Can Morality Save Us*
13) *Do You Know That You Are Saved*
14) *Assurance of Salvation*
15) *Christ as the Manifestation of God*
16) *Christ and Christianity*

17) *Christ as the New Life*

18) *Christ and the Christian*

19) *For What Did He Come?*, by Ruth Lee

20) *God Loves the World*, by W. Lee

21) *A Rich Man Perished* (Luke 16:19-31), by W. Lee

He also published a book of questions and answers on gospel truth, giving explanations on fifty aspects of the gospel.

2. Books for the Edification of New Believers

In his training on Kuling Mountain, Watchman shared a series of fifty messages for the edification of new believers. They are listed as follows:

1) Baptism; 2) Clearance of the Past; 3) Consecration; 4) Public Confession; 5) Separation from the World; 6) Joining the Church; 7) Laying On of Hands; 8) Abolishing of Distinctions; 9) Bible Study; 10) Prayer; 11) Rising Early; 12) Attending Meetings; 13) Kinds of Meetings; 14) The Lord's Day; 15) Singing Hymns; 16) Praising; 17) Breaking Bread; 18) Testifying; 19) Bringing People to the Lord; 20) Salvation for the Whole House; 21) After Sinning; 22) Confession and Recompense; 23) Restoring a Brother; 24) The Believer's Reaction; 25) Freedom from Sin; 26) Our Life; 27) The Will of God; 28) How to Handle Money; 29) Occupation; 30) Marriage; 31) Selecting a Mate; 32) Husband and Wife; 33) Parents; 34) Friends; 35) Entertainment; 36) Speech; 37) Clothing and Food; 38) Asceticism; 39) Illness; 40) Governmental Forgiveness; 41) The Discipline of God; 42) The Dealing of the Holy Spirit; 43) Resisting the Devil; 44) Head Covering; 45) The Way of the Church; 46) Oneness; 47) Loving the Brothers; 48) Priesthood; 49) The Body of Christ; 50) The Authority of the Church.

The intention was that every local church would use these fifty messages for the edification of new believers every week for one year and repeat them yearly.

The following thirty-five books were reprints of messages

published in *Notes of Scriptural Messages,* which Watchman
published for the use of young believers:

1) *Man's Only Sin*
2) *Confession*
3) *Forgiveness and Confession*
4) *The Other Aspect of the Trespass Offering*
5) *Salvation by Baptism*
6) *The Meaning of Baptism*
7) *The Mind of Christ*
8) *The Seal of the Holy Spirit*
9) *A Believer's Worth before God*
10) *The Numbering of Spiritual Days*
11) *The Four Ministers in the New Testament*
12) *Five Parables concerning Things New and Old*
13) *Our Lord's Sanctifying Himself*
14) *The Sympathy of the High Priest*
15) *The Power of Choosing*
16) *The Reason the Lord Was Not Disappointed*
17) *God Interrupting Man's Speaking*
18) *Loving God*
19) *Waste and Pragmatism*
20) *Four Things a Christian Should Pay Attention
     To*
21) *A Noble Deed*
22) *Mary* (John 20:16)
23) *"And Peter"*
24) *Tell Him*
25) *David and Mephibosheth*
26) *The Individual and the Corporate*
27) *The Widow, the Wife, and the Virgin*
28) *Leaking and Drifting*
29) *In Nothing Be Anxious*
30) *The Two Rests*
31) *The Pathway to Glory—through Jerusalem*
32) *How to Know the Will of God*
33) *Faith and Obedience*
34) *A Defeated Righteous Man*
35) *Tears*

3. Books of General Messages for Christians

The following nineteen books were published as general messages for Christians:

1) *The Messenger of the Cross*
2) *The Work of the Holy Spirit*
3) *Living by Faith*
4) *Living by Faith and the Course of Entering into a Truth*
5) *A Shallow Life*
6) *Authority and Submission*
7) *Spiritual or Mental*
8) *The Way to the Knowledge of God*
9) *Self-knowledge and God's Light*
10) *Man's First Sin*
11) *Universal Fatherhood: A Fallacy*
12) *Ministering to the House or to God*
13) *Worshipping the Ways of God*
14) *The Work of Prayer*
15) *The Prayer Ministry of the Church*
16) *Worship God,* by Ruth Lee
17) *The Kingdom of the Heavens,* by W. Lee
18) *Gleanings of the Genealogy of Christ,* by W. Lee
19) *Light on Dispensations,* by W. Lee

He also published one hundred forty-four messages in twelve volumes called *Twelve Baskets Full.* Thirty-five of these messages were reprints of the above-mentioned books, and seven were reprints of books on central messages. Of the one hundred two messages remaining, ten were given by Yu Cheng-hwa and twelve by Witness Lee. The remaining eighty were given by Watchman Nee.

4. Books on Central Messages

The Lord burdened and commissioned Watchman Nee with a specific testimony of Christ in His crucifixion, resurrection, ascension, return, and kingdom. His ministry, therefore, was focused on Christ's death and resurrection for the producing of the church in life to experience the victory of Christ that His kingdom might be ushered in. For this reason, he considered messages on these matters as the central messages. His burden to hold the overcomer conferences and to publish *The Present Testimony* was to present such central messages. He also translated books in this same category into Chinese. All the books in the other categories mentioned in the first part of this chapter were intended by him to prepare the believers to apprehend these central messages, which were mainly contained in the following twenty-two books:

1) *The Details of Spiritual Cultivation* (original English title: *The Christian Life and Warfare*) published in June 1927. This book was the initial step to writing *The Spiritual Man.*

2) *The Spiritual Man* in three volumes was published in the fall of 1928. This book was not only the central one but also the greatest one among Brother Nee's writings. It covers the following main points: 1) the three parts of man—spirit, soul, and body; 2) the distinction between soul and spirit; 3) the fleshly Christian; 4) the soulish believer; 5) the subjective aspect of the cross and the work of the Holy Spirit; 6) the spiritual man; and 7) the spiritual warfare.

After publishing two editions of *The Spiritual Man,* Watchman Nee realized that many of his readers became introspective. He also felt that the book was too perfectly written and too detailed. For these reasons he decided not to publish further editions. This was especially true after 1939 when he saw that spiritual warfare was not an individual matter but a corporate one. He told me that his view of spiritual warfare in *The Spiritual Man* was based mainly upon the writings and experience of Evan Roberts and Jessie Penn-Lewis. Roberts and Penn-Lewis saw only the individual aspect of spiritual warfare, and thus they presented it as a difficult matter. But over ten years after the publication of *The Spiritual Man,* Watchman began to realize that spiritual warfare, according to Ephesians 6, must be carried out by the Body of Christ in a corporate way. For this reason he made a final decision to discontinue the publication of this book. However, having later realized in Taiwan that with the exception of the chapter on spiritual warfare, this book could be quite helpful to believers in the matter of spiritual life, we decided to reprint it. Anyone who reads this book should keep in mind the above remarks.

3) *Having Been Made Dead to the Law* (Rom. 7:4, 15-19).

4) *The Extent of the Believer's Salvation*. This book tells us that God's salvation extends into our conscience (Heb. 9:14), heart (Matt. 5:8; Phil 4:7), soul, mind, and strength (Mark 12:30), thought (2 Cor. 10:5), speech (James 1:26), the lust of the body (Rom. 8:12-13), the members (Rom. 6:13, 19), and the ego (Gal. 2:20).

5) *The Overcoming Life* (1 John 5:12; Phil. 1:21).

6) *The Normal Christian Life*. This book contains messages on Romans 5, 6, 7, 8, and 12 given by Watchman Nee on his trip to Europe in 1938 and 1939. It was published in English and translated into Chinese.

7) *A Two-sided Truth* (Phil. 2:12-18). The twofoldness is this: On one hand God desires us to "work out" our salvation, and on the other hand, God "works in" us. We work out what God works within us.

8) *Two Principles of Conduct* (Gen. 2:9, 16-17). These are the principle of life and the principle of right or wrong. Christians should live by the first principle, not by the second.

9) *In Christ* (1 Cor. 1:30; Rom. 8:1-2; 2 Cor. 5:17; Col. 1:14; 2 Cor. 5:21; 1 Cor. 1:2; Col. 2:10; Eph. 1:3; John 16:33; 2 Cor. 12:2). We Christians are persons in Christ, enjoying redemption, life, peace, victory, and all spiritual blessings in Him.

10) *God's Masterpiece* (Eph. 2:1-10). The believers are God's masterpiece in Christ through His death, resurrection, and ascension.

11) *The New Covenant* (Heb. 8:6, 8-13). The new covenant is a better covenant, enacted with the redeeming blood of Christ and guaranteed and executed by the resurrected Christ in His eternal priesthood according to the power of an indestructible life.

12) *The Renewing of the Mind* (Rom. 12:2; Eph. 4:23). The believers' minds should be renewed that they may put off the old man and put on the new.

13) *The Power of Resurrection* (Phil. 3:10; Acts 2:32-33; Eph. 1:19-23; 2 Cor. 4:7). The power of resurrection is the

power of the Holy Spirit, in which the believers live, work, and overcome, and by which the church is built up.

14) *A Prayer for Revelation* (Eph. 1:15-23). The apostle Paul prayed in Ephesians 1 for the believers to receive revelation concerning the hope of God's calling, the riches of the glory of God's inheritance in the saints, the greatness of His power to the believers, and the church as the Body, the fullness of Him that fills all in all.

15) *Christ Is the Way, the Truth, and the Life.* This book is composed of five chapters: 1) Christ as the way, the truth, and the life (John 14:6); 2) Christ as the resurrection and the life (John 11:25); 3) Christ as the bread of life and the light of life (John 6:35; 8:12); 4) Christ as the "I Am" (John 8:24, 28, 58); and 5) Christ as the rock for the church (Matt. 16:16-18).

16) *Christ Is All Spiritual Matters and Things.* This book also comprises five chapters. The first three chapters are the same as the first three chapters of the preceding book; chapter four is on Christ being the matters and things of God (John 1:29; 6:35; 8:12; 11:25; 14:6; 1 Cor. 1:30; Col. 3:4; 1 Tim. 1:1; Psa. 27:1); and chapter five is on Christ versus matters or things (John 8:28; Col. 3:3-4; 1:16-20).

17) *Christ Becoming Our Wisdom* (1 Cor. 1:30). God has put us in Christ and has made Christ in us to be our wisdom for our righteousness, sanctification, and redemption.

18) *Christ Is Our Righteousness.* This book comprises three chapters: 1) the righteousness of God (Rom. 3:21-28); 2) Christ as our righteousness (1 Cor. 1:30); and 3) our being made the righteousness of God (2 Cor. 5:21).

19) *The Holy Spirit and Reality* (John 4:24; 16:13; 1 John 5:6). Reality is in the Holy Spirit. Everything that is in the Holy Spirit is reality.

20) *The Glorious Church* or *Holy and without Blemish* (Eph. 5:22-32). The messages in this book use Eve in Genesis 2, the wife in Ephesians 5, the woman in Revelation 12, and the bride in Revelation 21 to illustrate all the spiritual aspects concerning the church's being glorious, holy, and without blemish.

21) *The God of Abraham, Isaac, and Jacob.* This book is on

the three aspects of the full experience of a believer. The first aspect is to know God the Father and to experience Him as the source of all blessings, as portrayed by the experience of Abraham. The second aspect is to know the inheritance of the Son and to enjoy all the rich inheritance God the Father prepared in Christ for the believer, as portrayed by the experience of Isaac. The third aspect is to know the discipline of the Holy Spirit and to experience the dealings of the natural life and the Holy Spirit working Christ into the believers, as portrayed in the experience of Jacob.

22) *The Breaking of the Outer Man and the Release of the Spirit* (John 12:24; Heb. 4:12-13; John 4:23-24; 1 Cor. 2:11-14; 2 Cor. 3:6; Rom. 1:9; 7:6; 8:4-8; Gal. 5:16, 22-23, 25). This book stresses the breaking of our outer man, which is the natural man, that our spirit with the Holy Spirit may be released from within us.

5. Books on the Practicality of the Church

In his books on central messages, Watchman Nee covered the reality of the church. He was also burdened to put out five books on the practicality of the church:

1) *The Assembly Life.* This book comprises an introduction and four chapters. In the introduction he stressed the need of the church. The subjects of the chapters are as follows: 1) the authority of the church, the eldership; 2) the practice of fellowship among the local churches; 3) how to meet; and 4) the boundary of a local church being the boundary of the city in which the local church is.

2) *Rethinking the Work.* This book is Brother Nee's main work concerning the practicality of the church. It is composed of ten chapters mainly dealing with the following points: 1) who the apostles are; 2) how the local churches are established; 3) how the elders are appointed; 4) the ground of oneness and the ground of division; 5) the relationship between the work and the churches; and 6) the organization of a local church.

This book was translated into English under the title *Concerning Our Missions* and was reprinted under the title *The Normal Christian Church Life.*

3) *Further Talks on the Church Life.* This book is composed of the messages given by Watchman Nee in 1950 and 1951 after World War II and mainly deals with: 1) the ground of the church; 2) the content of the church; 3) the oneness of the church; and 4) the service of the church.

4) *The Orthodoxy of the Church.* This book comprises messages given by Watchman Nee on the seven epistles in Revelation 2 and 3 concerning the church life.

5) *Church Affairs.* This book contains a course of Watchman Nee's training at Kuling Mountain concerning the business affairs of the church.

6. Books on the Workers of the Lord

1) *The Ministry of God's Word.* The contents of this book are a training course of Brother Nee given at Kuling Mountain on the ministers of the Word of God and their ministry.

2) *The Character of the Lord's Worker* is also a training course given on Kuling Mountain dealing with the character of one who works for the Lord.

7. Books on Bible Study

The following are the publications on Bible study:

1) *Where Is Heaven?* (Heb. 8:1; 2 Cor. 12:2; Isa. 14:12-14; Psa. 75:6-7; 48:2; Ezek. 1:1, 4; Zech. 6:6, 8; Job 26:7).

2) *A Synopsis of the Book of Revelation* gives some crucial knowledge for studying Revelation and a full outline of its twenty-two chapters.

3) *Bible Studies for Beginners* contains twenty-six lessons.

4) *Study on Revelation* concerns the prophecies of the church, the Jews, the world, the great Babylon, and the New Jerusalem.

5) *Study on Matthew* concerns the kingdom of the heavens.

6) *The Song of Songs* concerns the stages of the spiritual life.

7) *The Way to Study the Scriptures* gives about forty different ways for studying the Bible.

8) *Abstracts of the Scriptures* is in four volumes and

contains the abstracts of forty-four books of the Bible from Genesis to Acts, leaving Romans to Revelation to be finished.

9) *Once a Year through the Bible* gives the subjects and the outlines of all the books of the Bible with assigned portions for daily reading.

10) *Fifty-two Basic Truths in the Scriptures,* by W. Lee, contains the following:

1) Condition of Man; 2) The Love of God; 3) The Redemption of Christ; 4) The Work of the Holy Spirit; 5) Repenting and Believing; 6) Forgiveness; 7) Cleansing; 8) Sanctification; 9) Justification; 10) Reconciliation with God; 11) Regeneration; 12) Eternal Life; 13) Freedom; 14) Salvation; 15) Assurance of Salvation; 16) The Security of Salvation; 17) Obeying the Sense of Life; 18) Living in the Fellowship of Life; 19) Consecration; 20) Dealing with Sin; 21) To Be Led; 22) Doing the Will of God; 23) To Be Filled with the Holy Spirit; 24) Preaching the Gospel; 25) Serving the Lord; 26) A Few Matters Related to a Believer's Life; 27) Knowing God; 28) The Faithfulness of God and the Righteousness of God; 29) The Election and Predestination of God; 30) The Union of God with Man; 31) The Person of Christ; 32) The Precious Blood of Christ; 33) Law and Grace; 34) In Adam and in Christ; 35) The Two Natures of a Believer; 36) Three Lives and Four Laws; 37) Union with Christ; 38) The New Testament Service; 39) Believers and Sin; 40) Receiving the Reward; 41) Entering into the Kingdom of the Heavens; 42) Sufferings; 43) The Church; 44) The Angels; 45) The Devil; 46) The World; 47) Sin; 48) Death and Resurrection; 49) Judgment; 50) Heaven and Hell; 51) The Rapture of the Believers; 52) The Second Coming of Christ.

8. Books Translated

In addition to all the above books, some spiritual books in English were translated under Brother Nee's publication ministry through the years.

1) The following eleven books were on the central messages, mostly translated by Brother Nee himself:

   (1) *The Cross of Christ,* chapter one by Andrew Murray and chapter two by Jessie Penn-Lewis
   (2) *Union with Christ in Death,* by Jessie Penn-Lewis
   (3) *The Way of Deliverance,* by Jessie Penn-Lewis
   (4) *The Meaning of the Gospel,* by T. Austin-Sparks
   (5) *The Three Main Principles of the Cross,* by T. Austin-Sparks
   (6) *A Manifested Mystery,* by T. Austin-Sparks
   (7) *Victorious Life Is a Real Fact,* by T. Austin-Sparks
   (8) *Resurrection Life and the Body of Christ,* by T. Austin-Sparks
   (9) *The Reigning Life,* by C. H. Usher
   (10) *Victory Is in the Union with Christ,* by Mackee
   (11) *God's Plan of Redemption,* by Mrs. Charles A. McDonough, translated by Yu Cheng-hwa

2) The following seven books on inner life were translated by Brother Yu Cheng-hwa. These books are helpful if they are used properly.

   (1) *Sweet Smelling Myrrh,* an autobiography of Madame Guyon
   (2) *Life out of Death—Spiritual Torrent,* by Madame Guyon
   (3) *A Short, Easy Method of Prayer,* by Madame Guyon
   (4) *Letters by Madame Guyon*
   (5) *The Practice of the Presence of God,* by Brother Lawrence
   (6) *Spiritual Maxims,* by Brother Lawrence
   (7) *Maxims of the Saints,* by Father Fenelon

3) The following eight books on general messages were translated by others:

   (1) *The Son of God,* by J. G. Bellett
   (2) *Straight Paths for the Children of God,* by A. M.

(3) *The Streams in the Desert,* by Mrs. Charles E. Cowman

(4) *Christianity or Religion,* by A. C. Gaebelein

(5) *How to Bring Men to Christ,* by R. A. Torrey

(6) *Seen and Heard,* an autobiography of James M'Kendrick

(7) *The Twofoldness of Divine Truth,* by Robert Govett, translated by Yu Cheng-hwa

(8) *Modern Science and the Long Day in Joshua,* by Harry Rimmer

J. Chart

Chart of Things to Come shows the outline of all prophecies concerning the future and depicts the raptures of the saints, the great tribulation, the coming of Christ, the judgment at the judgment seat of Christ, the millennium, the judgment at the great white throne, and the new heaven and new earth with the New Jerusalem.

K. Hymnals

Under Watchman Nee's publication ministry, three hymn books were published:

1) *Hymns:* A collection of one hundred eighty-four hymns. Most of the hymns were selected by Brother Nee out of over ten thousand hymns, songs, and poems, and were translated by him with some improvements and adjustments. A few were written by him, and one was written by Ruth Lee. Originally, it was called *Hymns for the Little Flock.* Later, this name was dropped because people used it to designate us as the Church of the Little Flock. The contents were classified as follows: words of praise, joy of salvation, springs of the valley of Baca, union with Christ, growth in grace, seeking in the spiritual pathway, consolation of the pilgrims, prayer meeting, consecration, spiritual warfare, the Holy Spirit, the work, the praise of the sucklings, and the trumpet of the gospel.

2) *Hymns:* A larger collection of 1,052 hymns compiled

and composed by Watchman Nee with the cooperation of some brothers.

3) *Gospel Songs:* A collection of one hundred songs and hymns compiled and composed by Witness Lee.

CHAPTER TWENTY-EIGHT

THE GOAL OF WATCHMAN NEE'S MINISTRY

Watchman Nee had a definite goal for his ministry. His ministry focused on Christ and was expressed in the local churches. The goal of his ministry was to establish local churches. He preached the gospel with the intention of producing material for the building of the churches. His Bible teaching, edifying the young believers, holding conferences, conducting trainings, and issuing publications were all with the goal and view of building a corporate testimony in the local churches. By reading his writings we can realize that he received a clear vision and a definite commission from the Lord concerning this goal.

HIS EMPHASIS ON THE GOAL

In the introduction of his book *The Assembly Life*, he stressed this goal emphatically:

...Before times eternal, God had a will and a foreordained plan of His own. His goal is to have a group of people containing His life who are like His Son. The goal of God was to establish not just the individual Christ, but also the corporate Christ. This corporate Christ is the church. From this we can know that it is the church which God pays attention to today. Unfortunately, it is not only the carnal believers who fail to emphasize what God stresses, but even the spiritual believers fail to emphasize it. They always replace the church of God with many works.

Today what Satan causes man to do is substitute the church of God with various kinds of work. However, we know that the purpose of God from beginning to end is to have a corporate Christ, which is the church, so that Christ might be the Head and the believers might be the members. Satan is determined to destroy this plan. This is why he causes man to pursue various works in order to replace the church.

Today some lay much stress on preaching the gospel, and by so doing they replace the church with gospel preaching. There are many today who can surely preach the gospel and save sinners. And preaching the gospel is good, but if gospel preaching replaces the church and causes men never to think about the church, then we are definitely deceived by Satan. What I have said is not too strong. God's intention in gospel preaching is merely to collect stones for the church. If gospel preaching substitutes for the church, that is wrong.

There are some who establish missions, encourage foreign evangelism, zealously donate money, form national councils, set up organizations for foreign evangelism, and send missionaries to foreign lands for evangelistic work. But why do many people today know only missions and not the church? The reason is because from eternity past God's emphasis was the church, but man's emphasis in this age is missions. Many have forgotten the church! Mr. Gordon has said, "God never sets up missions; He only establishes the church." However, men today set up mission boards, evangelistic organizations, schools, hospitals, humanistic societies, orphanages, charitable associations (as the Methodist Episcopal Church does), and even Sunday schools to help others. Are these good or bad? They are good, but if man uses these to replace the church of God, God will never be satisfied. Do you see Satan's craftiness? Satan's subtle method is to utilize works used by God and substitute them for the church, which God in His eternal will intends to establish. If your eyes are open, you will see that all these things should be dropped and that you should turn your attention to the church, because the church life, the life of the Body of Christ, is the goal of God.

Many Christians may say, "We have not established mission boards, humanistic societies, Sunday schools, schools, and hospitals." Please do not speak so fast. You may not have done these wrong things on the negative side, but what have you done on the positive side? Many would think, "As long as I am zealous, victorious, and a holy Christian, that is good enough." Brothers and sisters, I say a strong word; these are not what God is after; they are not His unique goal. I am by no means saying that zeal, victory, and holiness are insignificant. These are significant, but they are not God's ultimate goal. What God desires is the corporate church, the building, the spiritual house. He is not after fragmentary or individual pieces of brick, tile, wood, or stone. God desires a body, not a finger or any other member. What God wants is the church. His desire is for Christ to have the preeminence in the church and to be Head of the church as well. Although wood, stone, brick, and tile are necessary, they are by no means the goal of God. You have been a Christian for these many years, but how much time have you spent considering what God is after? Have you ever thought about this matter of the church? Or has your primary attention been paid to how to pray, how to overcome sin, how to help sinners be saved, and how to study the Bible well? Do you only think about these things, or have you really considered what the church is? What God wants is a church. Anything that falls short of this fails to meet the goal of God. I am by no means saying that these other things are not good, but I am saying that anything short of the church cannot be counted as the goal of God. If Sunday schools are merely for the sake of Sunday schools, orphanages merely for orphanages, humanistic societies merely for humanistic societies, and gospel preaching merely for gospel preaching, it is fine as long as they do not replace the church. For all these things fall short of the church of God. What God wants is the church. The death of the Lord Jesus was for the church, and the coming of the Holy Spirit was also for the church. From beginning to end, in the New Testament, one principle can be found: Everything is for the church. Take, for example, the fact that the Lord's death was for the church. The book of Ephesians tells us, "Christ also loved the church and gave Himself up for her." The Lord was raised from the dead to be far above all rule and

authority, and He is above all to be Head over all things
to the church. The Lord builds the church on this rock. The
work of the Holy Spirit for the past two thousand years
has been for the building up of the church. God saves
sinners and enables men to overcome in order to establish
the church. It is for the building up of the church that God
has given us apostles, prophets, evangelists, shepherds,
and teachers. Ephesians tells us that the Lord cleanses the
church by the washing of water in the word and sanctifies
her in order that He might present her to Himself a glorious church, not having spot or wrinkle or any such things,
but that she should be holy and without blemish. Here
again it is a matter of the church. God's ultimate goal
is to have the New Jerusalem, and what the New Jerusalem typifies is the church. God's goal as recorded in
the Old Testament, New Testament, the four Gospels, and
Revelation is to have the New Jerusalem, which is for
the church. I say strongly that unless our aim, work,
and living today are for the church—that is, for the accomplishment of what God is after—we are a big failure. May
the Lord have mercy on us and deliver us from our limited
vision into His goal and into what He emphasizes in the
Scriptures....

The church is God's goal. Today He places this goal
before man. God's ultimate desire is to have the New
Jerusalem. God intends to put the church, which repre-
sents the New Jerusalem, into every city as a unit. Before
the New Jerusalem descends from heaven, God's goal is
to have a miniature of the New Jerusalem in every city.
This means that God desires to have a church in every city
to express His eternal will. From beginning to end, the
most important work God desires to do is to build up
the Body of Christ. For this reason God establishes a local
church in every city. The local church is the miniature of the
magnificent church of God, a small-scale model expressing the New Jerusalem. The will of God is to establish the
church, the Body of Christ, the New Jerusalem. But this
scope is too vast; how can we touch the New Jerusalem,
which is in the new heaven and new earth? What shall we

do? We can never grasp this firmly. However, you can come to Shanghai to achieve this purpose. For in every city there is a miniature where God puts the saved ones and unites and assembles them together to become a local church and thereby express His will....

I am not here accusing you! I myself am guilty! In these many years of evangelistic work in China, very few have paid attention to God's emphasis. Roman Catholicism has been in China for more than three hundred years, and if we count from Nestorianism, Christianity has been in China for over a thousand years. Yet no one has ever paid attention to the expression of the eternal will of God on a small scale. But we also are the same. We only pay attention to personal victory over sins, overcoming experiences, work, and saving souls, but we have not yet seen how to express in a particular locality God's will concerning the church. May God be gracious to us and cause us to see that personal victory over sins, overcoming experiences, and the work of saving souls are merely things related to the local assemblies—they should not replace the church. God's center is fixed on the church in every locality, and everything else should be joined to this center. Therefore, our aim today is not merely to pay attention to overcoming experiences, victory over sin, preaching the gospel to sinners, and having prayers answered. Rather, we should go a step further and ask what we should do in order to be fitly framed together with other brothers and sisters....

The question today is not whether this piece of stone is good or bad, big or small, beautiful or ugly, but whether this piece of stone is properly fitted with other pieces of stone and whether these pieces of stone can be built into a house. Many Christians today are very good, and others are extremely shining and beautiful, but they cannot be framed together. They are either too big or too tall; they just cannot be fitly framed with other Christians. Every person who is saved is a living stone. Therefore, the question is not whether you are victorious, defeated, powerful, weak, good, or bad. The question is whether you can be joined with all the other living stones, properly fitted into the building. If you are a stone which leaves cracks between you and the other stones, you are not of much use in the house of God.

In an open letter published in the twelfth issue of *Collection of Newsletters,* July 1935, Watchman stressed this goal again with the following brief, strong word: "We are clear that God wants us to *manifest the life of Christ in the local churches.* Hence, the reality of our work is the life of Christ, and the outward expression of our work is the local churches."

HIS FAITHFULNESS TO THE GOAL

Watchman Nee's ministry was received by many Christians, but the goal of his ministry was rejected by the majority. They appreciated his ministry of life, but they would not care for his goal of building up the local churches. Some even considered him wrong in having such a goal. Actually, however, it was not that he was wrong, it was that they did not see that the Lord had revealed to him God's desire to have Christ expressed in local churches. Fairly speaking, at the time Watchman Nee was raised up by the Lord, among millions of Christians with all kinds of Christian work, where was there one proper church built up with Christ in oneness without any element of division? In a situation filled with division and confusion, he received the heavenly vision that the Body of Christ should express in one church in each locality what was in the heart of God. He was a man after God's heart, testifying to his fellow Christians the vision he had seen, but he was fully misunderstood and rejected in this matter. Because of their strong backgrounds in the denominational structures, his fellow Christians were veiled from seeing the clear vision of God's heart's desire. Some criticized him as being narrow-minded. Others considered him a "sheep-stealer." Others even accused him of being wrong in the matter of the church. Actually, he was neither narrow-minded nor wrong; he was faithful to his Master's goal and took that goal as the goal of his ministry. He knew the price and was willing to pay the price for this. He even paid this price at the cost of his life. He cared for nothing but his Master's heart's desire—the local churches expressing Him in a corporate way. He was not a "sheep-stealer," but a true witness of his Master, who loved the church and gave Himself for it. He had no intention whatsoever to build up his own "church" or to build up anything for himself. His concern was for God's heart's desire. He had a heart large enough to receive all the children of God, and he loved all the Lord's redeemed ones, even though he was misunderstood and rejected by many. His deep longing was that all would receive the light to see what the Lord was really after and seek the Lord according to His heart.

According to the Lord's own love for the church and according to the vision he had received from the Lord, Watchman Nee bore an anti-testimony to divided Christianity and sounded the trumpet that all the Lord's true seekers should leave denominational divisions and come back to the genuine oneness of the Body of Christ to express Christ corporately in each locality. This was the goal of his entire ministry, and he held this goal to the day he died.

CHAPTER TWENTY-NINE

THE ACCOMPLISHMENT
OF WATCHMAN NEE'S MINISTRY

In spite of the fact that he was despised, criticized, misunderstood, opposed, and rejected by the denominations, Watchman Nee's ministry still accomplished a number of things. His ministry made clear the matter of salvation by grace. It aroused believers both in and out of the recovery to love the Lord. It stirred up Christians to seek the truth. It ushered the seeking ones into spirituality. It brought the Lord's people into identification with Christ in His death, resurrection, and ascension. It established the local churches. And it ushered in and built up a ministry of supply. Let us consider each of these matters in turn.

MAKING CLEAR THE MATTER OF SALVATION BY GRACE

Since the time the gospel began to be preached in China, although it was enthusiastically and widely declared, salvation by grace never became adequately clear to the Chinese Christians until Watchman Nee's ministry was raised up. The first step in his ministry was to preach the gospel. As he began to preach the gospel, he discovered the need of some clear teaching concerning assurance of salvation. Along with his preaching of the gospel, he incorporated the clear word of the Bible concerning the assurance of salvation. In the twelve years between 1922 and 1934, through his labor this matter was made clear to the Chinese Christians. In the fall of 1933 I was invited to preach in a chapel of a Presbyterian hospital in the city of Soochow, Kiangsu. While telling the audience that they could know assuredly that they were saved according to the Bible, I noticed the pastor shaking his head, indicating that he did not agree. This incident depicted the ignorant situation of so many Christians concerning the matter of salvation in China at that time. Since 1934, however, up to this present moment, the two matters of salvation by grace and the assurance of salvation have become crystal clear to the Christians in the Far East, and it has become popular to preach these truths in all the denominations.

AROUSING BELIEVERS TO LOVE THE LORD

Through Watchman Nee's spoken and written ministry, many Christians were set on fire to love the Lord. This became a tide flooding over not only the unbelievers but also hundreds of Christians of different ages throughout China. Wherever his ministry went, it brought in a revival of seeking the Lord. This matter was neither superficial in its depth, nor did it mushroom overnight. It happened as slowly and solidly as a seed sown into the depths of many seekers and lovers of the Lord, causing them to be attached to Him and making them grow in Him. One brother in Shanghai testified that when he first heard Watchman speak, even when the Lord's name was mentioned, it was so sweet to him. Just a short prayer by Watchman in the Lord's name caught him for the Lord. Watchman Nee as a person and his ministry as the Lord's supply became a great magnet attracting people to follow him in loving the Lord with their whole heart. Through his ministry, people were not moved toward the Lord in a way of enthusiasm; rather, deep in their being, his ministry caused others to deeply touch the Lord in love. Many who came in contact with his ministry were fully captivated and captured by the Lord and led to consecrate themselves fully to Him for His move on this earth.

STIRRING UP CHRISTIANS TO SEEK THE TRUTHS

Watchman's ministry also had the characteristic that it stirred up his listeners to seek the truth according to the Scriptures. Before his ministry was raised up, not many Christians in China were interested in checking all truth with the Scriptures. Most Christians simply followed tradition both in teaching and in practice. Whatever the missionaries and pastors taught and practiced, the Christians swallowed without exercising much discernment of the Spirit and without checking it according to the holy Word.

Watchman Nee was a pioneer in questioning every doctrine, form, ritual, and sacrament of today's Christianity. He checked every item with the pure word of God in the Scriptures. In this way he discovered many truths in the Scriptures himself and created an atmosphere of seeking after the truth among seeking Christians. This questioning attitude became a constituent and characteristic of his ministry which spontaneously helped all who came in touch with him to drop the inaccurate and unscriptural teachings and practices. A love of studying the Bible was stirred up in the hearts of God's people. This became a great tide among the Christians in the Far East. Because of this ministry, many lives were changed, many marriages and families were adjusted, many were helped to grow in life, many were enlightened to know the will of God, and many were captured and turned to the Lord's recovery. Also many outward practices in many denominations which were not scriptural became adjusted. Terms such as "fellowship," "meeting time," "brother" or "sister," "the Lord's table," and many other terms not commonly used before became common practice through Watchman Nee's ministry. When I was a young man, I often heard my pastor use the term "denominations" in a formal and official way without any negative connotation. However, after Watchman's ministry sounded the trumpet against denominationalism, no one dared use the term "denomination" in a positive sense. Nearly all Christian leaders became convinced that denominations were doctrinally wrong. Although they would not give up their denominations, they did insist that in spite of their denominations they would not have the spirit of the denominations. But the denominations, they claimed, were still needed for the spread of the gospel and the edifying of believers. The trumpet sound of Watchman Nee's ministry against denominationalism has left an indelible impression upon the ears and consciences of all Christians in the Far East up to this very day.

USHERING THE SEEKING BELIEVERS INTO SPIRITUALITY

Watchman Nee's ministry was spiritual in nature and laid great stress on spirituality. Many seeking believers were helped to divide soul from spirit. Before the ministry of the word of God was manifested through him, few Chinese Christians knew how to discern the difference between soul and spirit. Now, since his ministry has been continuing for many years, emphasizing the importance of knowing the soul negatively and knowing the spirit positively, the matter of seeking spirituality has become commonplace among Christians in the Far East. Though many Christians in the Far East do not live according to the spirit but according to the flesh or the soul, they nevertheless have come to know through his ministry that there is a difference between a life and a walk which are fleshly and soulish and a life and a walk which are spiritual. What Watchman's ministry did was to pave the way for seeking Christians to live and work according to the spirit, rather than according to the flesh or the soul. His ministry in this aspect greatly uplifted the standard of Christian life in the Far East.

BRINGING THE LORD'S PEOPLE INTO IDENTIFICATION WITH CHRIST IN HIS DEATH, RESURRECTION, AND ASCENSION

The central point of Watchman Nee's ministry was Christ in His death, resurrection, and ascension. He himself bore this testimony both in his life and in his work. A good number of those who came in touch with him were brought into identification with Christ in His death, resurrection, and ascension. They were helped by his ministry to live by Christ in conformity to His death through His resurrection life. This was the central point of his ministry, and this was much deeper than all the previous items of his accomplishments. Such a life in union with Christ is the inner substance of the Lord's recovery, the hidden base of the church life, and the sustaining pillar of the Lord's testimony. It is this feature which produces the overcomers, who are joined to the Head to fight the spiritual warfare for the fulfillment of God's eternal purpose that His kingdom might be brought in.

ESTABLISHING THE LOCAL CHURCHES

The achievement of his ministry consummated in the

establishment of hundreds of local churches, mostly in the Far East. By the time he was arrested in 1952, approximately four hundred local churches had been raised up in China. Approximately one hundred of these were in the county of Ping-Yang in the province of Chekiang in southern China; over forty were in the province of Suiyuan in northwest China; approximately twenty were to the north in the province of Kiangsu; and over twenty were in the province of Taiwan. The rest were scattered in major cities and seaports throughout the provinces of China. If the situation had not changed, it is possible that these local churches under Watchman Nee's ministry could easily have evangelized the entire country of China.

In addition, over thirty local churches in the southeastern Asian countries of the Philippines, Singapore, Malaysia, Thailand, and Indonesia were directly or indirectly raised up through Watchman Nee's ministry.

BUILDING UP A MINISTRY OF SUPPLY

Although it was not his specific intention, a ministry of supply was spontaneously built up through his ministry, especially his publication ministry. In the last half century in the Far East, many Christian workers, including those who opposed him, used his writings for their preaching and teaching. His Gospel Bookroom eventually became a station of supply. Most of the seeking Christians in the Chinese-speaking world received spiritual food and life supply from his publications. Thus, even the opposing denominations were nourished through his written ministry.

CHAPTER THIRTY

A SEER OF THE DIVINE REVELATION IN THE PRESENT AGE

In conclusion, Brother Nee, as a unique gift of the age given by the Lord to His Body for His move of the recovery on the earth, should be considered as a seer of the divine visions in the present age according to what he had seen of the divine revelation. The major items of the divine visions he has seen are as follows:

I. The Triune God—the Divine Trinity:
   A. The Father as the source.
   B. The Son as the embodiment of the Father.
   C. The Spirit as the realization of the Son.
II. The eternal plan of God:
   A. God made, in eternity past, an eternal plan (economy) according to the desire of His good pleasure.
   B. To make Christ, the second of the Divine Trinity, the centrality and universality in God's creation and redemption for Him to have the preeminence in all things.
   C. To have a church to match Christ as His counterpart, His Body, and His fullness; as a new man in God's new creation; and as God's household, house, and kingdom.
   D. This Christ is to be the Savior, the Head, the life, and the element of the church.
   E. This Christ will be the Ruler of the millennial kingdom and will have His overcoming believers as His co-kings for one thousand years.
   F. This Christ will also be the center and reality of the New Jerusalem, the holy city, as a mutual dwelling of God and His redeemed to express the processed Triune God forever.

III. The incarnation of the Triune God:
    A. Of God the Father.
    B. In God the Son.
    C. With God the Spirit.
    D. To be the embodiment and the expression of the Triune God.
    E. To bring God into man, making God one with man as a God-man.
    F. To have God united with man.
IV. Christ as the Son of God:
    A. The embodiment of the Godhead.
    B. The centrality and universality in the divine dispensation:
        1. In creation.
        2. In redemption.
        3. In the church life.
        4. In the Christian life.
        5. Having the preeminence in all the above four items.
V. The death of Christ:
    A. Its redeeming aspect, crucifying all the negative and old things.
    B. Its life-releasing aspect, imparting the divine life into the believers.
VI. The resurrection of Christ:
    A. Overcoming death.
    B. Making Christ the firstborn Son of God.
    C. Making Christ the life-giving Spirit.
    D. Regenerating all the believers and making them the many sons of God and the brothers of Christ.
    E. Bringing man into God.
VII. The divine life:
    A. The life of God.
    B. The eternal life.
    C. The uncreated life.
    D. The overcoming life.
    E. The indestructible life.
VIII. The Spirit:
    A. The consummation of the Triune God.

B. The application of the Father in the Son to the believers.

C. The Spirit of life.

D. The life-giving Spirit.

E. The regenerating Spirit.

F. The indwelling Spirit.

G. The sanctifying Spirit.

H. The transforming Spirit.

I. The Spirit as the firstfruit of the taste and enjoyment of God, as the believers' eternal portion.

J. The Spirit of power upon the believers.

K. The reality of God.

L. The reality of Christ.

M. The reality of the truth.

N. The reality of the resurrection of Christ.

IX. The redemption of Christ and the salvation of God:

A. The redemption of God has been accomplished by Christ's vicarious death for the sinners.

B. The salvation of God is based upon Christ's redemption to save us from our past sins and from our present problems unto the ultimate enjoyment of the processed Triune God in the New Jerusalem forever.

C. The salvation of God is of God's grace, which is different from the law.

D. God's salvation is different from the Lord's reward. God's salvation is given to the believers today through their faith; the Lord's reward will be awarded to the overcoming believers at His coming back according to their overcoming life and work.

X. The believers:

A. As the tripartite men, with a spirit, soul, and body.

B. Regenerated with the divine life to be the sons of God.

C. To be the members, the constituents of the Body of Christ.

D. To be sanctified with the divine nature of God.

E. To be transformed by Christ as the Spirit.

F. To be glorified with the divine glory forever.

XI. The church:
- A. In its universal aspect—the unique universal church, as the universal expression of Christ.
- B. In its local aspect—the many local churches as the local expressions of Christ.
- C. As the kingdom of God.
- D. As the house, the dwelling place, the temple of God.
- E. As the Body of Christ.
- F. As the bride of Christ.
- G. As the increase of Christ.
- H. As the fullness, expression, reproduction, continuation, spread, growth, and surplus of Christ.
- I. As the new man:
  1. With Christ as his life.
  2. With Christ as his constituent.

XII. The New Jerusalem:
- A. As the tabernacle of God, the eternal dwelling of God.
- B. As the bride of Christ.
- C. As the ultimate consummation of the church, the Body of Christ.
- D. Composed with all the saints of the Old Testament and the New Testament.
- E. Constituted:
  1. With the nature of God as the transparent gold.
  2. With the redeeming Christ as the pearls.
  3. With the transforming Spirit as the precious stones.
- F. As the eternal dwelling of the redeemed, regenerated, transformed, and glorified saints.
- G. As the ultimate and eternal manifestation and expression of the Triune God united with the redeemed, tripartite men.

All the above twelve items are the most mysterious matters in the divine revelation according to the Scriptures.

Brother Nee was not only a seer of these divine visions, but also a pioneer in the experience and enjoyment of the contents of all these divine visions.

CHAPTER THIRTY-ONE

WITNESS LEE'S RELATIONSHIP
WITH WATCHMAN NEE
FROM 1925 TO 1935

INITIAL CONTACT

In the beginning of our history, a great geographical distance existed between me and Watchman Nee. He was in the southern province of Fukien, and I was in the northern province of Shantung.

He was saved in 1920 and I in 1925. My mother's maternal grandfather was a Southern Baptist, who in turn brought my mother into Christianity. She studied in the American Southern Baptist mission school and as a teenager was baptized into the Southern Baptist Church about 1885. I was born in 1905. She brought me in contact with her Baptist Church in Chefoo. I studied in the Southern Baptist Chinese elementary school and in the English mission college operated by the American Presbyterians in Chefoo. Though I attended the Southern Baptist Church services and Sunday school in my youth, I was not saved and was never baptized by them. Eventually, for about five years, I ceased attending any Christian services.

After my second sister experienced salvation, she prayed for me and introduced me to a very fine Chinese pastor of the Chinese Independent Church. This pastor paid me a number of visits, encouraging me to attend his Sunday morning services. After a long delay on my part, on the second day of the Chinese New Year in 1925, I decided early in the morning to attend the services of that Chinese Independent Church. After about two and a half months, they baptized me into their membership by sprinkling. But it was not until a short time later that I was actually saved and turned to the Lord through the preaching of Sister Peace Wang in April of the same year. At that time I was exceedingly ambitious as

a young man for my education and my future. But after I
was saved under Sister Peace Wang's preaching that afternoon, while I was walking home, I stopped and prayed to God,
according to Sister Wang's message, somewhat as follows:
"God, I don't like being usurped by Satan as Pharaoh, through
the world as Egypt; I would like to serve You and preach the
gospel of the Lord Jesus through the villages at any cost for
my whole life."

From that day I loved the Bible. The word of the Bible
became sweeter than honey, as mentioned in Psalm 19:10
and in Psalm 119:103. The Word nourished me, changed my
life, and caused me to love the Lord and follow Him. I
collected as many books on the Bible as possible.

Soon I was led to attend the Brethren Assembly (the
Benjamin Newton branch) in our town. The way they expounded the Bible and taught biblical truths attracted
me very much. From the year I was saved, I continuously
attended their meetings for seven years. I learned much from
them, especially in the matters of biblical types, prophecies,
and parables. Their teachings helped me to give up worldliness in its outward aspect and kept me from drifting away
from the Lord's pathway. However, I did not receive much
help from them in the matters of life, the Spirit, and the
church. I received a great deal of knowledge from their teachings but very little life.

While I was seeking to know the Bible in a thorough way,
there appeared in my hometown a Christian periodical
entitled *The Morning Star.* I obtained and read all available
issues of that paper. As I read, I frequently noticed articles
under the by-line of Watchman Nee. It was obvious that those
articles were the most outstanding ones on biblical truths.
They were the best in the whole paper. The more I read
them, the more I enjoyed reading them. From the way this
writer addressed his readers, I imagined he was an aged
Christian teacher, perhaps over sixty years of age. Actually,
he was a young man only two years older than I. Then an
issue of the paper was published with a notice saying that
Watchman Nee would publish his own paper, to be entitled
The Christian. Immediately, I subscribed to this magazine.

From 1925 through 1927 I received all twenty-four copies. When one issue would come, I would devour the whole thing in the same day if possible. Besides reading *The Christian,* I purchased all the books he published on the spiritual life. From these I received the greatest help in the matter of life. I greatly appreciated and highly treasured this magazine and these books.

At the same time, I was led to read Watchman Nee's article in *The Lamp unto My Feet,* a periodical published by the Newton Brethren in Chefoo. This article also deeply impressed me.

During these days I began to correspond with Watchman, and this initiated our first contact. I wrote, asking him questions about the Bible, all of which he answered. In one letter I asked him for advice concerning the best book on understanding the Bible. He answered that to his knowledge, the book which could be of most help in knowing the Bible was John Nelson Darby's *Synopsis of the Books of the Bible.* He added that unless I read it four or five times I would not be able to understand it well. Eight years later, while I was staying as his guest in Shanghai, he gave me this set of books as a gift.

After being saved, I still attended the Sunday morning services in the Chinese Independent Church for about two and a half years. But through the reading of Watchman Nee's writings, I began to realize that the denominations were wrong and that there was such a thing as a proper church. Though inwardly I was through with the denominations, yet I still remained there. In that denomination there was a young man who realized that I was different from others in seeking after the Lord. One day he asked, "How can we know that we are saved?" Taking the opportunity to help him with the assurance of salvation, I handed him a book on the subject by Watchman Nee. After reading it, he became clear and was saved. His name was Du Chung-chin. A relationship developed between the two of us, and that relationship was likened by our pastor to the one which existed between Joshua and Caleb. Later this brother was transferred by his business to Shanghai, and I encouraged him to attend a meeting where

Watchman Nee was ministering. Seven years later he became one of the first three elders of the church in Shanghai.

At the end of 1927, the Chinese Independent Church elected me to be a member of their board. This was an unusual distinction for such a young man as me. But I was forced at that time to tell them that I could not accept the position and would remain in their denomination no longer. I rather asked them to remove my name from their "book of life." Henceforth, I began to meet regularly with the Brethren Assembly, attending all their seven weekly meetings. I sat among them, earnestly absorbing all the doctrines they taught. I remained with them until 1932. While I was still with them, I was baptized by immersion in the sea by their leader, Mr. Burnet, in 1930.

One day in August 1931, as I was walking down the street, the thought suddenly occurred to me that all the teachings I had received in the Brethren Assembly were mostly doctrines. I considered how much knowledge I had accumulated and yet how dead I was. True, I never returned to the world, yet, though I attended seven meetings a week, I was utterly cold and fruitless. At this time I experienced a deep and real repentance.

The next morning at an early hour I climbed to the top of a small mountain near my home. I cried to the Lord and wept in desperation. Morning by morning I went there to pray. From that day on I cared little about talking; I only wanted to pray. This experience lasted for several months, from August until February or March of the following year.

During the time I was seeking the Lord, in September 1931, Watchman was about to have his second overcomer conference in Shanghai. At that time I corresponded with him and enrolled as one of the attendants in that conference. But because of the Japanese invasion into Manchuria, close to the province of Shantung, I was prohibited from attending that conference.

In the spring of 1932, Brother Du Chung-chin returned to Chefoo from Shanghai and came to see me. He told me of all the good meetings and all the good things of the church in

Shanghai. This made me all the more eager to travel to Shanghai and partake of the blessings there with the saints.

THE FIRST PERSONAL CONTACT

Brother Du and I then went to our former denomination and proposed that they invite Watchman Nee to come speak to them. Although we had left that denomination, we left them with a very good impression of us. They accepted our proposal and invited Watchman to come speak. When Du Chung-chin was returning to Shanghai, I asked him to extend my invitation to Watchman to come visit our town, which he did. At the same time the Southern Baptist Seminary in Hwang-Hsien, a city close to Chefoo, also invited Watchman to speak there. So in the summer of 1932, he came to speak at these two places. I, with others, went to meet the steamship on which he was arriving, and when the two of us saw each other, immediately we knew one another. We had corresponded with each other for some time, and there was a mutual recognition. He put himself into my hands and spoke with me of the things that were on his heart. He spoke to a large crowd for approximately one week in the auditorium of the Chinese Independent Church. I received much help from his messages, and following that conference I also accompanied him to the Southern Baptist Seminary in Hwang-Hsien.

In those years the Pentecostal movement was very strong in north China, and the seminary where Watchman spoke had come under the influence of this movement. In those meetings I saw for the first time the strange practices of the Pentecostals. Some were jumping, some were laughing, and some were shouting. There were many strange sights. After the presiding pastor, with some effort, calmed down the meeting, Watchman gave his message. He gave an inspiring word on the gospel of God's love from Luke 15.

Following the first meeting, Watchman and I walked home together. On the way I said, "What kind of way is this to have meetings—shouting, jumping, and rolling?" He replied that in the New Testament there are no ordinances telling us how we should meet. His word shocked me and made me

wonder whether he was agreeable with those strange practices of the Pentecostal movement. Eventually, I discovered
that he did not agree with that kind of practice, but neither
would he insist on any outward form.

I was staying in the seminary dormitory. One afternoon
while a Pentecostal meeting was being held in which Brother
Nee was not speaking, I stayed in my room to have some time
with the Lord. I read Isaiah 44:22 and deeply sensed as I
read, "Return unto Me, for I have redeemed you," that the
Lord was calling me to serve Him. I deeply felt that the Lord
gave me verse 21 as a promise: "You are My servant; you
will not be forgotten by Me." Also verse 23 seemed to be a
clear word to me concerning the goal of His calling: "Jehovah
has been glorified in Israel." The Lord's presence was very
real to me there, and I was thoroughly anointed, refreshed
with His Spirit, and filled with joy and encouragement.

Following the meetings at the seminary, Watchman returned to Chefoo and stayed in my home for two or three
days. We had some excellent fellowship concerning the Lord's
interest.

While staying in my home, he asked me to introduce him
to Mr. Burnet, the founder of the Newton Brethren Assembly
in my hometown. Mr. Burnet was an aged man and an
excellent Bible teacher who had learned at the feet of the
Brethren teacher Benjamin Newton. At the time the three
of us came together, I realized that Mr. Burnet did not
appreciate Watchman's testimony for the Lord. Mr. Burnet
stressed the accuracy of biblical knowledge, while Watchman
emphasized the necessity of life.

My time with Watchman during those days deeply
impressed me with the sweetness, loveliness, attractiveness,
and newness of the Lord. Those days provided a new start
for me in following the Lord and caused me to have a basic
turn from knowledge to life. Because of those days with
Watchman Nee, I began to have fellowship with the Lord in
a more intimate way. The Lord became more precious to me.
That experience was even greater than my experience of
salvation. Those days with Watchman affected my pathway
in the Lord throughout all the following fifty-nine years, since

1932. For eternity I can never forget those days! What a mercy and grace it was to me.

The day before he left, Watchman charged me to do nothing after his departure; otherwise, others would think I was following him. I replied, "How could I do anything? In this town no one is standing with me."

But on the day of his departure, something happened. In the evening a brother who was a member of the board of the denomination I had left came to ask Watchman if he would help another believer in distress. When I told him that Watchman was gone, we agreed to have a time of fellowship together. It was summer, so we went down to the beach. After a lengthy time of fellowship, about ten o'clock that night, this brother turned to me and said, "You must baptize me tonight in the sea." After much hesitation, I did it. Through this event a meeting started in my home. I wrote to Watchman explaining what had taken place. He came in April of the following year to confirm and strengthen us in the Lord's recovery and was a guest in my home for about ten days. He ministered to us in our meeting hall in the evenings and spoke to the denominational Christians in the Chinese Independent Church auditorium in the mornings. His messages greatly edified all the attendants and helped the building up of the church there in the Lord's recovery.

At this time I related how the Lord had called me to serve Him when I was with him in Hwang-Hsien the year before. To this he made no comment.

RELATIONSHIP IN THE LORD'S CALLING

Just as I desired to spend my life preaching the gospel on the day I was saved, so after I graduated from college, the Lord reminded me of this same thing. But I took the excuse that I had to help my younger brother finish his college education. After he graduated from college, I was again reminded by the Lord that I should give up my occupation and spend my full time preaching the gospel. At that time I knew that my destiny was to give my life to serve the Lord. However, I did not have a faith bold enough to perform it.

After the church in my hometown was raised up, I still

kept my occupation and at the same time cared for the meetings. By 1933, just one year after the church began, the work
was booming. There was a great demand upon my time. During the three weeks between August 1 and August 21, I
struggled much with the Lord. I deeply sensed that He was
calling me to give up my occupation and serve Him by faith,
but I dared not take definite action because of the lack of
faith.

Among all the brothers in the church at that time, only my
younger brother and I made what would be considered good
money in our occupations. For this reason most of the needs of
the church were taken care of secretly by the two of us. Therefore, when the call of the Lord came to give up my occupation,
I considered all the needs. Not only would the amount being
offered to the church be lessened if I gave up my employment,
but others would have to care for me. So I was struggling with
this matter.

After three weeks of struggling with the Lord, I simply
could not go on; so in the evening of August 21, following
the prayer meeting, I explained my situation to the two
leading ones and asked them to pray for me. After eleven
o'clock that night, I went to the Lord and knelt before Him
in my reading room. The Lord immediately rebuked me: "You
have an evil heart of unbelief in falling away from the living
God!" (Heb. 3:12). I said in my heart, "I have a wife and
three children to take care of." The Lord responded, "Your
heavenly Father knows that you need all these things...and
all these things will be added to you" (Matt. 6:32-33). At that
time I became clear that I had to spend my full time serving
the Lord. The only factor which caused me to hesitate was
lack of faith. I deeply sensed that the Lord was there. His
presence was so real that I could not deny it. But up to this
point I could not pray. Then He warned me, "If you will take
My word, take it; otherwise, I am through with you."
Immediately following that word, I felt that the Lord
departed. I could pray no more; I could not even say Amen.
Tears filled my eyes. Finally I said, "All right, this is it."
There was no other way. The next morning both of the two
leading ones came to me and told me that after praying they

felt it was of the Lord that I should leave my occupation and give my full time to serving the Lord.

The next day I went to resign my job. After resigning, I went to the post office and found a letter awaiting me from Ch'ang-ch'un, the capital of Manchuria under Japanese occupation. Opening it, I found to my surprise the first invitation I ever received in my entire life calling me to go to another place to speak for the Lord. It was immediately after my resignation that I received this letter. It seemed to be a definite confirmation of the Lord regarding my resignation, and I was much strengthened and encouraged. I accepted the invitation and went. Through my visit an assembly was raised up there. The preacher, the elders, the deacons, and others of the Presbyterian denomination, close to twenty, all turned to the Lord's recovery and were baptized by me in the river in one day.

I spent seventeen days in that place. While I was there, a letter arrived from the general manager of the company in which I had been employed, telling me that they would not let me go but would promote me and increase my salary. The time was late September. I began to consider; it was the policy of our company to give the employees a bonus at the end of the year. I was tempted by the thought that if I would work for only a little more than three months I could still get that bonus and then quit.

Upon returning to my hometown, a letter was awaiting me from Watchman Nee. I looked at the envelope, noticing it was mailed from Shanghai. I opened it and read it. It was dated August 17, exactly in the midst of the time I had been struggling with the Lord. The letter said, "Brother Witness, as for your future, I feel that you should serve the Lord with your full time. How do you feel? May the Lord lead you." It is impossible to tell what strong confirmation I received by receiving that short note from him. That little note simply annulled the letter from my general manager. I was leaping in my heart. I said to myself, "This matter is settled. Even if someone would offer me the whole world, I would not take it. Tomorrow I will go to the office and tell the general manager that I reject his good offer." The next day I did exactly that. Then I felt that I must go to Shanghai to see Watchman Nee and discover why he wrote me that note at that particular time, August 17.

In Shanghai Watchman related to me the following story. He told me that while he was returning to China from Europe his ship was sailing on the Mediterranean Sea. One day while in his cabin, burdened and praying for the Lord's work in China, he felt he should write me a note telling me that I should spend my full time serving the Lord. When he told me that, I was fully convinced that he was a person wholly with the Lord. Otherwise, how could I be thousands of miles away struggling with the Lord and he be on the Mediterranean Sea receiving a burden to write me concerning this matter at the very instant God was dealing with me? I was persuaded that he was a man of God. He did not need to ask me to work with him; I had already made the decision. I had to follow him and work with him. This incident I have just related became the basic factor in our working together for the Lord.

RELATIONSHIP IN ENTERING THE WORK

While in Shanghai in October 1933, Watchman received me as his guest. I stayed with him for about four months, and during that time he did a number of things to perfect me. Concerning some of these things, I was clear what he was doing, and concerning others I was not clear at the time. I spent much time with him. We were together for many hours, and I always gave him the opportunity to speak. I would not speak, for I realized that the more I spoke, the more foolish I was. I gave all the time to him. He never talked with me about vain things but always took the opportunity to speak with me mainly about four matters.

First, he helped me know the Lord as life. Before I stayed with him, I loved the Lord and had already obtained a great deal of doctrinal knowledge of the Bible. But I was not clear concerning life. It was not until I spent time with him that my eyes were opened to see the matter of life.

One afternoon as we sat together, neither of us said a word. I was seated on a sofa and he in a rocking chair. While he was rocking, he began to ask me, "Brother Witness, what is patience?" I was puzzled. The question was too simple. Surely we all know what patience is. But since this question came from his mouth, it had to be of considerable import. I dared not answer. While he was rocking, he continued, "What is patience?" I did not understand what his intention with me was at that time. He had a burden, but I did not comprehend it. Eventually I said, "Well, patience to me is a sort of endurance. When people ill-treat you and persecute you, yet you endure the suffering, that is patience." He shook his head and said, "No!" Then I said, "Please tell me, what is patience?" He answered, "Patience is Christ." I could not understand it. It sounded like a foreign language to me. I asked, "Brother, what do you mean by saying that patience is Christ? Would you explain it to me?" He only continued rocking. He offered not a word of explanation. "Patience is Christ," he repeated. I was not only puzzled but deeply bothered. We remained in that state for a long time. I would not raise any other question, and he would say nothing else. I was very eager to know what he meant, but after a long period with no explanation forthcoming, I was fully disappointed. It was late in the afternoon, and eventually I said, "Brother Nee, the time is gone; I must return to have my dinner." He replied, "All right."

When I returned to the guest house, I was really troubled. I went to my room and prayed, "Lord, what does it mean that patience is Christ?" The Lord spoke to me in those days, and my eyes were opened. I saw that Christ Himself is my patience. Real patience is not a kind of behavior, but just Christ lived out from me. I saw it! It was in this way that Watchman helped me so greatly in the matter of life.

Second, during these times of fellowship Watchman also related to me the history of the Lord's move with him from the year he was saved up to that day. I was not fully in the church, nor was I in the work in those first ten years of the Lord's recovery; so he used hour after hour to convey the things to me concerning the Lord's move in those years, not in a brief way but in full detail. At the time I did not understand his reason for relating those things to me, but later I knew. He purposed to perfect me and build me up. He was laying a good foundation.

Third, he instructed me in matters concerning church history from the first century to the present. He recounted all the main things which occurred concerning the church, and the way he did it was deeply significant. He did it from the aspect of the Lord's recovery and with the goal of the Lord's recovery in view.

Fourth, he also helped me grasp the living way to know the Bible. I had been helped by the Brethren to know the Bible in the way of letters, but he helped me know the Bible in the way of life. In all our conversations together, I received much help from him in these four matters. A good foundation was laid for my work, even up until the present time, in the matters of life, the church, and the work.

One afternoon while I was studying, he came to my room and threw two sets of used books on my bed. He said, "Here are some books for you," and immediately left. One group of books was John Nelson Darby's five-volume *Synopsis of the Books of the Bible,* and the other group was a four-volume set of Henry Alford's *New Testament for English Readers.* I realized that his purpose in giving me these two sets of books was to perfect me in knowing the Word of God.

In addition, he also put me into a position where I could participate in the work and minister in the local church in Shanghai. This afforded me an excellent opportunity to learn how to serve the Lord. Before putting me into such a situation, however, he tested me. His way of testing was secret. In the beginning I did not know what he was doing; I did not realize that I was being tested. In the previous years while we were corresponding, he did not really know me. But when we stayed together for a longer period of time, he was observing and secretly putting me to the test. First, immediately after arriving in Shanghai, I was asked to speak in the general Sunday morning meeting. This caught me by surprise, but I gave a rather long message on the pathway to glory from Matthew 13:53—17:8.

At that time the church in Shanghai met in two halls. The main hall was hall one while hall two was somewhat secondary. Not long after I arrived in Shanghai, the brothers arranged for me to hold a conference in hall two. I believe that this was according to Watchman's instructions in order to test me a little. I spoke every night and was exposed to all. I was on the test for about a week. Watchman was not there, but whatever I said found its way to him. I must have passed the test for I was later charged to speak regularly in the first hall.

One day Watchman brought me a bundle of letters from various places. Various persons had written him asking questions about the church, church practice, life, and about the interpretation of the Bible. He said, "Witness, I am too busy. I do not have time to devote to all these things. Would you reply to these letters and answer all their questions for me?" I never imagined that this could be a test, but it was. I said to him, "There are probably some questions to which I will not know the answer." He replied, "That does not matter; if you have questions, just ask me." By the Lord's mercy I answered all of the letters. The longest answer I wrote was on sects and the structure of the church. Watchman appreciated it very much and published it in the fourth and fifth issues of *Collection of Newsletters*. Watchman's third overcomer conference was held in Shanghai in January 1934. Many co-workers and saints attended the conference from different places throughout the country. It started on a Monday. Nearly all the outsiders arrived on the Lord's Day before the conference began. On the morning of the Lord's Day, while we were all waiting for Watchman to come and speak, a short note was delivered to me from him asking me to speak in that meeting. Both I and the attendants were all surprised that he did not show up in that meeting. But I spoke in the meeting according to his request and acquired some new experience.

During that ten-day conference, I received much help from his messages. They were indeed marvelous, marking a real turn in both my Christian life and in my church life. My eyes were opened to see Christ in His preeminence in all things according to God's eternal plan. I took brief notes on all his

messages, which he eventually published in the March and
April issues of *The Present Testimony* in 1934.

One day before the conference, we were having fellowship
together. At that time he asked me how I daily studied the
Bible. I replied that I was in Acts and Colossians. Immediately he said that these two books were a very good match.
At first I did not understand what he meant, but eventually
I was helped to see that Acts reveals to us how Christ
ascended to the heavens and was made both Lord and Christ
(2:36), whereas Colossians reveals that Christ should have
the preeminence in all things and should be all and in all in
God's economy (1:18; 3:11). There was never another person
in my entire Christian life who helped me know the Scriptures in such a profound and living way, especially regarding
the revelation of Christ with the church.

On one occasion the first hall in Shanghai arranged to
hold a gospel meeting, but no one knew who the speaker
would be. Many thought that Watchman would speak. I
was feeling quite relaxed and prepared to hear a message
from him. I hoped also to learn more concerning how to
preach the gospel. About an hour before the meeting, there
was a knock at my door, and a note was passed on to me.
It said, "Brother Witness, you give the message on the gospel
tonight." It shocked me! What should I do? At any rate, I had
to speak.

That night I spoke from John 16 concerning the Spirit
convicting the world of sin, of righteousness, and of judgment.
I pressed the people with the matter of sin because we were
born of Adam, of righteousness because we can believe in
Christ, and of judgment because we follow Satan. I told the
people that here are three persons—Adam, Christ, and Satan.
We were all born sinners in Adam, but now God has offered
us the opportunity to get into Christ to be justified by taking
Him as our righteousness. By believing in Christ we are
transferred out of Adam into Christ. However, if we do not
believe in Christ, we will remain sinful in Adam, and one
day we will be together with Satan sharing God's judgment
upon him. As I delivered this message, I could not see
Watchman in the meeting. I did not know where he was, and

no one told me where he was. But after a period of time had elapsed, one day as we were walking down the street, he suddenly turned to me and said, "Brother Witness, not many in this country can give a message from John 16 on the three points of sin, righteousness, and judgment and on Adam, Christ, and Satan as you did. I encourage you to go on." When I heard this, I said to myself, "How did he know this?" Eventually, I discovered that while I was speaking he was standing behind the door listening to my word. He heard everything. By that time I was aware that he was continually testing me.

In 1934, after I had been in Shanghai for about four months, Watchman came to see me one day. He said, "Brother Witness, we the co-workers here all feel that you should move your family to Shanghai and work together with us. Bring this matter to the Lord, and see how He will lead you." I brought the matter to the Lord, and at this time my eyes were opened to see a very significant matter. I saw from the book of Acts that there was only one flow, one current on the earth; it began from the throne of grace and came down to Jerusalem. From Jerusalem it took its course through Samaria, traveling to the north to Antioch; then from Antioch it turned westward to Asia Minor and to Europe. I saw that in the entire book of Acts there was only one current of the Lord's work on this earth and that there was no record of the work of anyone who was not in the current. When Barnabas separated from Paul and began another current, the account of his work in Acts terminated (Acts 15:36-41). The later co-workers, such as Timothy and Apollos, after being raised up by the Lord for His work, all were merged into one flow of the Lord's move, though they did not need to go to Jerusalem for this purpose (Acts 16:1-3; 18:24-28). The Lord revealed to me that the flow of His work in China must be one. Since it had begun from Shanghai, I should not go to the north and keep another flow. If the Lord was going to do something in the north, I must first enter into the flow in Shanghai; then eventually the flow in Shanghai would travel to the north. Although a work was already started in the north, I became crystal clear concerning the one flow. With this vision in view, I returned to the north following Watchman's conference, stayed for awhile, and then returned to Shanghai to stay and work with him. Hence, there was one flow and one current of the Lord's work in China.

CHAPTER THIRTY-TWO

WITNESS LEE'S RELATIONSHIP WITH WATCHMAN NEE FROM 1934 TO 1936

RELATIONSHIP IN THE ASSIGNMENT OF WORK

While I was away in the north, Watchman conducted a series of meetings with the church in Shanghai in February 1934 following his conference. The meetings also included the conference attendants who stayed on after the conference, and the purpose of the meetings was to study the Bible concerning the assembly life. I came back to Shanghai from Chefoo in May. The day after my arrival, Watchman came to my place, threw a bundle of articles to me, and said, "Please write a preface for these articles." When I opened the bundle, I was so happy to see that the articles were composed of the messages given by him in the Bible study meetings while I was away. I could not stop until I had finished reading all four chapters. The most striking point in all the chapters concerned the boundary of the local church. After reading the chapters, I wrote a preface to them. They were published as a book under the title *The Assembly Life*.

During the period after I returned to Shanghai, Brother Nee's health was not good. During most of the meetings, he either rested or was away elsewhere. He spoke mostly during the conference times. The burden for the ministry in the regular meetings was left to me.

Brother Nee bore the main responsibility for two publications: *The Present Testimony* and *The Christian*. The publication of *The Christian* was suspended for a period of seven years, during which he published only *The Present Testimony*. In 1934 the decision was made with many co-workers to resume the publication of *The Christian*, and I was asked to edit it. I bore this responsibility until 1940.

From the end of 1933, Watchman Nee also issued a paper

with news of the work and the churches entitled *Collection of Newsletters*. The eldest sister co-worker among us, Ruth Lee, was appointed to be acting editor of that paper. When she was away from Shanghai, I had the responsibility of editing that paper also.

Through all these responsibilities, a tremendous opportunity was opened to me to learn how to work for the Lord in His recovery, how to help others grow in life, how to build the church with life, and how to care for the publication ministry. Having been sovereignly placed under Brother Nee's leadership, by the Lord's mercy and grace, I learned many lessons in the matter of life, in the practice of the church, and in caring for the work in a living way. What I learned during this time laid a solid foundation for my future. How I thank the Lord for this! How grateful I am to Brother Nee for his perfecting work and for his gracious and wise dealings with me.

With all of us staying in Shanghai together, we were enabled to have much helpful contact. On one occasion the two of us were driving to a dairy ranch in a suburb of Shanghai to visit some brothers. During our ride we fellowshipped about the situation between us and the denominations. As we were considering the fact that the denominations were rejecting our testimony, he said, "From now on we must turn to the Gentiles like the apostles did in Acts 13:46." This opened my eyes to see something more of the Lord's way.

In the summer of 1934, he traveled with four of us brothers, driving the car himself, to visit four provinces, Kiangsu, Chekiang, Kiangsi, and Anhwei, to look into the situation in these places regarding the Lord's move. While traveling with him on this trip, I realized that he was a person who loved the Lord with his whole heart, and that he was also a person who had deep insight and foresight concerning many things. We five brothers from five different provinces, ranging from the far north to the far south, traveled and lodged together for a number of days. We enjoyed Brother Nee's helpful building-up fellowship and the Lord's presence with the oneness and harmony in the spirit.

I could never forget the precious and sweet experiences of those golden days in the heavenlies!

In the summer of 1934, Sister Ruth Lee visited the churches in Kwangtung province and Hong Kong. Therefore, during this time I was charged to care for the editing of *Collection of Newsletters*. During the same time Brother Nee went to Foochow, his hometown, for rest. While resting there in Foochow, he wrote me the following letter concerning that publication, which was published in *Collection of Newsletters*, issue nine:

July 6, 1934

Dear Brother Witness:

...Concerning the articles for *Collection of Newsletters*, I personally hope that in the future there will be more news about how the brothers and sisters have consecrated to the Lord, about how they have obeyed the Lord and have taken the Lord as Head over all things, about how they have overcome their dryness and entered into the more abundant life, and about how they were delivered from a sinful life and have overcome sin. These spiritual aspects are much more important than outwardly leaving the denominations.

What is our center? Is our work to preach Christ as Lord or to preach leaving the denominations? I am really fearful that in every locality there are brothers who, being limited in understanding and spiritual experiences before God, only have a little knowledge about outward matters such as baptism, head covering, and denominations, and exhaust their effort to publicize these matters. By doing so, they cause outsiders to misunderstand us, thinking that we only emphasize these outward things and that we do not exalt Jesus Christ as Lord.

We know that if anyone follows the Lord, he will certainly take care of these outward matters. But it does not mean that anyone who practices these outward things is necessarily following the Lord completely. We must emphasize again and again for the sake of the ignorant brothers among us, that although we believe in these outward matters, yet our testimony, that which makes us different from others, is not in these outward things.

Another matter which is continually on my heart is the matter of the co-workers. We thank God that many who had rank and position in the denominations have seen the truth of the church. But this is also a problem! Many have seen only the error of sectarianism among the denominations, but have not perceived the wrongness of the system in the denominations. Therefore, while they may have left the denominations, they have not rejected the system. Consequently, they think that since they were workers in the denominations, they can continue in the same way after they have come out of the denominations. They simply do not care whether or not they are gifted or whether or not they have been called by God. Although they have left their particular denominations, they have never left the work which these denominations afforded them. This will cause us to be filled with many unsuitable workers.

I believe God's will is this: Unless one is clear that he has been called and is definitely gifted, after he leaves the denominations, he should seek a proper occupation and witness for the Lord there. He should never have the thought that since he has been a worker before, he can therefore go ahead and begin a work in any locality. This is the most dangerous thing in our midst. We would prefer a locality be without any worker or work than to be doing something in a loose way. Oh, the flesh must be dealt with!

I am grateful to God that many have obeyed in these outward matters, yet their obedience is not merely restricted to these matters. These matters are but a part of their obedience to God's will. Unless it emanates from within, anything outward is worthless....

Peace be unto you.

Your brother,

Watchman Nee

During this same period of time while traveling in the south, Sister Ruth Lee wrote Watchman and me a letter concerning the church. Watchman asked me to publish it in issue ten of *Collection of Newsletters* with his comment as follows:

July 13, 1934

The following letter was written to Brother Witness and me by Sister Lee while she was traveling and working in southern China. She specifically requested that we not publish her letter in *Collection of Newsletters* because it is contrary to the position of head covering for a sister to talk about church matters. But feeling that this letter is profitable to the believers in each locality, we publish it. Brother Lee and I assume full responsibility for its content and anything pertaining to it.

Watchman Nee

Ruth Lee's letter reads:

Dear Brothers Watchman and Witness:

...All work must pass through fire to prove its value. What can one do apart from the Lord?

At this time, in the various places, through personal fellowship with the brothers and sisters and from what I have seen and heard, I have much for which to be grateful to the Lord. Yet I also have some fear and sighings. Most of the brothers and sisters in Swatow are like a sheet of white paper—all that is needed is some good writing. They are also like a piece of good ground—all they need is proper sowing. Within a year's time, about twenty brothers and forty to fifty sisters have actually begun meeting together, not including those who only come for the messages. The sisters in Taishan labor incessantly and offer themselves to the best of their ability. These are good signs.

I wish that from now on the brothers would pay attention to the following matters:

1) If the brothers in a certain locality desire to have the Lord's table, they should at least know what the church is and the reason for the table. If some presume that simply because they have no name they are not a sect, and yet in many activities they are a sect in another form, and if they consider that only they are the church and are better than anyone else, then inevitably they will become the worst sect.

2) The brothers and sisters in a locality who are lacking in gift should procure proper jobs and serve God with their jobs. Otherwise, they simply become dead preachers sitting in their parishes, where neither sinners are being saved nor brothers and sisters are growing in life. Consequently, the place is full of spiritual death. We may ignore any derision from the denominations, but what about our testimony? If a place is without a worker, it is best for the brothers and sisters there to pray livingly, remember the Lord, and give personal testimonies. It is not necessary to adhere to a set form. If a brother or sister professes to be called by the Lord yet is not gifted, then in the eyes of others, this calling is questionable. The problem with this kind of worker is that he is either presumptuous or lazy. Sometimes problems also arise in regard to material supply—those who are pure may suffer hardship, while others may make godliness a means of gain.

3) If a brother or sister is gifted, it is best for him or her to serve God according to what he or she has. For anyone to go beyond their gift when they minister will unavoidably be unreal or in error.

4) Even though we are standing on the "right" side, nevertheless, it would be best that our messages would emphasize what is in the Bible, without saying explicitly that this denomination or that denomination is right or wrong. We should let any seeking one, after hearing the truth and realizing the error in which he is, be willing to pay the price to follow the Word. Avoid arguing over minor points. To be divided because of different interpretations of the Bible, is not this the way of the Brethren?

More and more I feel that every time as we break the bread, although our eyes can only see a certain number of brothers and sisters, yet, through the bread, what we actually see are all the saved ones. Otherwise, the testimony of Ephesians 1:23 is lost.

5) When the authority of a local church is in the hands of the sisters, and the sisters are not clear, then the brothers should be frank to admonish them concerning this. But if the sisters intentionally refuse to stand on the proper position, then the brothers will not have a standing there. However, there are some places where the sisters are very good, while the brothers are old, formal, and dead. In such cases there is need for some enlightened brother to deal with these brothers. If the brothers will not listen, then one cannot blame the sisters for backsliding or being disjointed. In cases like this, the brothers are still a sect, only with the word "free" added to it. It is excusable to be in this situation if one is unclear, but if he is disobedient after knowing, then it becomes a matter of motive.

The reason why I have said so much is not that the brothers in Shanghai have any strong points or special authority; I am only hoping that in your speaking or writing you would pay attention to these aspects. I am a sister, and in this letter I am simply conversing with you as a member of the family giving you a report of these matters.

The brothers in Swatow are very burning for the gospel, preaching twice weekly with two brothers responsible each time. In this matter I will be honest to say that the brothers in Shanghai are behind.

I really ask the Lord to supply the work and the need of the workers in each of these localities. Recently quite a few brothers and sisters in each locality were out of jobs, while the others mostly had only average jobs. Although many brothers and sisters have given their utmost, there is still a lack for the work and the workers. On the one hand, the workers should never tell the brothers and sisters directly or indirectly of their need by giving hints or speaking through others. Yet on the other hand, often some brothers and sisters either regard the responsible worker as a rich man, or sometimes care only for the work and not the worker. I say this not because I have a need, but because of my observation.

Pardon me for writing about so many things.

Peace in the Lord!

Sincerely yours,

Ruth Lee

Greetings to all the brothers and sisters in Shanghai.

In the same summer, Watchman wrote *Some Words from the Responsible Brothers* and asked me to sign it with him and publish it in the tenth issue of *Collection of Newsletters*. It read as follows:

Collection of Newsletters is a publication for the circulating of news within the family. It is absolutely not for the public and is available only to those brothers who walk with us. We mail it to you because we trust that you are having fellowship with us and are sharing the responsibility of intercession with respect to the news contained in it. We mail it to you because we trust that you will not publicize it to the ordinary people "outside the circle" but will call upon God for its sake "within the veil"!

We also believe you understand that our work is spiritual and that our emphasis is life. We are clear that God wants us to *manifest the life of Christ in the local churches.* Hence, the reality of our work is the life of Christ, and the outward expression of our work is the local church. In this present time, when the outward church is desolate, we do not have the slightest intention to start a new "movement," "group," "organization," or "denomination." We dare not even call ourselves the churches in the various places. We stand only on the *position* of the local church. This publication, therefore, carries the news of the assemblies which are standing on the position of the local church in each locality. As to its content, there is nothing but Christ.

We have no headquarters. Concerning the localities, we have neither the power to control any of them nor the right to interfere with any of their activities. All that they have, they each have received from their Head, the Lord Jesus. The fellowship of prayer and the direction in various matters are all mutual. This prayer and direction come about because of the need and through the Lord granting us the strength. The answers to all questions are spiritual, not official, and their source is gift, not position. We do not wish to be the "Diotrephes" among God's children, nor do we wish to become the class of Nicolaitans.

All brothers who go out to work are sent by the Lord. We are co-working with them. We hope that you can bear some spiritual responsibility with us.

Watchman Nee
Witness Lee

When he returned to Shanghai from Foochow, I was invited to visit the churches in Ping-Yang County of Chekiang province. Watchman encouraged me to go, so I went. In October of that year, he went to Hangchow for the fourth overcomer conference and I traveled there from Ping-Yang to attend the conference. Again, this was another glorious time!

RELATIONSHIP IN SUFFERINGS

During the conference at Hangchow, Watchman's mother and the eldest sister co-worker, Ruth Lee, both urged Watchman to get married during that conference time. They considered it to be a good time since all the co-workers from the entire country were present. Watchman agreed with the condition that I would be his best man and that Philip Luan would be master of ceremonies at the wedding. Sister Lee fellowshipped with both of us concerning this matter. We told her immediately that we would be more than happy to do what Watchman desired and felt honored to be asked by him.

At the wedding Mrs. Samuel Chang was the maid of honor.

All the co-workers and local saints attended the wedding. It was a happy time for all of us.

Following the wedding I traveled to Chefoo for a rest. While I was there, the big turmoil against Watchman's marriage transpired. Since I had been best man and Philip Luan had been master of ceremonies, we two were considered to be the ones best qualified to bear responsibility for handling the situation. Hence, Brother Luan cabled me and charged me to return to Shanghai to care for the situation. Immediately I cabled Watchman with the word of Deuteronomy 23:5: "Jehovah your God turned the curse into a blessing for you." I arrived in Shanghai on New Year's Day 1935. Philip Luan and I, with the help of Peace Wang, did our best to calm down the turmoil. All of our efforts seemed in vain because of the strong attack from the opponents. Eventually, because of his sickness and tiredness, Philip Luan returned to his home in Hangchow to rest. This left me alone in that difficult situation.

During that trying period, one morning Watchman came to me with the newspaper of the day and said, "In my entire life I never saw a marriage publicly attacked by printing an open advertisement in large characters in the country's leading paper." He said this with much sorrow. After that, he left Shanghai and traveled to the southwestern provinces of China.

At the same time Ruth Lee departed from Shanghai to visit the central part of China. The only help I had came from Sister Peace Wang. The situation was becoming difficult. By the Lord's mercy, Sister Wang and I decided to know nothing, do nothing, and say nothing concerning this problem. We simply continued on positively with the meetings. Praise the Lord, eventually He gained the victory and brought us through.

Before Watchman left Shanghai, he did not say a word to me concerning the work there. But following his departure, I discovered from one of the elders that his instruction to them was that the responsibility of the work there had been committed to me.

After three or four months, Watchman returned, and by

May of 1935, although the storm was still present, it had calmed somewhat. Then Ruth Lee suggested to me that since Watchman would not minister, we must find a way to urge him to minister. But regardless of how much we urged him, he would not minister. Then one day Ruth said to me, "Let us beg him to hold a study with us on the Song of Songs." We therefore went to tell him that we were really eager to know the Song of Songs, and we asked him to accompany us to West Lake in Hangchow for a couple of weeks' rest and at the same time to have a study with us on the Song of Songs. He was happy about it and did it. Only four brothers and three sisters, who were all co-workers, went and stayed with him. The studies given by him at that time are now published in the book entitled *The Song of Songs*. Again, I received great help through these studies in the stages and turns of life. After that, Watchman began to minister regularly again.

From 1933, when Watchman returned from his trip to visit the Brethren in England, the Brethren had written us several letters concerning our fellowship with them. Up to the time of Watchman's wedding, we had not had time to respond to those letters. But since the wedding was over and the turmoil had subsided, Watchman began to consider how best to answer the letters of the Brethren concerning our fellowship with them. He asked me to care for this matter, but I did not take his word. Eventually, he did it himself and asked me, another co-worker, and the three elders in Shanghai to sign the letter with him.

RELATIONSHIP IN THE SPREADING OF THE WORK

At the end of May 1935, I returned to Chefoo. Watchman had decided to visit England, but before departing to England, he and his wife planned to come to Chefoo and stay in my home for some rest. Sister Nee came first in July, and Brother Nee came a little later. They were my guests for over one month. For a number of days Watchman went to stay in Tsinan with Brother Stearns, who was an American Presbyterian doctor. This doctor received much spiritual help from him and frequently came with his family from Tsinan to Chefoo for summer vacation.

At that time Watchman and the churches were somewhat depressed. One day after reading an article on revival in a Christian magazine, he said, "We need such a revival." Not long after this, one evening while seeking the Lord in the tennis court of the house where Dr. Stearns stayed, he experienced once more the outpouring of the Holy Spirit. Following this, he held a conference with us on the overcoming life of Christ. That conference brought a revival to the church in Chefoo, and I myself obtained the greatest help in experiencing Christ as the overcoming life.

Because of the revival, Watchman canceled his trip to England and returned to Shanghai. Since the Lord had caused a revival, the decision was made that the co-workers were to go out to the major cities to spread the Lord's recovery. I was assigned to work in the north and went to Tientsin, the largest port of northern China near the old capital, Peking. This was done under the direct instruction of Brother Nee. At that time I traveled to Shanghai to see him concerning this matter.

In January of 1936, I, together with Peace Wang, a young sister under instruction, and two young brother co-workers, were sent there. After a short time, Watchman came to Peking and Tientsin to strengthen the start of the work there. We arranged a week of special meetings for him to preach the gospel to the upper class. After those special meetings, Watchman returned to Shanghai and continued to work there for the Lord's recovery.

In May of the same year, a high official of the provincial government of Honan, a Christian brother, being zealous for gospel preaching among his colleagues, invited Peace Wang to preach the gospel to them and then invited Watchman and me to do the same. We both went according to his request and stayed in his home for about a week. We preached the gospel to the governor and all his high officials with their wives and friends in that brother's courtyard in the evenings. The meetings were quite prevailing. During the daytime Watchman and I spent our time in fellowship. He was again somewhat depressed, and one day he said to me, "If Sister M. E. Barber were still alive, our spiritual condition would be uplifted." This made me realize that he was seeking some spiritual help.

In the fall of that year, I took the initiative to contact the Pentecostal movement in Peking and began to speak in tongues, at the same time helping others to do the same. When the news of this arrived in Shanghai, Watchman sent me a cable with the word from 1 Corinthians 12:30: "Do all speak in tongues?" That simple cable helped me a great deal in that situation.

CHAPTER THIRTY-THREE

WITNESS LEE'S RELATIONSHIP
WITH WATCHMAN NEE
FROM 1937 TO 1950

RELATIONSHIP IN NEW REVELATIONS

At the end of December 1936, I received a cable from Watchman Nee asking me to come to Shanghai immediately for an urgent conference of all the co-workers. Peace Wang, Chang Yu-tzu, a third co-worker, and myself arrived at Shanghai early on the morning of January 1, 1937. Watchman met us at the station, and the conference started the same day. In that conference, messages were released which now form the substance of the book entitled *The Normal Christian Church Life*. During the conference he became ill with a cold. He called me to his bedside and charged me to deliver the message which he intended to release on Acts 13. After receiving all the points from him, I did as he desired and delivered the message, but I must confess that it was very inadequate. Eventually, after he recovered, he gave that message again himself.

One day during this conference time, he took me to see the construction work of the training center he had planned to build at Chenru, a suburb of Shanghai. He related to me how he was burdened to pass on to the Lord's young seeking ones some practical training on life, on the church, and on the work. The construction work of the training center was damaged by the invading Japanese in August 1937 before it was completed.

At that time the decision was made that I should travel throughout all the provinces of northern China to preach and teach in the denominations. We felt at that time that we should pass on all the light the Lord had given us to the denominations. In the summer and in the fall of that year, I did much traveling in the northwestern provinces of

Suiyuan, Shansi, and Shensi with Sister Peace Wang and others.

In that summer Japan invaded China, and many of the co-workers fled from the coast to the interior. At Sian, the last station of our journey in the northwest, we received a cable from Watchman Nee that we should go to Hankow in the central part of China to meet with him and the co-workers for a co-workers' conference. Peace Wang and I proceeded there by train. While waiting in Hankow for Brother Nee to arrive, I received a cable from the elders in Chefoo urging me to return to care for my family because of the Japanese invasion. After I left Hankow, Watchman arrived and delivered the messages of *The Normal Christian Church Life* the second time in the co-workers' conference. After returning to Chefoo, I could not leave again because of the war, so for a period of time I was retained in northern China while most of the other co-workers were in the interior.

In August 1939, after Watchman Nee came back to Shanghai from London to hold a conference concerning the Body of Christ, he cabled me to attend this conference. At that time I was traveling and working in the central part of my province with four young co-workers. All five of us proceeded to Shanghai for the conference. In all the meetings of the conference, I was invited by Brother Nee to read the Scripture verses before he spoke. It was during that conference in 1939 that my eyes were opened to see the Body of Christ.

As his guest at this conference, I was again brought into close contact with Watchman. He related portions of his European trip to me, making me clear concerning the real situation of the Lord's interest in England and in northern Europe.

Following the conference I returned to Chefoo, intending to come to Brother Nee's training in Shanghai. The following April, I and a few others attended the training and stayed there for approximately two months.

One day while walking with him down the stairway of the meeting hall, he said to me, "We have the blueprint of God's plan in our hand." That puzzled me. "What is 'the blueprint'?"

I said to myself. As time went on I discovered what he was practicing in Shanghai concerning the practicality of the church life. I took "the blueprint" back to the north and put it into practice in Chefoo for about two years.

RELATIONSHIP IN REVIVALS

A revival came to Chefoo in 1942 through practicing that blueprint. Because of that revival I suffered persecution and was imprisoned for one month in May 1943. After I was released from prison, I was severely ill of tuberculosis of the lungs. It was through that persecution, imprisonment, and sickness that I was forced to leave my hometown in 1944. I went to Tsingtao, resting and recuperating there for about two years. After Japan surrendered in August of 1945, I was invited to visit the church in Nanking in June of the next year, where I met Ruth Lee again after an absence from each other of over six years. From Nanking I proceeded to Shanghai to meet the invitation of the church there, staying there for about three weeks. I held a conference with the restored church in Shanghai on the tree of life and had much contact with Peace Wang and Yu Cheng-hwa, the eye specialist. In the same summer Watchman returned from Chungking to Shanghai and located there for his pharmaceutical business. He had still not resumed his ministry, but I had opportunity to visit and fellowship with him during this time.

Following my stay in Shanghai, I returned to Tsingtao. In the fall my wife and children were able to join me there from Chefoo. Based on the invitation and encouragement of the leading brothers in Nanking and Shanghai, I moved with my family to work in their district in October of 1946.

By being in Shanghai again, I had much opportunity to see Brother Nee after a separation of more than six years. While I was in the north, he had been in the western interior. We had had no correspondence during the war years, and I was somewhat concerned whether my practice in Chefoo had been right or not. Also, at this time Peace Wang and I were concerned for the recovery of Watchman's ministry. For this reason we both took every opportunity to have fellowship with him. Many times we had fellowship concerning life, the

Spirit, the work, the churches, and the Lord's move in the recovery. In all these matters he helped us very much. In our fellowship I related to him all the things I had practiced during our years of separation. His response was to encourage me to carry out the same things in the other churches. We presented to him the urgent need to resume his ministry because of the restoration of the church in Shanghai and the wide doors opened in new fields. I asked him to resume his ministry, but he told me that because of certain rebellious brothers, his ministering spirit would not allow him to minister to the church in Shanghai. I realized from this that in order to recover his ministry, there was the crucial need of a revival among us.

He was fully open to both Peace Wang and me and gave us instructions concerning the Lord's work. In his fellowship with us, he stressed again and again the need to have the outer man broken that our spirit with the Holy Spirit might be released in our public ministry and personal contact with others. This was a great help to me.

After staying in Shanghai for a short time, a revival began to come in among the saints, and the number of attendants in the meetings greatly increased. Many who were distracted by the storm in 1942, which caused the church in Shanghai to be closed, were recovered. The news spread rapidly to all the churches throughout the country. The churches in the provinces of Fukien and Kwangtung urgently invited Peace Wang and me to visit them. Co-workers and leading ones from throughout the country were coming to Shanghai for fellowship. The decision was made that in April of 1948 a conference would be held for all the seeking ones throughout the country who could come and fellowship concerning the Lord's recovery.

At the end of December 1947, Sister Peace Wang, Sister Rachel Lee, and I first visited the church in Hong Kong and then proceeded from there to visit the churches in Canton, Swatow, Amoy, and Foochow, Watchman's hometown. During our three-week stay with the church in Foochow, a revival came in.

Before returning to the south, I composed and compiled

The Chinese Gospel Hymnal. While we were staying in Foochow, Watchman inspected the manuscript and polished some of the gospel songs, especially the one entitled "You Need Jesus."

Following the conference in Foochow, we stayed with Watchman another two weeks to fellowship with him that the recovery of his ministry must be sped up. When the other co-workers and leading ones heard about this fellowship, they also would not leave, but asked us to obtain permission from Watchman that they might also participate in the fellowship. At first he would not give his permission, but on further entreaty, he agreed for them to be present on the condition that they would sit a distance away from him in another section of his spacious living room. Only Peace Wang, Rachel Lee, and I sat together with him for fellowship. I opened the fellowship by asking him why all the churches in the provinces of Fukien and Kwangtung were filled with confusion. Immediately he responded by releasing a message on the line of Jerusalem. The word poured out of him for over an hour. We sat there astonished. To our surprise a sister sitting among those far away burst out, "Why should we not do it right now according to Brother Nee's message?" Brother Nee responded, "If you wish to do it, you must all hand yourself over to the work (the ministry). Sign a note indicating your consecration, and pass it on to Brother Lee." This they all did.

When the leading brothers of the church in Foochow heard about this, they came that evening and handed over both themselves and the church to the work. This stirred up all the saints in town, and Watchman decided to call a meeting of the whole church. He asked me to speak at that meeting, but I told him strongly that if he would not go and speak, I would not even attend the meeting. He therefore took up the burden and spoke at that meeting. All of us realized that this was the beginning of the recovery of his ministry. Hundreds of us rejoiced over this. These events transpired in March 1948.

I then told him that over forty co-workers and seeking ones would be attending a conference in Shanghai in April, which had already been scheduled. I asked him if he would take care of this conference, and he agreed.

In one of the conference meetings in Shanghai, he requested that we sing the spiritual prose on the life of the grapevine. His desire after so many years of suffering was to express his spiritual sentiment through the singing of that prose. I then put it into meter, and we sang it in the meeting.

That conference broadened the revival which had already been brought into Shanghai. Also through that conference Watchman's ministry was fully recovered. At that time he decided to have a six-month training in the training center on Kuling Mountain. Peace Wang, Ruth Lee, and I were assigned to stay in Shanghai to care for the church and the supply of the training.

By 1948 the number of attendants in the church in Shanghai had greatly increased. It was, therefore, necessary to build a larger meeting hall, and a piece of land was purchased for that purpose on Nan-Yang Road. The cost was two hundred ten gold bars, equivalent to one hundred five thousand dollars in U.S. currency, to be paid in three equal installments. At that time the church had on hand only half of the initial installment.

One day Watchman asked me to come to his home. After I arrived he handed me thirty-seven gold bars, the equivalent of eighteen thousand five hundred dollars, which was more than sufficient to pay the other half of the initial installment. He told me that he had purposely kept that amount of gold aside to be applied on a meeting hall site for the church in Shanghai.

Also at this time he realized that the Lord's recovery would spread to Taiwan, and he was burdened to buy some land in Taipei, the capital of Taiwan, for this purpose. A brother who was a businessman in Taipei promised to take care of this matter for him, and Watchman sent that brother some money for this purpose. When that brother attended the conference in Shanghai, Sister Peace Wang and I were deeply impressed that he might not be faithful in money matters. On a certain day when Watchman invited me to help him send a further amount of money to that brother,

Peace Wang and I took the opportunity to express our feeling to him concerning that brother. He replied that the Lord knew that Judas was stealing from the purse, but He still allowed him to care for the money. I responded, "I cannot understand this point." But he gave no explanation.

Later, when I was sent to Taiwan, Watchman instructed me to visit that brother, and he gave me full authority to settle the account with him. I took one of the Taipei elders with me and asked the brother about the account. He presented a bundle of interest bills to us showing that Brother Nee still owed him a good amount of interest. I sent the report of this conversation back to Watchman in writing, but I received no further instruction from him regarding this matter.

One day while fellowshipping about the Lord's work, he asked me why I had gone to a certain place. My answer was that I wanted to help the church there solve its problems. He said that that was playing politics. He continued by saying that to do anything with a purpose, regardless how good, spiritual, or scriptural it might be, is to play politics. Only to follow the Lord's leading is not politics. As long as you are unable to say that your going there is following the Lord's leading, you are playing politics. In this same year, 1948, because of the heavy responsibility of the church in Shanghai, he appointed me as an elder there to help the situation.

RELATIONSHIP IN BEING SENT OUT FROM CHINA

In November 1948, Brother Nee called an urgent conference of all the co-workers in Shanghai to pray, fellowship, and seek clear guidance concerning whether we should stay or leave China. At that time I was in Hangchow holding a migration conference with the church there. On the last day of the conference, I received a cable from Brother Nee asking me to return immediately to Shanghai. Upon arriving in Shanghai, I found him eagerly waiting to hold the meetings. In the opening meeting he did not first have fellowship with us; rather, he simply announced that since everyone knew the political situation, Brother Lee must leave the country. He said, "Regardless of whether he likes it or not, he must be asked to go abroad." It was a serious time. Hardly anyone said a word. There was prayer, and Watchman closed with these words: "Let us bring this matter to the Lord and see how the Lord will lead us." That was the decision.

Because of the change in the political situation in northern China, Brother Nee fellowshipped with me that Chang Wu-cheng, Sen Feng-lu, and Liu Hsiao-liang in Tsingtao should migrate with their families to Taiwan for the spread of the Lord's recovery. The two of us sent these brothers a cable to that effect.

Following the co-workers' conference, Watchman still charged me to stay in Shanghai to oversee the building of the new meeting hall. In February of the following year, in the opening of the second co-workers' conference, concerning the matter of staying or leaving, Watchman repeated his announcement of the previous conference to the effect that I must leave the country. This time, after some prayer, he announced to all the rest that his feeling was that he and they must stay and prepare themselves to sacrifice everything for the Lord's work.

Following the meeting, while dinner was being prepared, Watchman and I took a walk. I asked, "Brother, why have you decided that I must leave the country, while you and all the rest stay and sacrifice everything for the Lord's work? Does this mean that you think I am not worthy?" He explained, "Brother, you must realize that although in this desperate situation we trust in the Lord, it is possible that the enemy will one day wipe us out. If this happens, you will be out of China, and we will still have something left. So you must go." I told him, "If this is the case, I will take your word and go." Then he asked whether I would go to Hong Kong or Taiwan. I answered, "I have no idea; I haven't given it a thought. Whatever you say, I will do." That was all.

At this time Watchman and I wrote a letter to Brothers Chao Ching-hwai, Chang Wu-cheng, Sen Feng-lu, Liu Hsiao-liang, and Chang Yu-lan in Taipei, appointing them as elders of the church there for its full establishment.

After this I remained on in Shanghai, attempting to finish

the building of the new hall, and Watchman went to Foochow to carry out his second training.

Two months later, I received a cable from Watchman at his training center, saying that I must turn over all responsibilities in Shanghai to the local leading ones and come to him immediately. This I did. After I arrived in Foochow and stayed in his training center for a short time, the situation required me to go to Taiwan. This took place in May 1949.

Following his second training, Watchman assigned three of his trainees, one brother and two sisters, to come to Taiwan to help me in the Lord's work. The brother came to Taiwan and, after investigating the situation there, dropped Brother Nee's assignment. The two sisters, however, came and worked in Taiwan according to Brother Nee's intention. Watchman wrote me a long letter of recommendation regarding them, especially concerning the change in their disposition.

LAST CONTACT

Early in 1950 Watchman Nee visited Hong Kong from the China mainland. Because a revival was brought there through his ministry, he cabled me in Taiwan, asking me to meet him there before he returned to China. I replied that I was in the midst of an important conference in Taipei and would not be able to arrive in Hong Kong before he left. His response was that as soon as I was free I should go to Hong Kong, regardless of whether he was still there or not, to arrange the service of the church there. Eventually, on February 16, I went to Hong Kong and stayed there for one and a half months.

The following is a testimony of Brother Hsu Jin-chin, an elder in the church in Hong Kong during that period of time:

On the evening of February 15, 1950, Brother Nee told us, "This afternoon I received a cable from Brother Lee. He will be here tomorrow to fellowship with the elders and the responsible brothers. I have also asked him to take the lead here. Tomorrow he will arrive. At that time I hope that you will receive him at the airport." By then, I was an elder already, and I arranged to have the brothers and sisters receive him at the Kai-Tak airport the next day.

On the morning of the day after I arrived, Brother Nee took me to the meeting of co-workers and leading ones. In the presence of all, he said, "Brother Witness, according to the authority the Lord has given you, please make arrangements for all the service of the co-workers, the elders, and the deacons in the church here." This was an assignment of tremendous responsibility, to lay a good foundation for the church service in Hong Kong.

In the evening he took me to the special meeting of the revival and asked me to speak. I said, "As long as you are present, I have no burden to speak." He then continued to minister in those special meetings.

In the revival in Hong Kong, some brothers and sisters handed over their possessions to the work for the Lord's recovery. Watchman asked me to share the responsibility with him in the arrangement for their disposal.

The following is the testimony of Brother Hsu Jin-chin concerning one of the meetings:

On February 9, I attended a meeting, and the word of the meeting greatly touched me. At the end of the meeting, I stood up and offered a prayer and consecrated myself with loud weeping and tears. I sang the hymn "When I Survey the Wondrous Cross." My whole being was filled with unspeakable joy. The attendance that evening was over two hundred. The meeting was originally scheduled to end at 9:30 in the evening. But after some had started to pray, the Holy Spirit continued to work, and over twenty people consecrated themselves one after another. The meeting went on until 10:45.

As a result of this consecration, Brother Hsu and his wife wrote down the following declaration:

February 9, 1950, 9:30 p.m.

To the gracious Lord who has loved us:

We thank You and praise You. Because of Your calling and mercy, we gladly offer up our bodies as living sacrifices, and we hand over our children, our job, our time, our future, and everything we have to Your hands. We will gladly serve You in coordination with all the brothers and sisters in the church. Accept us, and may Your grace and love be with us all. Amen.

Recipients of grace,

Hsu Jin-chin
Chao Lai-ying

In response to their handing themselves over to the work for the Lord's recovery, Brother Nee and I wrote the following reply to them:

March 18, 1950

"While it remained, was it not your own? And when it was sold, was it not under your authority?" Acts 5:4

Dear Brother Jin-chin:

We have read the paper you have handed to us. After fellowshipping over the matter twice, we feel that according to your present spiritual condition, the time has not yet come for you to work together as "stewards." Hence, concerning your future, we feel that you should proceed according to the following methods:

1) As much as possible, everything in your possession that you have no use of should be sold. Try to gather up everything together. Half of these proceeds should be given to the elders of the church for the building of the meeting hall in Hong Kong. The other half should be sent away through the elders for use of the work in Shanghai.

2) Your business is returned to you for your own management. The profit you gain should be handed over

to the elders for the use of the work in the Hong Kong region.

We hope that you can be faithful in this matter and that you can give a good account before the Lord as a faithful steward on that day. Moreover, we hope that you will advance more in your stewardship in financial matters.

Peace be to you.

Your brothers,

Watchman Nee
Witness Lee

The following are two more letters written by Brother Nee and me to another sister concerning the disposal of material possessions.

March 15, 1950

Dear Sister I-Tien:

Peace in the Lord!

We have read the letter regarding the handing over of your possessions. How we thank the Lord that He has touched you regarding this matter and given you the enabling grace to meet His demands.

We notice that you are the wife of a brother, and we are reminded of the record in Acts 5 in which the intimate relationship between husband and wife regarding consecration is revealed. Although that couple in the Bible failed, it shows even more how important it is to overcome. It is further revealed there that while the husband may be defeated, the wife alone may be victorious.

In the light of this, we hope that you will be able to help your husband overcome with you.

Very often when a husband is wavering regarding his consecration, if he has a wife who is fixed in her consecration, he can be saved through her influence. We trust that

you will be faithful either together with your husband or
alone by yourself.

Your brothers,

Watchman Nee
Witness Lee

March 15, 1950

Dear Sister I-Tien:

Peace in the Lord!

Concerning the valuables which you have given, please
manage them as follows:

1) Deliver the sewing machine to the brothers who are
working together.

2) Regarding the surplus money you have each month,
please give it to the elders of the church in Hong Kong,
requesting them to keep half for the church in Hong Kong
and to distribute the other half to Hangchow, Chungking,
K'un-ming, and Foochow for the Lord's work.

We feel this settlement is in accordance with the Lord's
will. May the Lord be with you and bless your future.

Your brothers,

Watchman Nee
Witness Lee

P.S.

1) The letter which we have written is to point out
where your responsibility lies. But you still may follow the
leading of the Holy Spirit and either put the money into the
offering box or send it to other work units. We do not wish
that our specific indication would nullify the leading of the
Holy Spirit.

2) When you deliver the money to the elders according
to our designation, please mark "Wife" on the wrapper so
that the elders will know what to do.

Before I went to meet Watchman in Hong Kong, while still in Taiwan, I finished the compiling and composing work on the second Chinese hymnal. I presented him with the manuscript, and he polished the hymn on the life of the grapevine, adding a few stanzas to it. It now appears as Hymn #635 in our English hymnal.

At that time I related to him that I had also composed sixty lessons on the basic truths of the Scriptures and that there was the need to reprint the first Chinese hymnal and some others of his publications. At this time he made the following arrangements regarding the bookroom and literature work:

1) The Gospel Bookroom should be set up in three places: Shanghai, Taipei, and Hong Kong. Watchman would personally manage the one in Shanghai; I would be responsible for the one in Taipei; and Brother Weigh would be responsible for the one in Hong Kong. Further, I was asked to assist the bookroom in Hong Kong regarding literary and editorial responsibility.

2) All three bookrooms would share the same copyrights.

(In 1975, Brother K. H. Weigh and I with other related brothers rearranged, due to the situation at that time, the matter of copyright as follows: All the Chinese books would be published by the Gospel Bookroom in Taipei; all the English books would be published by the Living Stream in the U.S.A.; the Hong Kong Church Bookroom would be used only for the distribution of our publications in Hong Kong.)

While in Hong Kong I shared with Watchman Nee how the Lord had blessed the work in Taiwan. He therefore encouraged me to return and remain there for the Lord's work.

Since I was much concerned for his return to the mainland, I had long fellowship with him one day regarding this matter. I said to him, "What the Lord's will is I dare not say. The matter is too great and serious." He said to me, "What shall we do with so many churches on the mainland? I must return to take care of them and stand with them for the Lord's testimony."

Concerning this matter, Brother Hsu Jin-chin testified to the following:

Before Brother Nee left Hong Kong, Brother Lee advised him many times not to return to the mainland. But Brother Nee said, "If a mother discovered that her house was on fire, and she herself was outside the house doing the laundry, what would she do? Although she realized the danger, would she not rush into the house? Although I know that my return is fraught with dangers, I know that many brothers and sisters are still inside. How can I not return?" Brother Lee escorted him three times back from the bus stop to his home in Diamond Hill....

In spite of others' advice, one day in the middle of March, Brother Nee asked his brother-in-law, Samuel Chang, to send him to the railway station to depart for the mainland. He did this without letting any others know. Soon afterwards, on April 1, I returned to Taipei.

That was the last time I saw him. From that time we had no correspondence and, of course, never saw each other again. We only received indirect news regarding him from his relatives until he went to be with the Lord.

IMPRESSIONS OF CONTACTS

Through all the twenty-five years I knew Watchman Nee, from 1925 to 1950, I was deeply impressed with certain characteristics of his.

Absolute toward the Lord

He loved the Lord as his first love. To him the Lord came first in everything. He never compromised regarding the Lord's interest, nor did he sacrifice any truth for the sake of convenience. He also did not follow the Lord halfway. His commitment to the Lord was absolute.

Well-balanced

In knowing the Bible and in his church practice, he was

very well-balanced. He did not follow any teaching or any practice in an unbalanced way as so many Christians in denominations do. He would frequently compare one view of a certain thing with other views that he might be kept from falling into some extreme. In his daily Christian life, he practiced the same principle.

All-inclusive

From reading many classical Christian books, he picked up all the good scriptural points of many different Christian groups, gathering them all into the practice of the church life. He never rejected a good scriptural point simply because it came from the wrong source. He even picked up some good items from extreme Pentecostalism. In this way he was able to bring into the present practice of the church all the riches which Christ had given His Body in the past centuries. Through him we are now able to participate in all these riches in the local churches, not in a narrow way, nor in a sectarian way, but in an all-inclusive way.

Knowing the Bible

In my entire life I have never met another person who knew the Bible as deeply as Watchman Nee. He received much help from many of the finest Christian writers of past centuries, but he also stood upon their shoulders, seeing more things from the Scriptures than they did. He not only knew the letter of the Bible, but he also knew the Spirit of the Bible. He probed into the depths and touched the Spirit of the Scriptures. His knowledge of the Bible was filled with light and saturated with life. He had not only the objective view of the Scriptures but also the subjective experience of God's Word.

Knowing the Lord

He was truly a man of God, knowing the Lord in a full way. He knew the Lord in His acts as well as in His ways. He knew the Lord not only according to His love, mercy, grace, righteousness, and holiness, but also according to His eternal purpose and His present economy. He had both the full, objective knowledge and the living, subjective realization of the Lord. He knew the Lord personally, as well as in the church, His Body.

Knowing Life

He knew that the Lord as the living Spirit lived in his spirit, and he knew how to exercise his spirit. He practiced rejecting the mind, emotion, and will of his soul, and he also practiced behaving and acting in the spirit. In this way he lived by the Lord as his life. He cared little for work; he continually cared for life more than work. He said repeatedly that the work should be the outflow of life. His ministry was not one of work but one of life, carried out by life. He paid much more attention to what he was than to what he did. He was truly a man of life.

Knowing the Church

He saw clearly that the church as the Body of Christ was Christ's expression with Him as its life and content. He also saw that the church could only be practical with the existence of local churches. He saw too that only churches in localities could carry out God's eternal purpose to have the church built up in a way which the gates of Hades could not prevail against. He thoroughly realized that to recover the proper church life on the proper ground is God's present economy. He did not teach mere doctrines concerning the church. He received a full revelation from the New Testament, not only regarding the content and reality of the church, but also regarding the practicality of the church. Through the years in his ministry, he not only stressed the experience of Christ but also emphasized the practice of the church life. His vision was not only Christ, but Christ and the church. Christ was his life, and the church was his living. He suffered for the church more than for Christ. The persecutions which came upon him from the denominations came mostly because of his emphasis on the church. He was burdened to carry out his vision concerning the practicality of the church life. He desired to see a local church in every city in China.

A GIFT OF THE AGE

I consider Watchman Nee to be a unique gift given by the Head to His Body for His recovery in this age. I fully respect him as such a gift. I have the full confidence and assurance that it was absolutely of the Lord that I followed this gift for the Lord's interest in His present move on this earth. I feel no shame whatsoever in saying that I followed a man—a man that was the unique gift and the seer of the divine visions in this age.

I am more than grateful to the Lord that immediately after being saved I was brought into such a profitable relationship with Watchman Nee and put into the closest relationship with him in the work of His recovery through so many events over a long period of time. The revelations concerning Christ, the church, the spirit, and life which I saw through Watchman Nee, the infusions of life which I received from him, and the things concerning the work and the church which I learned from him will require eternity to evaluate their true worth.

FACSIMILES OF LETTERS

PHOTOGRAPHS

MAP OF CHINA

19　年　月　日　第　页共　页

品琼大嫂：

　　　　明日是蕙妹逝世半周年之期（五月七日）。
这半年来，变化实在太大。回首前尘，展抚遗物，
叫我不能不一直心感悲痛。二十年来，不能一次
伺候她，总是终身遗憾。一切都是我对她不起，
实她因唯。我病已缠绵，经常反复。出殡我从望
简单化，~~回家二岳也地~~，~~另图～己葬以地埤~~，以免麻烦人家。
病中实在也想念你为亲属，想要和他们一起。但我
恢服环境去排。十余日来深思蕙妹不能自已。—
　　　　　　保身体为何？时常在挂念之中。年老的人，
有多加保重。你还想南边来，不想？我不知道如何说才好。
~~我也有~~　祝你好。

　　　　　　　　　　　　　　　　　述祖
　　　　　　　　　　　　　　　　　五月六日

1. Letter Two, chapter twenty-one (p. 183), from Watchman Nee to his
sister-in-law on May 6, 1972.

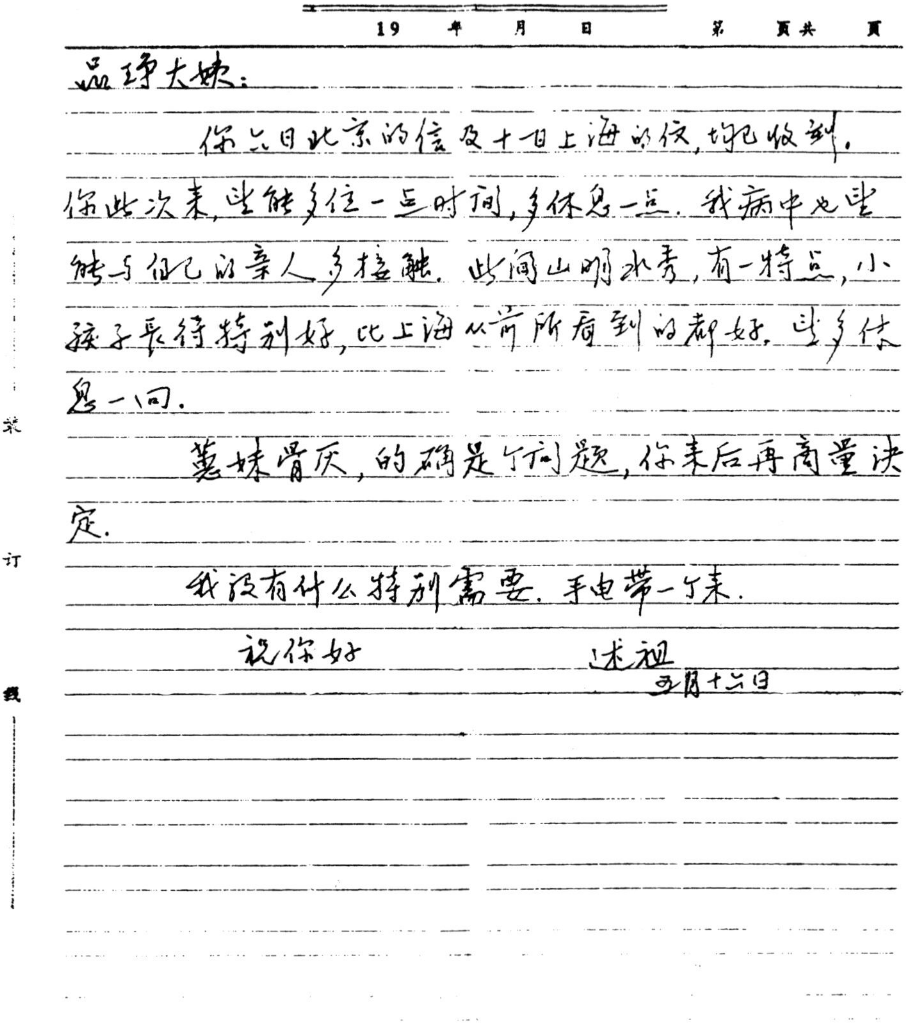

19　年　月　日　　第　页共　页

品瑾大姊：

你六日北京的信及十日上海的信，均已收到。你此次来，望能多住一点时间，多休息一点。我病中也望能与自己的亲人多接触。此间山明水秀，有一特点，小孩子长得特别好，比上海以前所看到的都好。望多休息一回。

蕙妹骨灰，的确是个问题，你来后再商量决定。

我没有什么特别需要。手电带一个来。

祝你好

述祖
五月十六日

装 订 线

2. Letter Three, chapter twenty-one (p. 184), from Watchman Nee to his sister-in-law on May 16, 1972.

3. Letter Four, chapter twenty-one (pp. 184-185), from Watchman Nee to his sister-in-law on May 22, 1972.

兴涛 妊婿：

　　我的情况，我想媾儿在世之日，一定对你谈。

　　你知道我是有大姊等家用的，所以生活没有问题。近我年老病多，极想到你们的亲人那里去。落叶扫根可以寻个归宿之处。我迫切希望，你能替我负责办妥这件事情。一切方面，全待靠你。

　　媾姐去世至今二个月半，我五内俱摧，过日为难，我希望你勉力为之，将证件寄到此处。媾姐生前多次提到楚宜及其孩子。不知孩子们现在如何行？念。

　　听说到浙江去，粮票有问题。我想，我吃很少，有解决方法，不要紧。

　　廿多年来通信，带生兑中。

　　祝你好

　　　　　　　　　　　　述祖白
　　　　　　　　　　　　五月廿二日。

4. Letter Five, chapter twenty-one (pp. 185-186, from Watchman Nee to his nephew-in-law on May 22, 1972.

19 年 月 日 第 页共 页

品琤大姨：

我将于明早调离枫树岑到 山下坡
农场去. 你来的时候不要买票到枫树岑, 要
买票到山下坡下車. 比枫树岑再远一点点.
进去第二站我曾蒙发一信给你, 比这封早, 不知
收到没有. 些早见面.
　　　祝 你好

述祖
五月廿五日

5. Letter Six, chapter twenty-one (p. 187), from Watchman Nee to his
sister-in-law on May 25, 1972.

兴涛：

　　我在枫树岭时，请友给你一信，坐你能替我办到公社的一张证明书，说明你们愿意收纳我，保证我的生活。(你知道我有太姊寄家用)你们态度要坚决明朗。

（— — — — — — — —）

　　我于今日从枫树岭调至白云山修养组，坐你努力而为，给我一封回信，证明要直接寄给白云山农场第十四队，抬头是由公社写给安徽广德县白茅岭农场，但是你寄来时要寄到安徽广德县白云山农场第十四队收。

　　我极望回到自己亲人那里去，请你努力。

　　　　　祝你好

　　　　　　　　述祖白

　　　　　　　五月廿六日

6. Letter Seven, chapter twenty-one (p. 188), from Watchman Nee to his nephew-in-law on May 26, 1972.

品珍大妹：

我调到山下坡十四队，这里离开车站还有十里路，还要翻一座山。你来实在不便当。可以不必来了。

我病中心仍喜乐，请你不必挂心，我仍尽力保傀自己，不要因病痛难过。

品蕙骨灰请你处理，一切都拜托你，我都同意。

纸短情长 祝你好

述祖白
三月廿日

7. Letter Eight, chapter twenty-one (p. 189), from Watchman Nee to his sister-in-law on May 30, 1972.

老韓送上海區工作用。

長老韓壽出去，專為香港區工作用。

（二）你的事業仍舊歸你自己辦。所得盈餘交

盼望你在這些事上能忠心，在那日能像一個忠心

的管家在主面前交賬。更盼望不久你在處理財物

的事上能有更大的進步。祝你

平安！

弟兄　倪柝聲
　　　李常受謹啟

三月十八日

8. Letter from Watchman Nee and Witness Lee to Hsu Jin-chin in Hong Kong on March 18, 1950 (chapter thirty-three, p. 323).

「田地還沒有賣不是你自己的嗎？
既賣了，價銀不是你作主嗎？

行傳五章四節

駿卿吾兄～

你交出來的單子，我們已經讀過。並且經過三次談
話之後，我們感覺按你們的屬靈情形，你們合作作
「家宰」的時候還沒有到。所以關于你們的前途，我
們覺得你們目前談以下辦法安排：

（一）一切不用的東西能賣多少者賣多少，能集
中多少者集中多少，將一半送交教會長
老作為香港造聚會所之用另一半送長

Photographs of Watchman Nee

Watchman Nee at his wedding: The bride and groom (above); the wedding photograph (below), with Witness Lee (holding certificate) standing to the right of the bridegroom, Mrs. Samuel Chang as maid of honor standing to the left of the bride, and Watchman's parents to the right of Witness Lee.

Another picture of Watchman Nee (above); the tomb of Watchman Nee and his wife in Soochow (below), [Watchman Nee's tomb at the right].

MAP OF CHINA

MONGOLIA

HEILUNGKIANG

MANCHURIA

INNER MONGOLIAN AUTONOMOUS REGION

KIRIN

• Harbin

• Ch'ang-ch'un

• Shen-yang

LIAONING

Teng-k'ou •

• Hu-ho-hao-te

KANSU

Yin-ch'uan •

NINGSIA

• Peking

• Tientsin

HOPEH

Shih-chia-chuang •

• Chefoo

T'ai-yuan •

SHANSI

• Tsinan

SHANTUNG

• Tsingtao

Hsi-ning •

TSINGHAI

Lan-chou •

SHENSI

• Sian

• Cheng-chou

• Kaifeng

HONAN

KIANGSU

• Nanking

• Wusih

• Soochow

• Shanghai

Ho-fei •

ANHWEI

Kwang-te •

Hangchow •

• Haining

SZECHUAN or SZECHWAN

Ch'eng-tu •

HUPEH

Hankow •

• Wu-ch'ang

CHEKIANG

• Chungking

Nan-ch'ang •

KIANGSI

• Pingyang

Ch'ang-sha •

HUNAN

• Kien-ou

KWEICHOW

Kuei-yang •

FUKIEN

Chuenchow or Chuanchow

• Foochow

• Taipei

TAIWAN

K'un-ming •

YUNNAN

KWANGSI

KWANGTUNG

Amoy •

Kulangsu •

• Swatow

Nan-ning •

Taishan •

• Canton

• Hong Kong

HAI-NAN

PHILIPPINES